Flags World

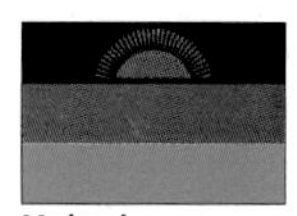

Libya | Liechtenstein | Lithuania | Luxembourg | Macedonia, FYRO | Madagascar | Malawi

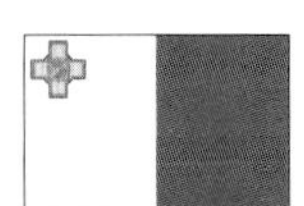

Malaysia | Maldives | Mali | Malta | Marshall Islands | Mauritania | Mauritius

Mexico | Micronesia | Moldova | Monaco | Mongolia | Morocco | Mozambique

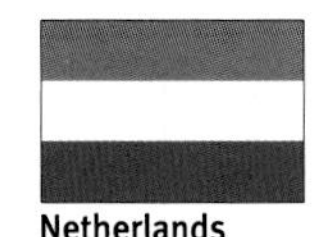

Myanmar | Namibia | Nauru | Nepal | Netherlands | New Zealand | Nicaragua

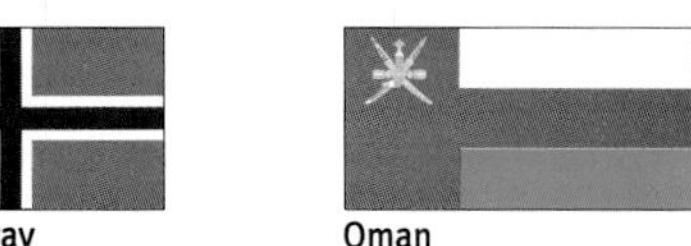

Niger | Nigeria | Northern Marianas | North Korea | Norway | Oman | Pakistan

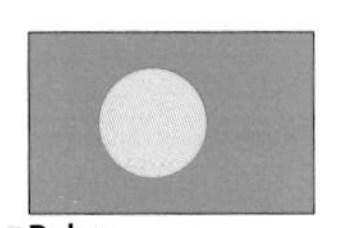
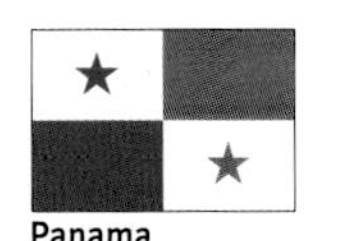

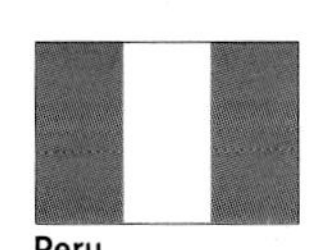

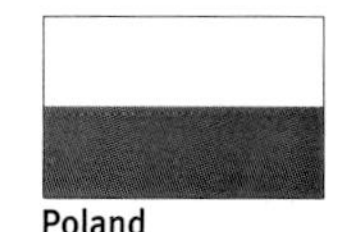

Palau | Panama | Papua New Guinea | Paraguay | Peru | Philippines | Poland

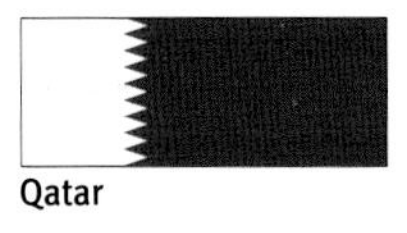
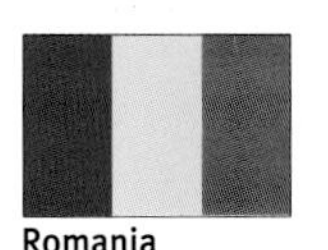

Portugal | Qatar | Romania | Russian Federation | Rwanda | St. Kitts and Nevis | St. Lucia

St. Vincent & the Grenadines | Samoa | San Marino | Sao Tomé and Principe | Saudi Arabia | Senegal | Serbia and Montenegro

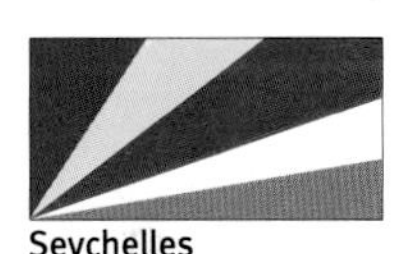

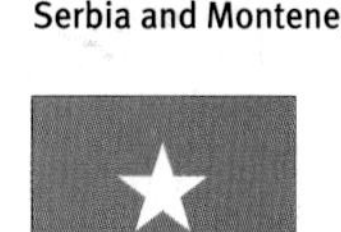

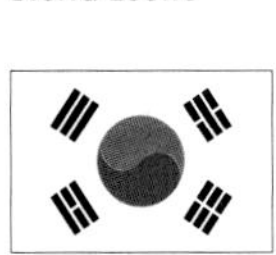

Seychelles | Sierra Leone | Singapore | Slovakia | Slovenia | Solomon Islands | Somalia

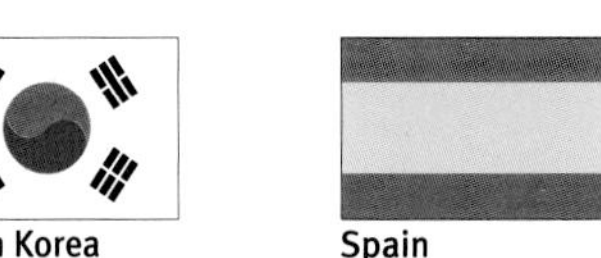

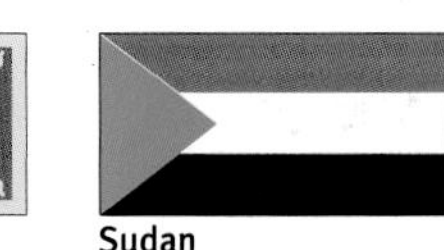
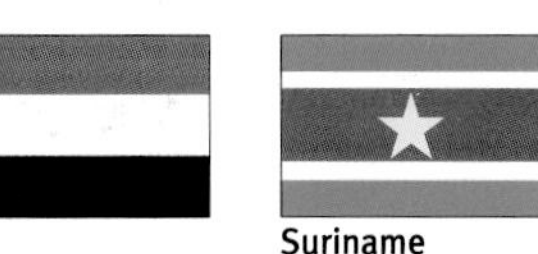

South Africa | South Korea | Spain | Sri Lanka | Sudan | Suriname | Swaziland

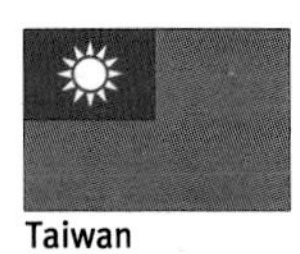
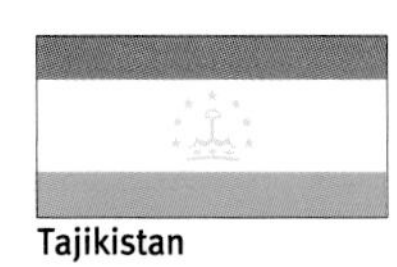

Sweden | Switzerland | Syria | Taiwan | Tajikistan | Tanzania | Thailand

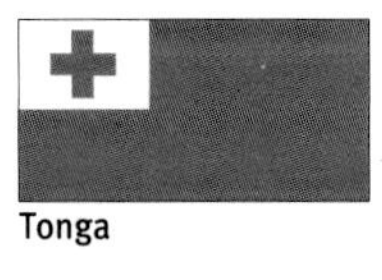

Togo | Tonga | Trinidad and Tobago | Tunisia | Turkey | Turkmenistan | Tuvalu

Uganda | Ukraine | United Arab Emirates | United Kingdom | United States of America

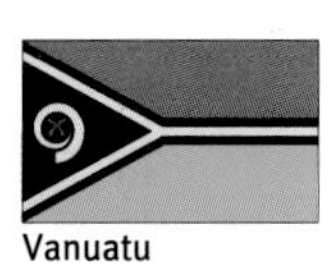

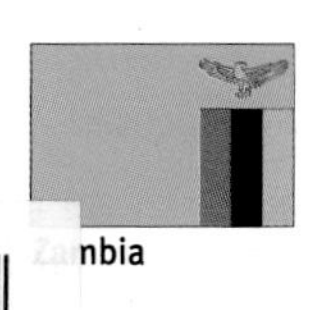

Vanuatu | Venezuela | Vietnam | nbia | Zimbabwe

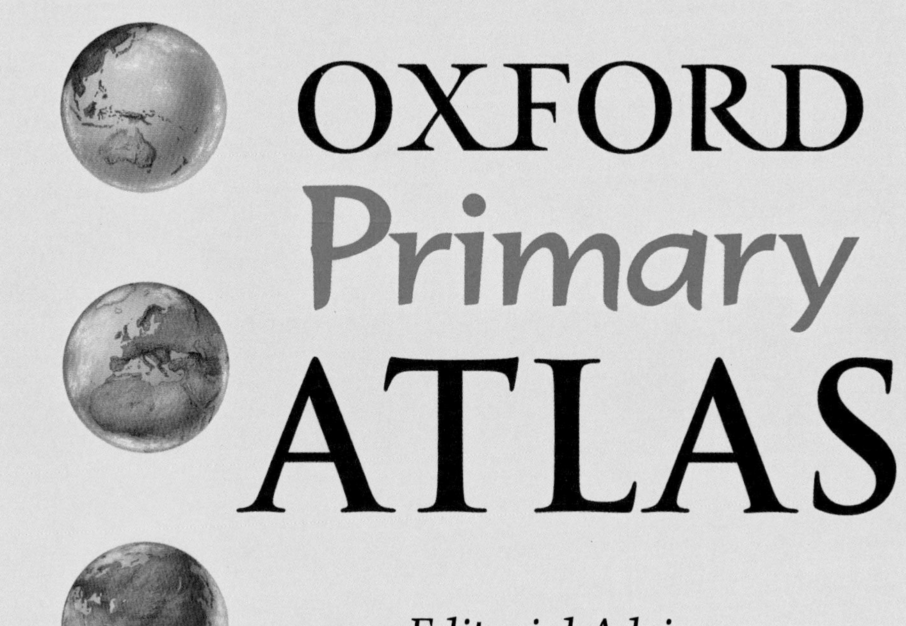

OXFORD Primary ATLAS

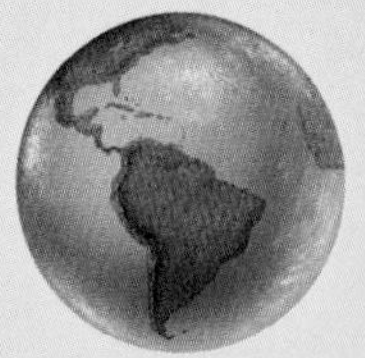

Editorial Adviser

Dr Patrick Wiegand

OXFORD
UNIVERSITY PRESS

Great Clarendon Street, Oxford OX2 6DP

Oxford University Press is a department of the University of Oxford. It furthers the University's objective of excellence in research, scholarship, and education by publishing worldwide in

Oxford New York

Auckland Cape Town Dar es Salaam Hong Kong Karachi Kuala Lumpur Madrid Melbourne Mexico City Nairobi New Delhi Shanghai Taipei Toronto

With offices in

Argentina Austria Brazil Chile Czech Republic France Greece Guatemala Hungary Italy Japan Poland Portugal Singapore South Korea Switzerland Thailand Turkey Ukraine Vietnam

Oxford is a registered trade mark of Oxford University Press in the UK and in certain other countries

First published 2005

ISBN 0 19 832160 0 (hardback)

ISBN 0 19 832159 7 (paperback)

3 5 7 9 10 8 6 4 2

Printed in Singapore

Acknowledgements

Illustrations by:
Julian Baker p 20; Adrian Barclay pp 31, 35, 41, 51, 54, 55; Mark Duffin pp 7 (compass), 23tl, tr & br, 24 (bricks), 26, 59; Nick Hawken pp 24 (settlements), 32, 33, 36, 37, 38, 39, 42, 43, 45, 46, 47, 48, 49, 52, 53, 55; Tracey Learoyd and Adrian Smith p 20 *and thereafter* (landscape pictograms); ODI p 24 *and thereafter* (population figures); Harry Venning p 60

The publishers would also like to thank the following for permission to reproduce the following photographs:
Alamy pp 20t (Robert Harding Picture Library), 20ct (The Photolibrary Wales), 20c (Geogphotos), 20cb (Worldwide Picture Library), 22tr (Leslie Garland Picture Library), 24t (David Crausby), 24c (Elmtree Images), 26t (David Martyn Hughes), 26b (Gina Calvi), 29ct (Jon Arnold Images), 29cb (Ian Thraves), 39t (Robert Harding Picture Library), 48t (ImageState), 60cr (Steve Bloom Images), 60l (TH Foto), 60r (Guy Somerset), 64tc (Robert Harding Picture Library), 64bl (ashfordplatt); Corbis pp 20b (Chinch Gryniewicz), 22tl (David Paterson), 23tl (Neil Beer), 26c (Jason Hawkes), 28t (Martin Jones), 33b (ML Sinibaldi), 36t (Lindsay Hebberd), 36b (Richard Bickel), 42br (Charles Lenars), 52t (Jeremy Horner), 64tr (Ron Watts), 65tr (Richard A. Cooke), 65bc (Galen Rowell), 65bl (Wolfgang Kaehler); Frank Lane Picture Agency pp 29b (Chris Demetriou), 42br (Derek Hall), 43ct (Peter Davey), 43br (David Hosking), 64tl (Minden Pictures); Getty Images/Photographer's Choice p 46l (James Randklev); Getty Images/Stone pp 24b (Patrick Ingrand), 29tr (Tony Page), 33t, 42t (Will & Deni McIntyre), 43l (Daryl Balfour), 46r, 52b (Pascal Rondeau), 58br; Getty Taxi pp 28b (Richard Cooke), 39b, 47r (B & M Productions), 48b (Tom Bean); Getty Images/The Image Bank pp 47l, 58bl (Image Makers), 64br, 65tl, 65br (Frans Lemmens); Heritage Image Partnership © The British Museum p 28ct (Institution Reference: M&ME, 1939,10-10,93); Powerstock p 28cb (Superstock); Science Photo Library pp 8 (NRSC Ltd), 59l (Earth Satellite Corporation), 59r (Planetary Visions Ltd), 60cl (David Vaughan); © UK Perspectives p 27.

The page design is by Adrian Smith.

The publishers are grateful to the following colleagues in geography education for their helpful comments and advice during the development stages of this atlas:

Jeremy Bullock, Susan Butler, Claire Condie, John Dewis, Tracey Ellis, John Halocha, Joan Huckle, Richard Jefferies, Pat Kelway, Amanda Lightfoot, Trevor Mason, Vanessa Richards, Vicky Stevenson, Emma Wells, Niki Whitburn, Brenda Whittle.

The publishers would also like to thank Phoenix Mapping and Suzanne Williams for their help during the production of this atlas.

Contents

- Atlas literacy 4–5
- Atlas numeracy 6–7

The United Kingdom

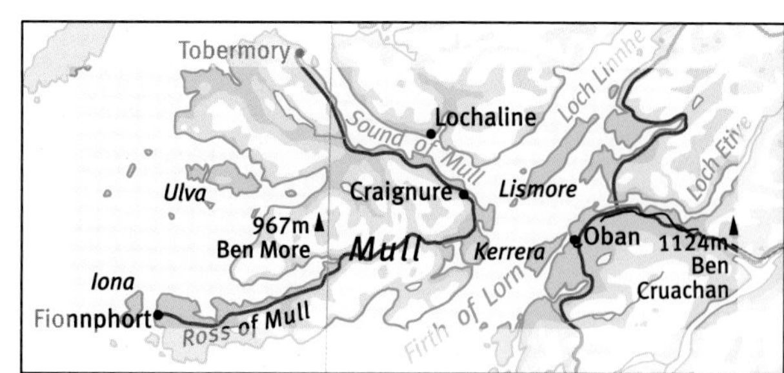

Tobermory
Lochaline
Sound of Mull
Loch Linnhe
Loch Etive
Ulva
Craignure
Lismore
967m
Ben More
Mull
Kerrera
Oban
1124m
Ben
Cruachan
Iona
Fionnphort
Ross of Mull
Firth of Lorn

United Kingdom and the Republic of Ireland 8–9

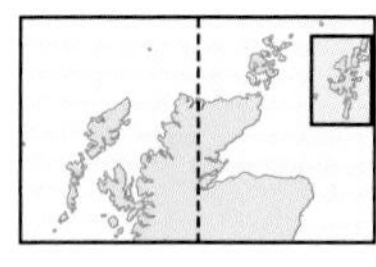
Northern Scotland 10–11

Northern Ireland and Southern Scotland 12

Southern Scotland and Northern England 13

Wales 14

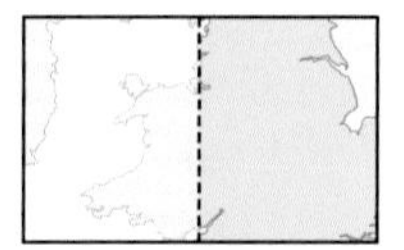
Midlands 15

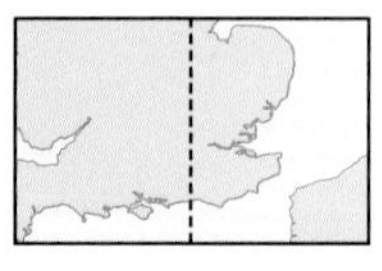
South East England 16–17

South West England 18–19

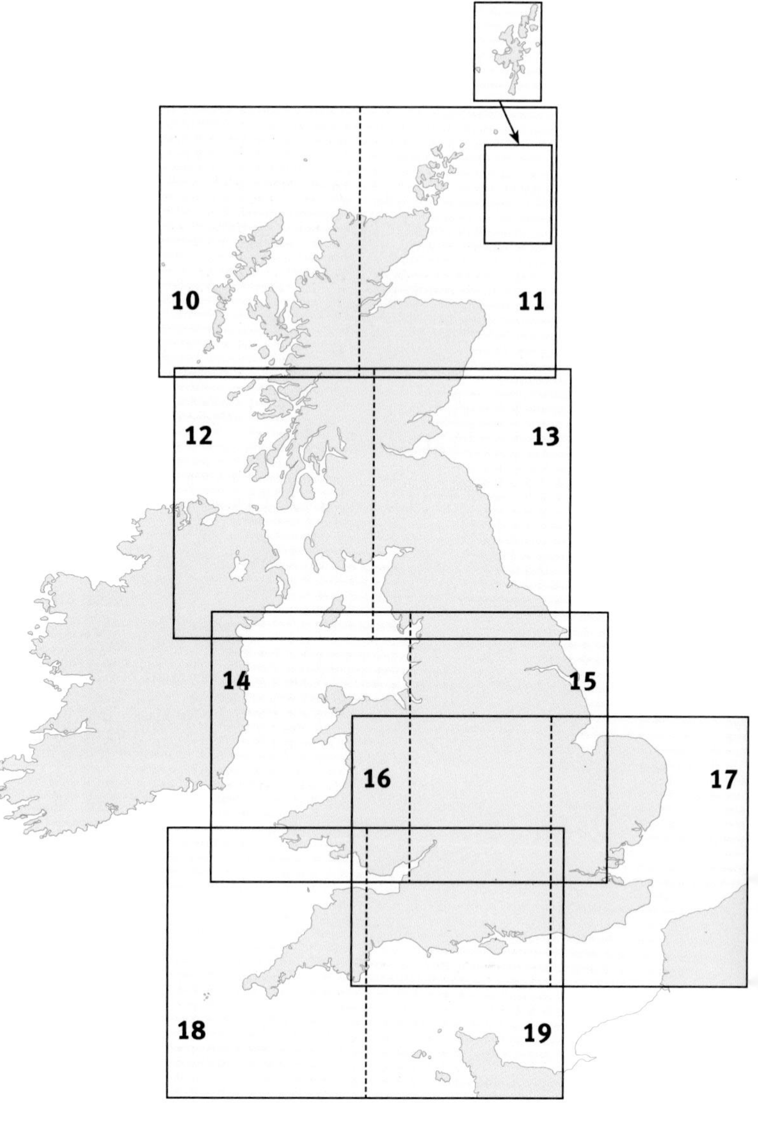

10
11
12
13
14
15
16
17
18
19

Landscapes and rivers 20–21

Weather, climate and water 22–23

People and settlements 24–25

Connections 26–27

Tourism 28

Conservation 29

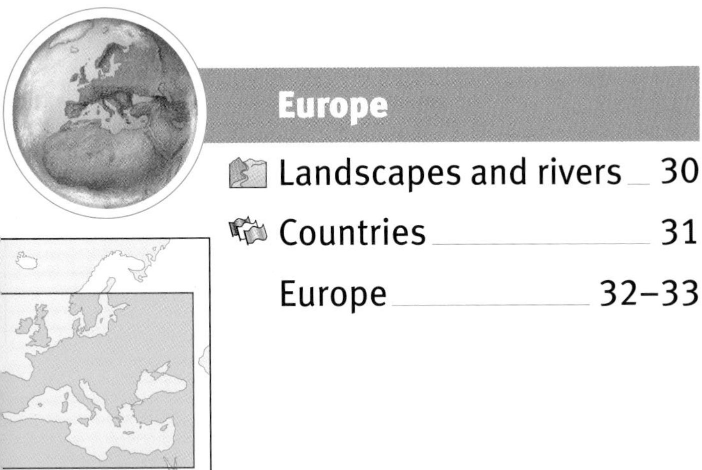

Europe

Landscapes and rivers 30

Countries 31

Europe 32–33

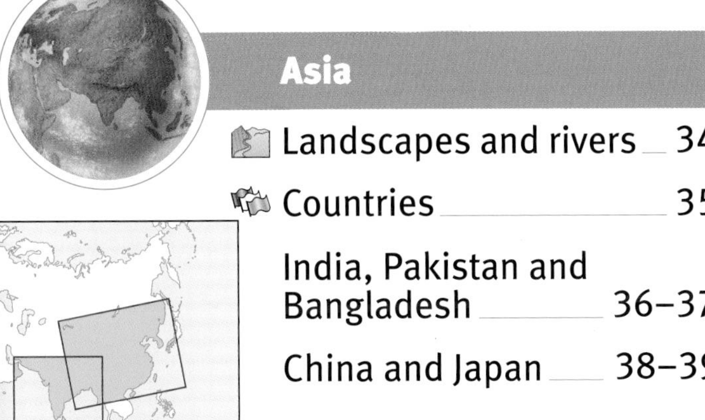

Asia

Landscapes and rivers 34

Countries 35

India, Pakistan and Bangladesh 36–37

China and Japan 38–39

Africa

Landscapes and rivers 40

Countries 41

Egypt 42

Kenya 43

North America

Landscapes and rivers 44

Countries 45

USA 46–47

The Caribbean and St. Lucia 48–49

South America

Landscapes and rivers 50

Countries 51

Brazil, Peru, Bolivia 52–53

Oceania

Landscapes and rivers 54

Countries 54

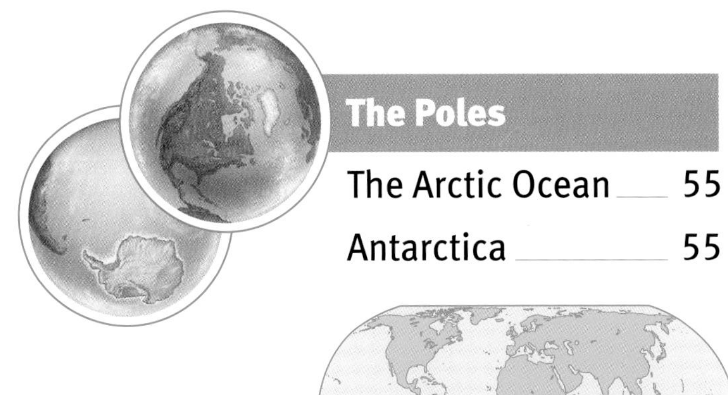

The Poles

The Arctic Ocean 55

Antarctica 55

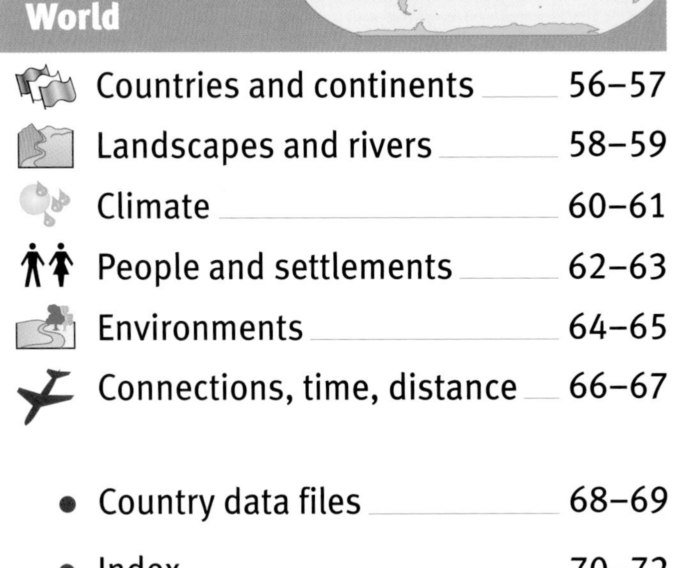

World

Countries and continents 56–57

Landscapes and rivers 58–59

Climate 60–61

People and settlements 62–63

Environments 64–65

Connections, time, distance 66–67

- Country data files 68–69
- Index 70–72

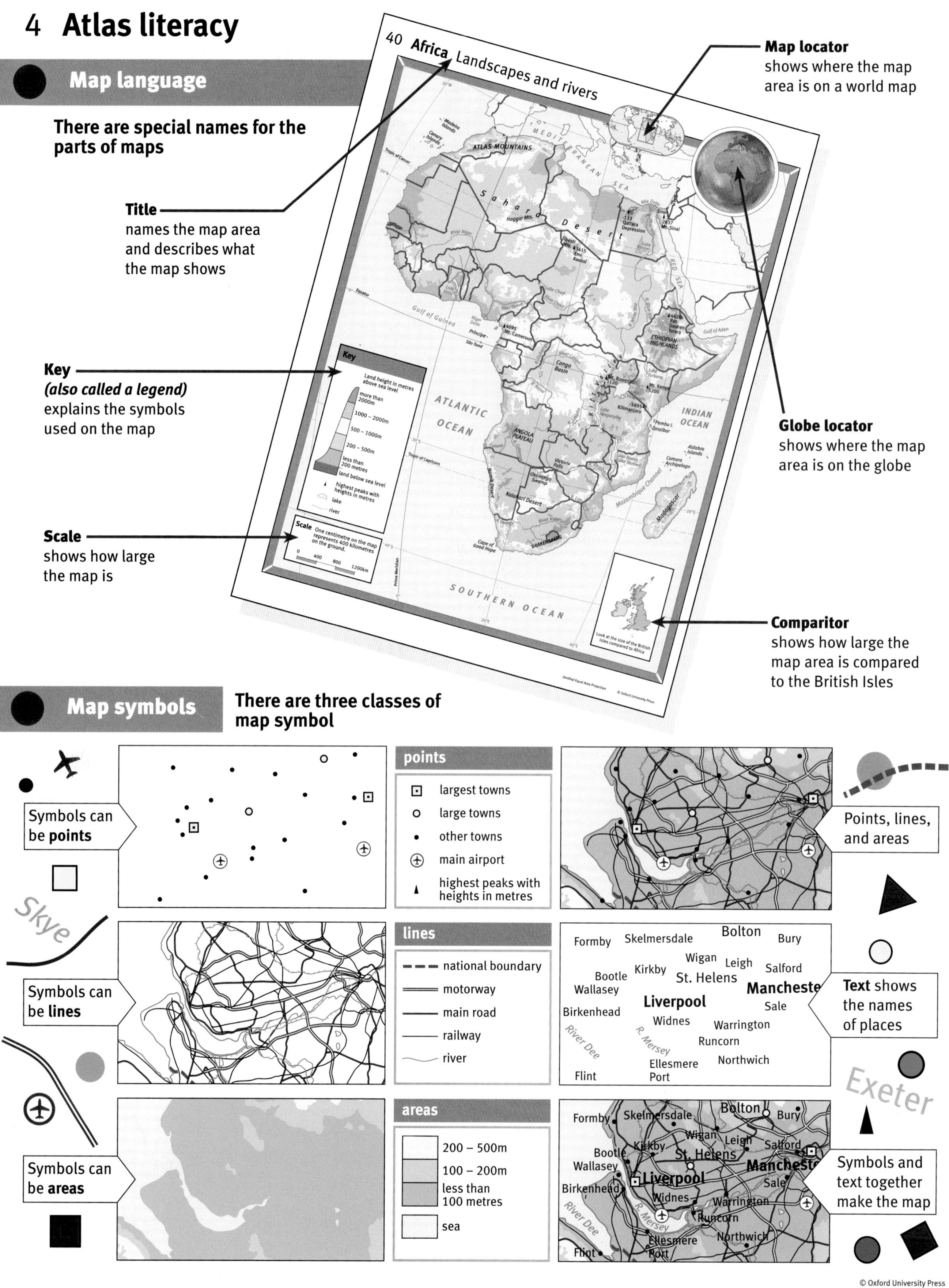

4 Atlas literacy
Map language
There are special names for the parts of maps
Title
names the map area and describes what the map shows
Key
(also called a legend)
explains the symbols used on the map
Scale
shows how large the map is
Map locator
shows where the map area is on a world map
Globe locator
shows where the map area is on the globe
Comparitor
shows how large the map area is compared to the British Isles
40 Africa Landscapes and rivers
ATLAS MOUNTAINS
MEDITERRANEAN SEA
Sahara Desert
RED SEA
Gulf of Guinea
ATLANTIC OCEAN
INDIAN OCEAN
SOUTHERN OCEAN
Congo Basin
ETHIOPIAN HIGHLANDS
ANGOLA PLATEAU
Kalahari Desert
Madagascar
DRAKENSBERG
Key
Land height in metres above sea level
more than 2000m
1000 – 2000m
500 – 1000m
200 – 500m
less than 200 metres
land below sea level
highest peaks with heights in metres
lake
river
Scale
One centimetre on the map represents 400 kilometres on the ground.
0
400
800
1200km
Look at the size of the British Isles compared to Africa
Map symbols
There are three classes of map symbol
Symbols can be points
Symbols can be lines
Symbols can be areas
points
largest towns
large towns
other towns
main airport
highest peaks with heights in metres
lines
national boundary
motorway
main road
railway
river
areas
200 – 500m
100 – 200m
less than 100 metres
sea
Points, lines, and areas
Text shows the names of places
Symbols and text together make the map
Skye
Exeter
Formby
Skelmersdale
Bolton
Bury
Wigan
Leigh
Kirkby
St. Helens
Salford
Bootle
Wallasey
Manchester
Liverpool
Sale
Birkenhead
Widnes
Warrington
River Dee
R. Mersey
Runcorn
Ellesmere Port
Northwich
Flint
© Oxford University Press

Ben Nevis
GRAMPIAN MOUNTAINS
NORTH SEA
SCOTLAND
UNITED KINGDOM
NORTHERN IRELAND
Ireland
REPUBLIC OF IRELAND
PENNINES
York
Manchester
Snowdon
ENGLAND
WALES
Great Britain
Dover
English Channel

Type on maps

The way text is printed on maps gives an important clue to what the words mean

Great Britain *Ireland*	islands
UNITED KINGDOM **REPUBLIC OF IRELAND**	countries
ENGLAND SCOTLAND WALES NORTHERN IRELAND	parts of the United Kingdom
PENNINES GRAMPIAN MOUNTAINS	physical features
Ben Nevis Snowdon	mountain peaks
NORTH SEA *English Channel*	sea areas
Manchester York Dover	settlements

Map abbreviations

An abbreviation is a shortened version of a word or a group of words

R. River
Mt. Mount
Is. Island
Pen. Peninsula

Some country names are abbreviated using the first letters of each word

UK United Kingdom
USA United States of America
UAE United Arab Emirates

El Faiyum
Beni Suef
R. Nile
El Minya

Lhaze
Mt. Everest 8848m
Kathmandu
Shiliguri

Country names and adjectives

There are patterns in the way some country names make adjectives

Australia	*Australian*	Ireland	*Irish*
India	*Indian*	Poland	*Polish*
Nigeria	*Nigerian*	Sweden	*Swedish*
Zambia	*Zambian*	Turkey	*Turkish*

China	*Chinese*	Brazil	*Brazilian*
Japan	*Japanese*	Canada	*Canadian*
Malta	*Maltese*	Egypt	*Egyptian*
Taiwan	*Taiwanese*	Italy	*Italian*

Bangladesh	*Bangladeshi*
Iraq	*Iraqi*
Israel	*Israeli*
Pakistan	*Pakistani*

Other country names make adjectives with no pattern

Cyprus	*Cypriot*	Greece	*Greek*	Peru	*Peruvian*
France	*French*	Iceland	*Icelandic*	Slovakia	*Slovak*
Germany	*German*	Netherlands	*Dutch*	Thailand	*Thai*

Map punctuation

A country name in brackets shows that a place is part of that country

Corsica is part of France

ITALY
Corsica (France)
Ajaccio
Rome
Sássari
Sardinia (Italy)
TYRRHENIAN SEA
Cágliari

The *Bulgarian* flag

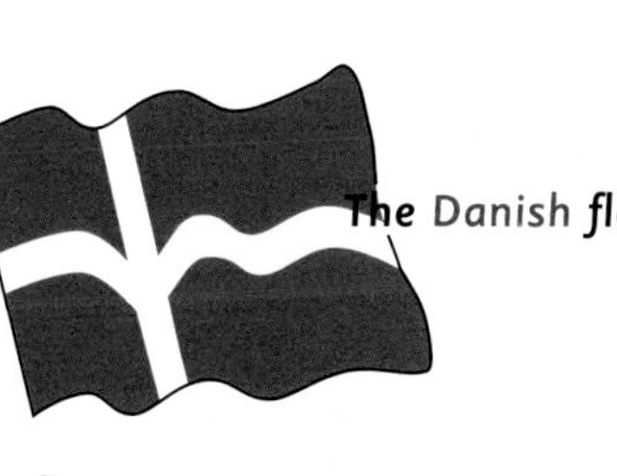

The *Danish* flag

The *Argentinian* flag

The *Senegalese* flag

6 Atlas numeracy

The Earth is a sphere*.

Two sets of imaginary lines help us describe where places are on the Earth.

All the lines are numbered and some have special names.

* It's actually slightly flattened at the north and south poles.

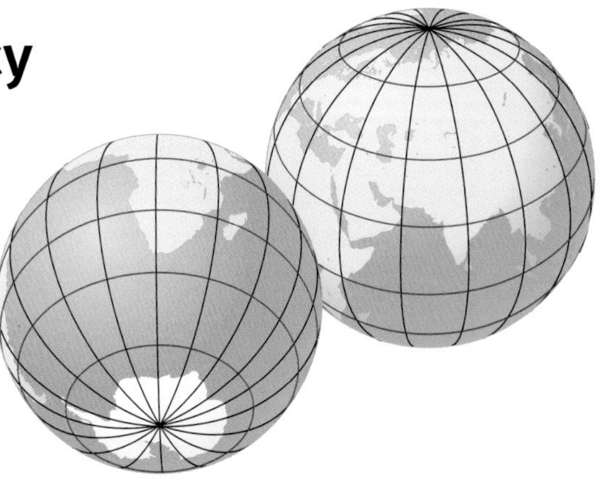

Longitude

Lines of longitude measure distance east or west of the Prime Meridian.

The **Prime Meridian** (also called the Greenwich Meridian) is at longitude 0°.

The **International Date Line** (on the other side of the Earth) is based on longitude 180°.

Latitude

Lines of latitude measure distance north or south of the equator.

The equator is at latitude 0°.

The poles are at latitude 90°N and 90°S.

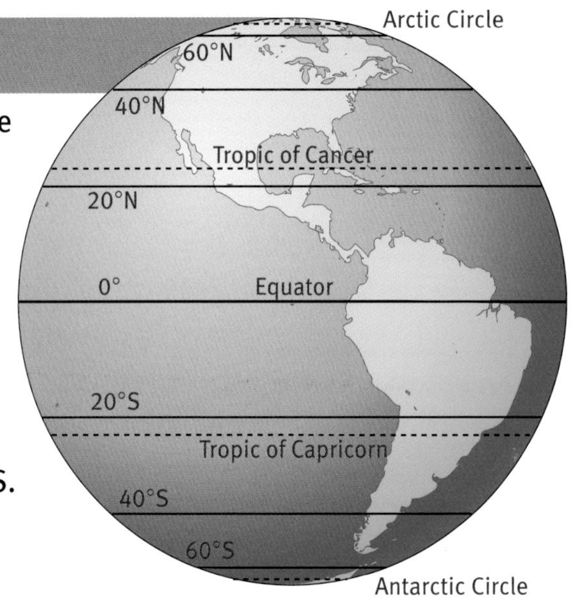
Arctic Circle
60°N
40°N
Tropic of Cancer
20°N
0°
Equator
20°S
Tropic of Capricorn
40°S
60°S
Antarctic Circle

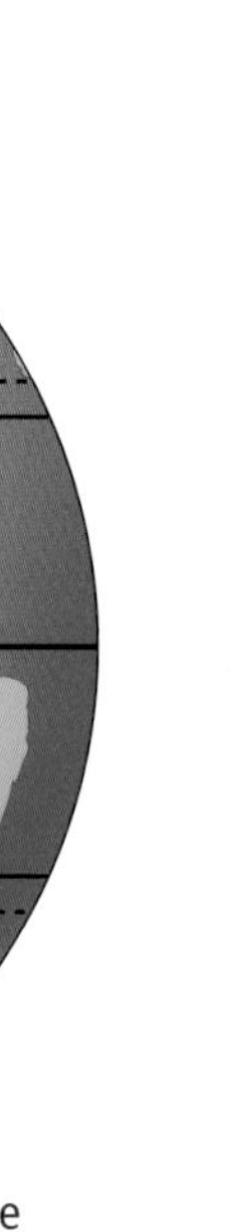

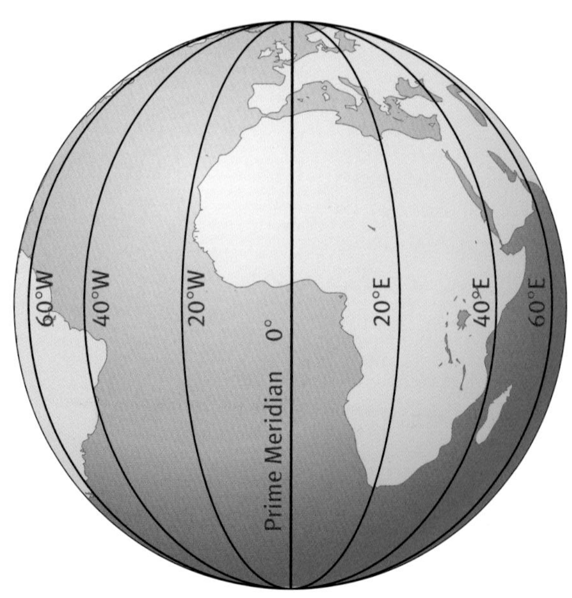
60°W
40°W
20°W
0°
Prime Meridian
20°E
40°E
60°E

Map projections

There are many ways of showing the Earth on a flat map.

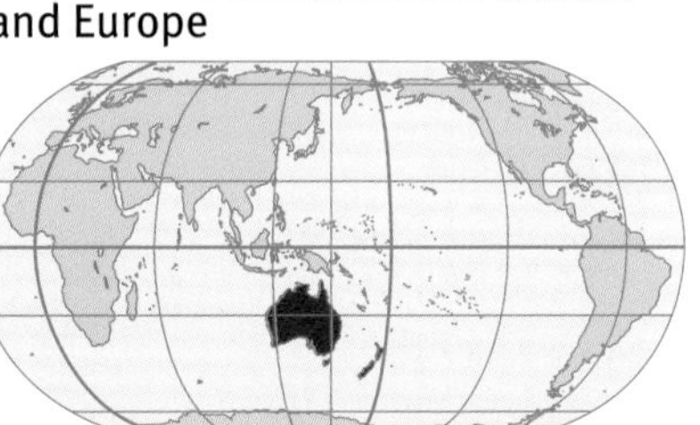

World map used in the United Kingdom and Europe

World map used in Australia and New Zealand

Grid codes

In this atlas, the lines of latitude and longitude are used to make a grid.

The columns of the grid have letters.

The rows of the grid have numbers.

Numbers and letters together make a grid code that can be used to describe where places are on the Earth.

Abuja is in B4 Durban is in C2

A
B
C
D
5
4
3
2
1
MEDITERRANEAN SEA
Casablanca
MOROCCO
Tripoli
Cairo
EGYPT
ALGERIA
LIBYA
Tropic of Cancer
MALI
NIGER
CHAD
Khartoum
SUDAN
ETHIOPIA
Abuja
Monrovia
Mogadishu
Equator
KENYA
DEMOCRATIC REPUBLIC OF CONGO
TANZANIA
Dodoma
INDIAN OCEAN
ATLANTIC OCEAN
Prime Meridian
Luanda
ANGOLA
ZAMBIA
MADAGASCAR
Tropic of Capricorn
NAMIBIA
BOTSWANA
REPUBLIC OF SOUTH AFRICA
Durban
Cape Town
SOUTHERN OCEAN
20°W
0°
20°E
40°E
20°N
20°S
40°S

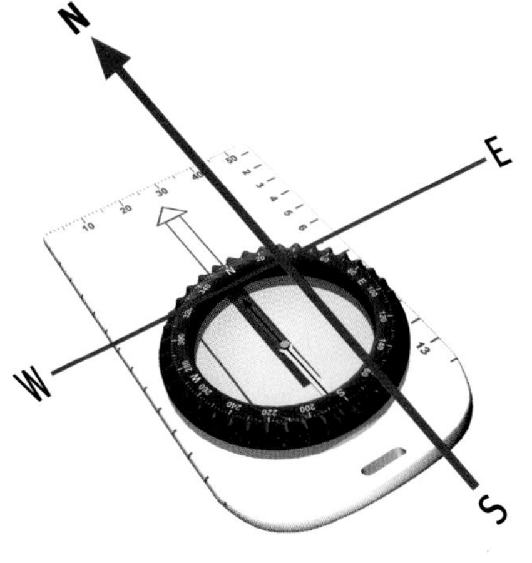
N
E
W
S

Direction

A compass is used for finding direction.

The needle of a compass always points north.

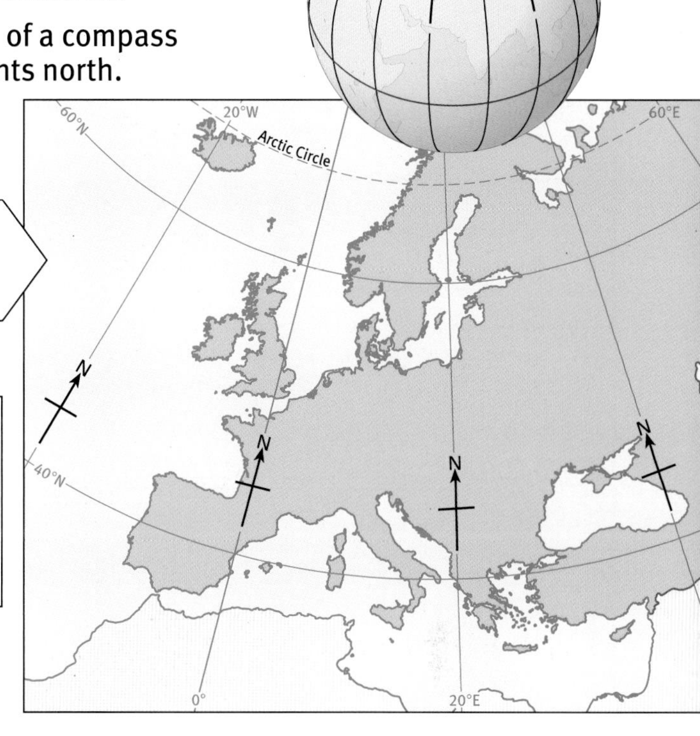
20°W
60°N
Arctic Circle
60°E
40°N
0°
20°E
N

North on atlas maps follows the lines of longitude.

N
London
Reading
Portsmouth
Brighton

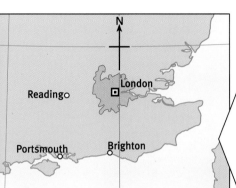

London is north of Brighton.
Brighton is south of London.
Reading is west of London.
Portsmouth is south west of London.

Scale

Maps are much, much smaller than the countries they show.

A few centimetres on the map stand for very many kilometres on the ground.

Each division on the scale line is one centimetre. The scale line shows how many kilometres are represented by one centimetre.

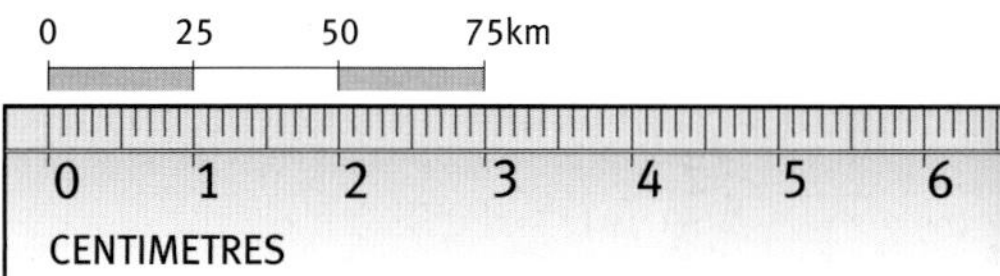
0
25
50
75km
0
1
2
3
4
5
6
CENTIMETRES

Anglesey
Holyhead
Llandudno
Colwyn Bay
Flint
Bangor
Caernarfon
Llanrwst
Betws-y-Coed
Snowdon 1085m
Blaenau Ffestiniog
Corwen
Llangollen
Pwllheli
Barmouth
892m Cadair Idris
CAMBRIAN MOUNTAINS
Welshpool
Aberystwyth
Rhayader
Aberaeron
Builth Wells

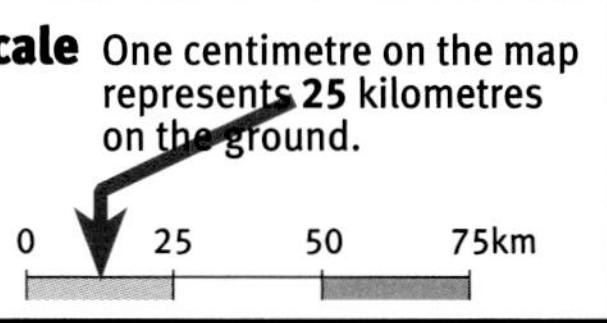
Scale One centimetre on the map represents 25 kilometres on the ground.
0
25
50
75km

The distance between Bangor and Betws-y-Coed is about 25km

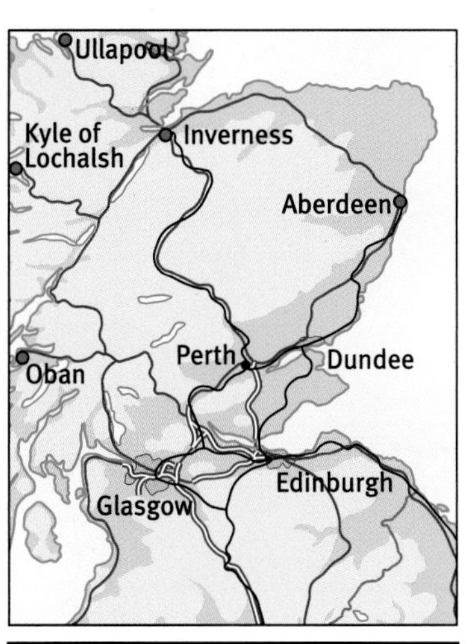
Ullapool
Kyle of Lochalsh
Inverness
Aberdeen
Oban
Perth
Dundee
Glasgow
Edinburgh

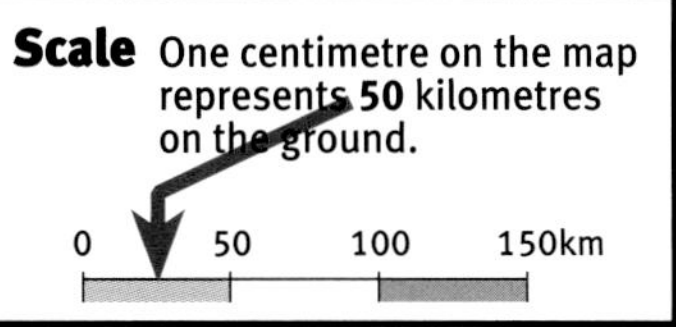
Scale One centimetre on the map represents 50 kilometres on the ground.
0
50
100
150km

The distance between Perth and Edinburgh is about 50km

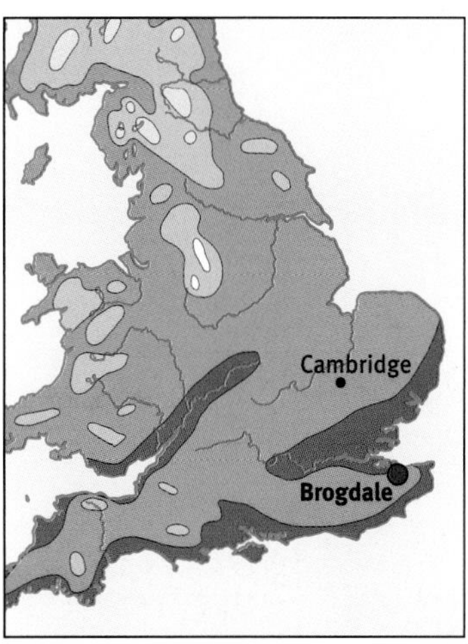
Cambridge
Brogdale

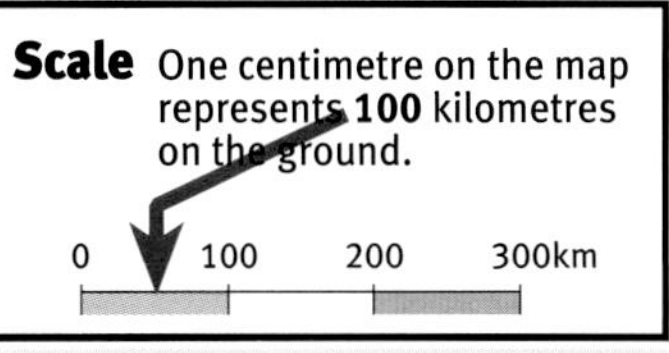
Scale One centimetre on the map represents 100 kilometres on the ground.
0
100
200
300km

The distance between Cambridge and Brogdale is about 100km

Larger scale smaller area more detail

Smaller scale larger area less detail

HONDURAS
Tegucigalpa
NICARAGUA
Managua
San José
COSTA RICA
PANAMA
Panama City
ST. VINCENT AND THE GRENADINES
ST. LUCIA
BARBADOS
GRENADA
TRINIDAD AND TOBAGO
Caracas
VENEZUELA
Georgetown
GUYANA
SURINAME
Paramaribo
Cayenne
French Guiana (France)
Bogotá
COLOMBIA
Equator
Quito
ECUADOR
BRAZIL
PERU
Lima
Brasília
La Paz
BOLIVIA
PARAGUAY
Asunción
Santiago
CHILE
Buenos Aires
ARGENTINA
URUGUAY
Montevideo
Falkland Islands (UK)

On world maps the scale is only true along the equator.

United Kingdom and the Republic of Ireland

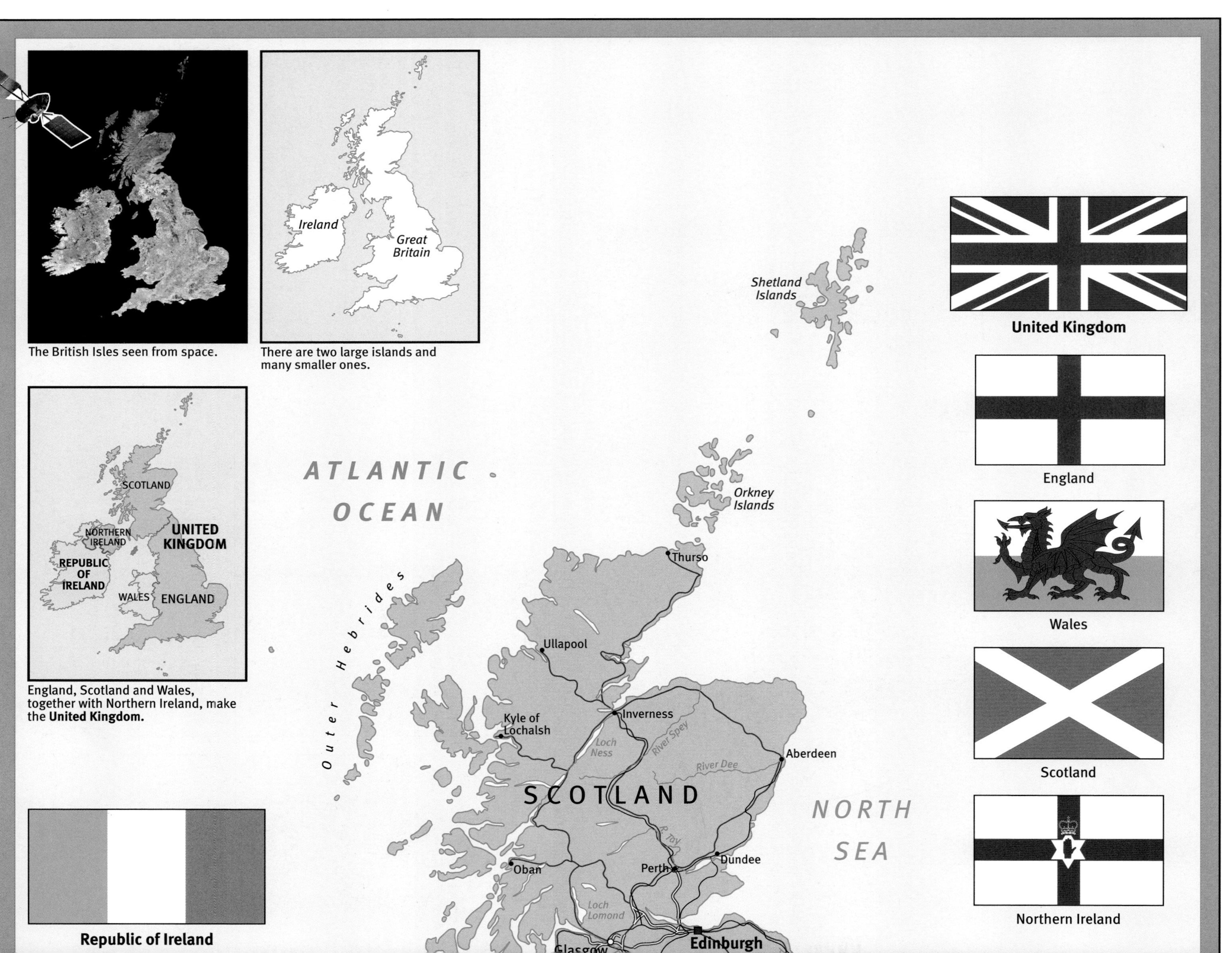
Ireland
Great Britain
SCOTLAND
NORTHERN IRELAND
UNITED KINGDOM
REPUBLIC OF IRELAND
WALES
ENGLAND
ATLANTIC OCEAN
Outer Hebrides
Shetland Islands
Orkney Islands
Thurso
Ullapool
Inverness
Kyle of Lochalsh
Loch Ness
River Spey
River Dee
Aberdeen
SCOTLAND
R. Tay
NORTH SEA
Oban
Perth
Dundee
Loch Lomond
Glasgow
Edinburgh
United Kingdom
England
Wales
Scotland
Northern Ireland
Republic of Ireland

The British Isles seen from space.

There are two large islands and many smaller ones.

England, Scotland and Wales, together with Northern Ireland, make the **United Kingdom.**

Transverse Mercator Projection

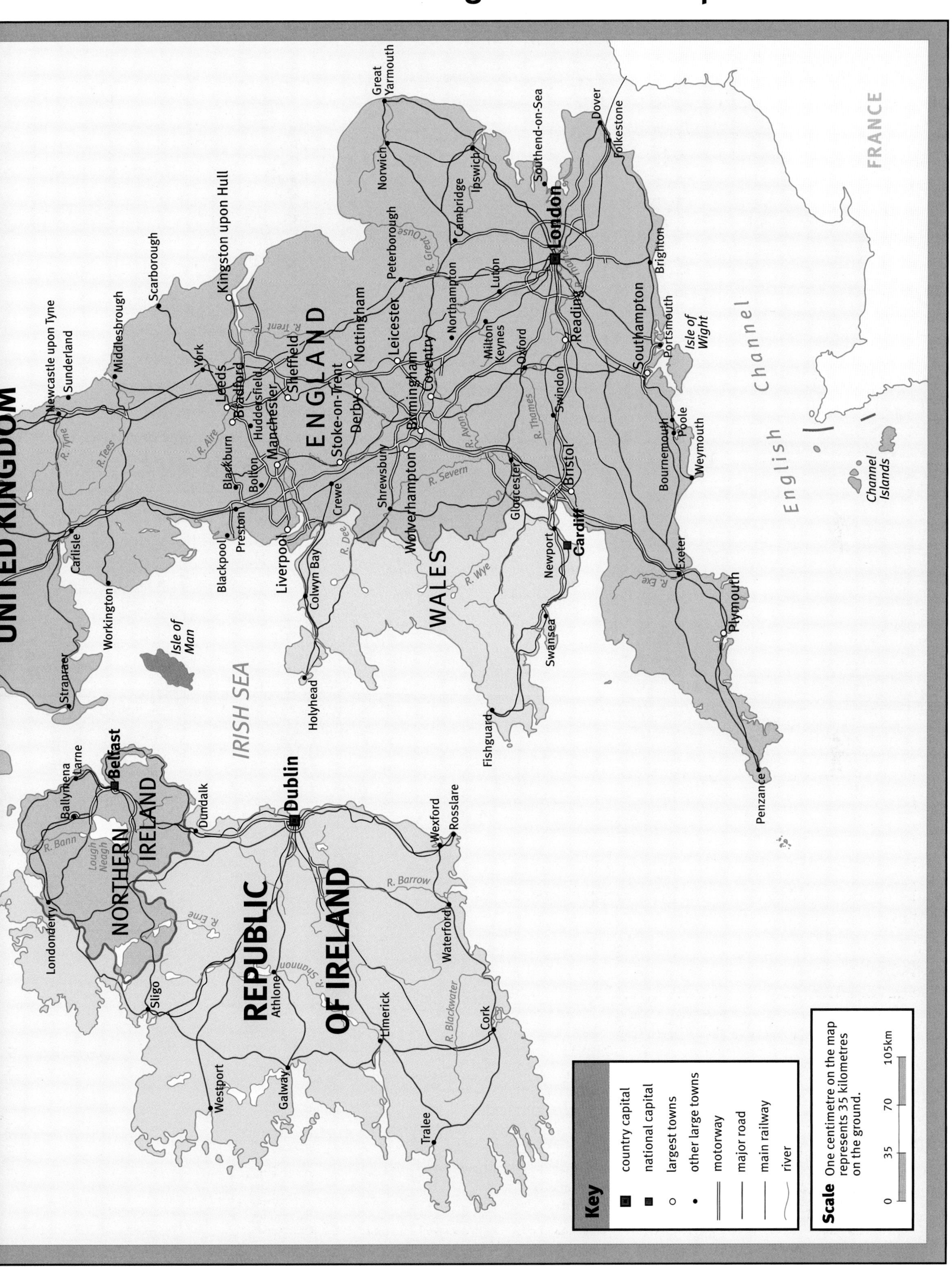

UNITED KINGDOM
Newcastle upon Tyne
Sunderland
Middlesbrough
Scarborough
Kingston upon Hull
Great Yarmouth
Norwich
Ipswich
Southend-on-Sea
Dover
Folkestone
FRANCE
London
Cambridge
Peterborough
R. Great Ouse
Northampton
Luton
Brighton
Southampton
Portsmouth
Isle of Wight
Reading
Milton Keynes
Oxford
Leicester
Nottingham
ENGLAND
R. Trent
York
Leeds
Bradford
Huddersfield
Sheffield
Manchester
Stoke-on-Trent
Derby
Coventry
Birmingham
Wolverhampton
Shrewsbury
R. Severn
Swindon
R. Thames
R. Avon
Bristol
Gloucester
Cardiff
Newport
Bournemouth
Poole
Weymouth
English Channel
Channel Islands
Exeter
R. Exe
Plymouth
Penzance
Swansea
Fishguard
WALES
R. Wye
Crewe
R. Dee
Colwyn Bay
Holyhead
Liverpool
Blackpool
Preston
Blackburn
Bolton
R. Aire
R. Tees
R. Tyne
Carlisle
Workington
Isle of Man
Stranraer
IRISH SEA
Belfast
Larne
Ballymena
NORTHERN IRELAND
Lough Neagh
R. Bann
Londonderry
R. Erne
Dundalk
Dublin
REPUBLIC OF IRELAND
Wexford
Rosslare
R. Barrow
Waterford
Sligo
Athlone
R. Shannon
Limerick
R. Blackwater
Cork
Westport
Galway
Tralee
Key
country capital
national capital
largest towns
other large towns
motorway
major road
main railway
river
Scale One centimetre on the map represents 35 kilometres on the ground.
0
35
70
105km

Northern Scotland

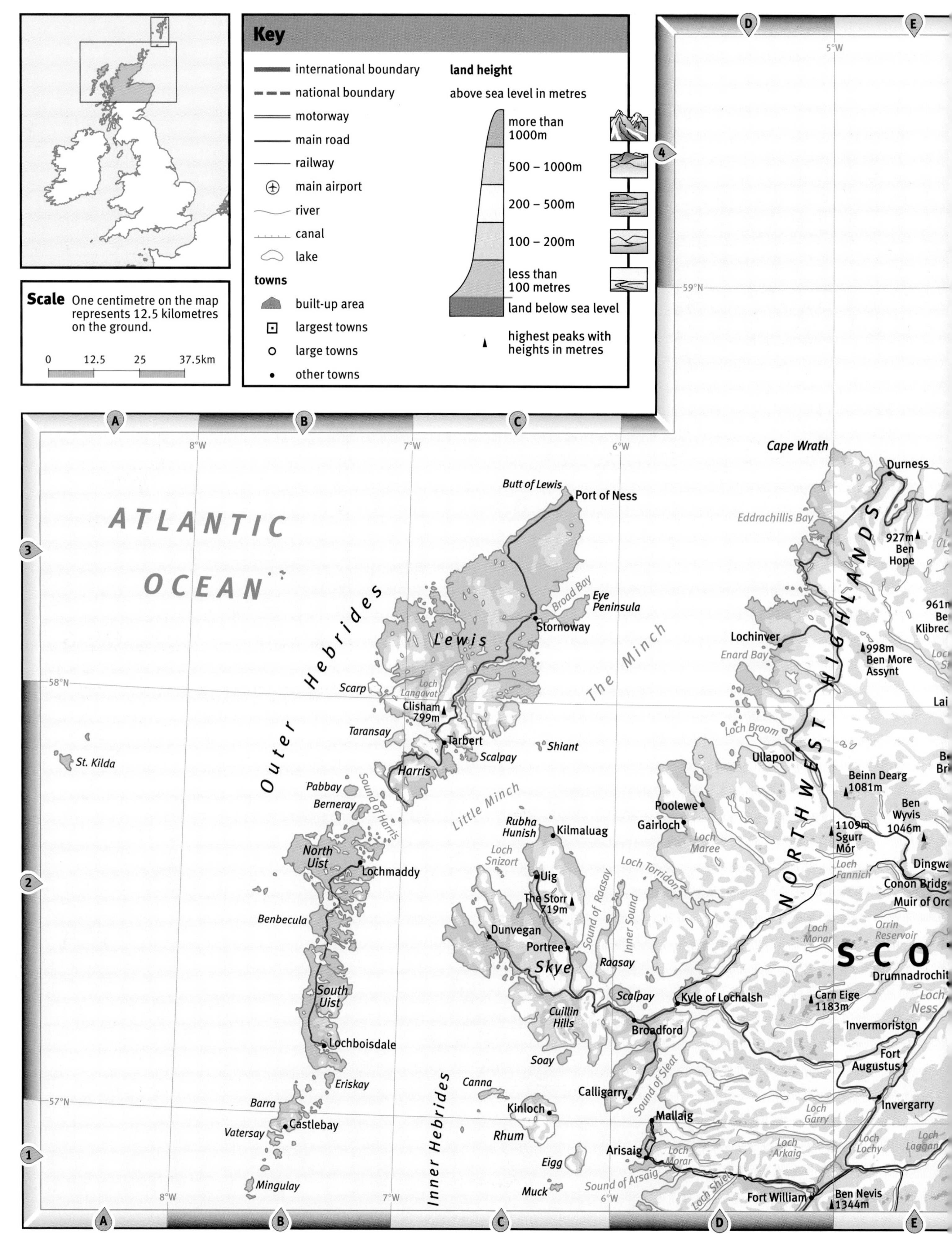

Key
international boundary
national boundary
motorway
main road
railway
main airport
river
canal
lake
towns
built-up area
largest towns
large towns
other towns
land height
above sea level in metres
more than 1000m
500 – 1000m
200 – 500m
100 – 200m
less than 100 metres
land below sea level
highest peaks with heights in metres
Scale One centimetre on the map represents 12.5 kilometres on the ground.
0
12.5
25
37.5km
ATLANTIC OCEAN
Outer Hebrides
Inner Hebrides
Butt of Lewis
Port of Ness
Broad Bay
Eye Peninsula
Stornoway
Lewis
Scarp
Loch Langavat
Clisham 799m
Taransay
Tarbert
Shiant
Scalpay
Harris
St. Kilda
Pabbay
Berneray
Sound of Harris
Little Minch
The Minch
North Uist
Lochmaddy
Benbecula
South Uist
Lochboisdale
Eriskay
Barra
Castlebay
Vatersay
Mingulay
Rubha Hunish
Kilmaluag
Loch Snizort
Uig
The Storr 719m
Dunvegan
Portree
Skye
Sound of Raasay
Inner Sound
Raasay
Scalpay
Cuillin Hills
Broadford
Soay
Canna
Kinloch
Rhum
Eigg
Muck
Calligarry
Sound of Sleat
Mallaig
Arisaig
Sound of Arsaig
Loch Morar
Loch Shiel
Fort William
Ben Nevis 1344m
Cape Wrath
Durness
Eddrachillis Bay
927m Ben Hope
961m
Lochinver
Enard Bay
998m Ben More Assynt
Loch Broom
Ullapool
Beinn Dearg 1081m
Ben Wyvis 1046m
Poolewe
Gairloch
Loch Maree
Loch Torridon
1109m Sgurr Mór
Loch Fannich
Dingwall
Conon Bridge
Muir of Ord
Loch Monar
Orrin Reservoir
NORTHWEST HIGHLANDS
SCO
Drumnadrochit
Loch Ness
Kyle of Lochalsh
Carn Eige 1183m
Invermoriston
Fort Augustus
Invergarry
Loch Garry
Loch Arkaig
Loch Lochy
Loch Laggan
8°W
7°W
6°W
5°W
59°N
58°N
57°N
A
B
C
D
E
1
2
3
4

Transverse Mercator Projection

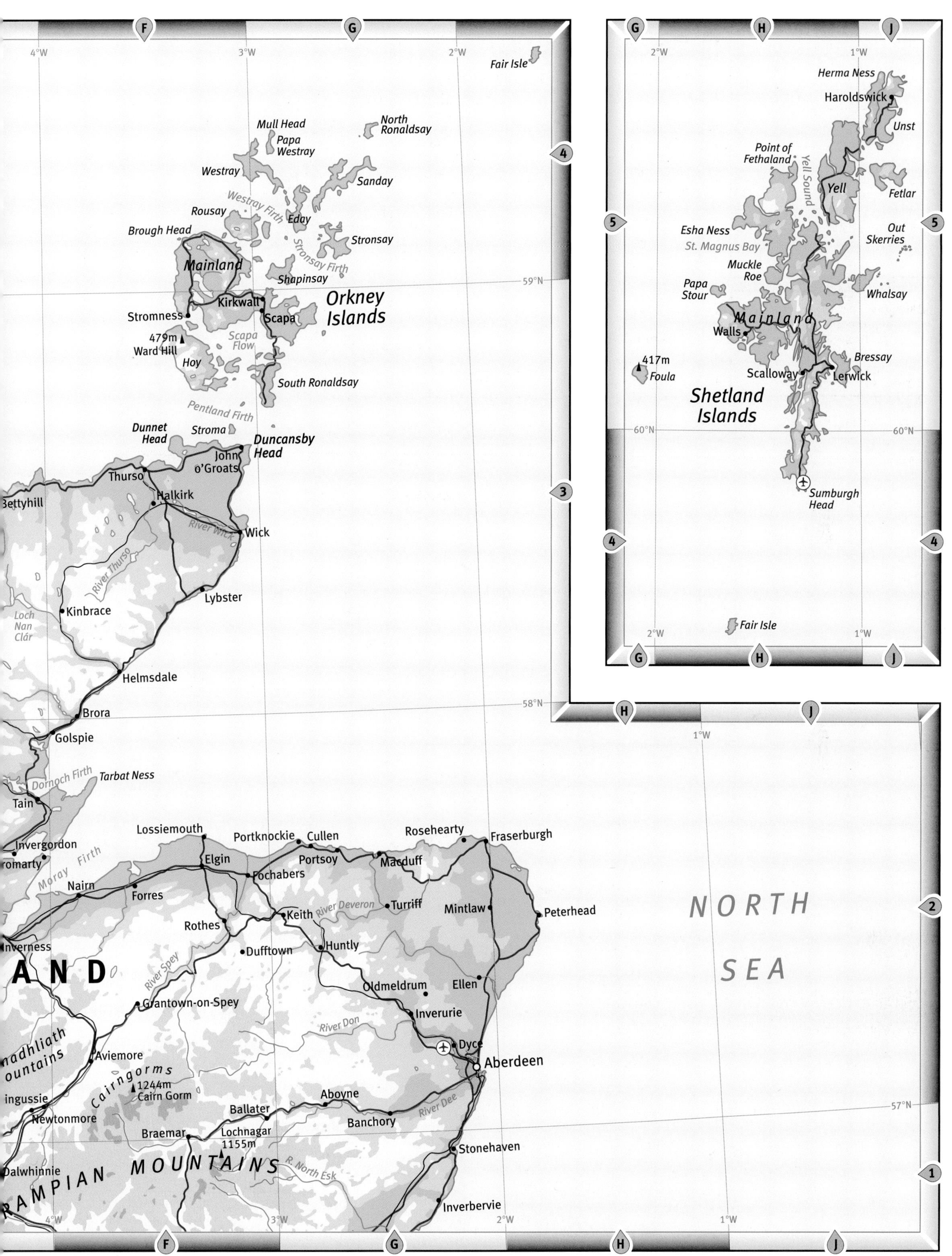
Fair Isle
Mull Head
North Ronaldsay
Papa Westray
Westray
Sanday
Westray Firth
Rousay
Eday
Brough Head
Stronsay
Stronsay Firth
Mainland
Shapinsay
Orkney Islands
Kirkwall
Stromness
Scapa
479m Ward Hill
Scapa Flow
Hoy
South Ronaldsay
Pentland Firth
Dunnet Head
Stroma
Duncansby Head
John o'Groats
Thurso
Bettyhill
Halkirk
River Wick
Wick
River Thurso
Lybster
Kinbrace
Loch Nan Clár
Helmsdale
Brora
Golspie
Dornoch Firth
Tarbat Ness
Tain
Invergordon
Cromarty
Moray Firth
Lossiemouth
Elgin
Portknockie
Cullen
Portsoy
Rosehearty
Fraserburgh
Macduff
Fochabers
Nairn
Forres
Turriff
River Deveron
Mintlaw
Peterhead
Keith
Rothes
Inverness
Dufftown
Huntly
AND
River Spey
Oldmeldrum
Ellen
Grantown-on-Spey
Inverurie
River Don
Dyce
Aviemore
Aberdeen
Monadhliath Mountains
Cairngorms
1244m Cairn Gorm
Kingussie
Aboyne
Ballater
Newtonmore
Banchory
River Dee
Braemar
Lochnagar 1155m
Stonehaven
Dalwhinnie
GRAMPIAN MOUNTAINS
R. North Esk
Inverbervie
NORTH SEA
Herma Ness
Haroldswick
Unst
Point of Fethaland
Yell Sound
Yell
Fetlar
Esha Ness
Out Skerries
St. Magnus Bay
Muckle Roe
Papa Stour
Whalsay
Mainland
Walls
417m Foula
Bressay
Scalloway
Lerwick
Shetland Islands
Sumburgh Head
Fair Isle
4°W
3°W
2°W
1°W
59°N
58°N
57°N
60°N
F
G
H
J
1
2
3
4
5

Northern Ireland and Southern Scotland

Scale One centimetre on the map represents 12.5 kilometres on the ground.

0 12.5 25 37.5km

SCOTLAND
NORTHERN IRELAND
GRAMPIAN MOUNTAINS
Fort William
Ben Nevis 1344m
Kinlochleven
Tobermory
Lochaline
Craignure
Oban
Tyndrum
Crianlarich
Inveraray
Furnace
Strachur
Lochgilphead
Helensburgh
Dumbarton
Greenock
Glasgow
Paisley
Clydebank
Dunoon
Rothesay
Tarbert
Kennacraig
Craighouse
Port Askaig
Port Ellen
Portnahaven
Campbeltown
Southend
Brodick
Lochranza
Arran
Islay
Jura
Mull
Kintyre
Largs
Ardrossan
Saltcoats
Irvine
Kilmarnock
Prestwick
Ayr
Maybole
Girvan
Ballantrae
Cairnryan
Stranraer
Glenluce
Newton Stewart
Wigtown
Whithorn
Drummore
Mull of Galloway
Malin Head
Inishowen Peninsula
Slieve Snaght 615m
Buncrana
Creeslough
Kilmacrenan
Letterkenny
Londonderry
Limavady
Coleraine
Portrush
Bushmills
Ballycastle
Ballymoney
Antrim Mountains
Carnlough
Larne
Ballymena
Antrim
Randalstown
Carrickfergus
Newtownabbey
Belfast
Bangor
Donaghadee
Newtownards
Lisburn
Lough Neagh
Cookstown
Magherafelt
Maghera
Dungiven
Strabane
Lifford
Ballybofey
Sperrin Mountains
Sawel 683m
Newtownstewart
Omagh
Donegal
Dungannon
Coalisland
Irvinestown
Enniskillen
Manorhamilton
Lisnaskea
Clones
Monaghan
Aughnacloy
Armagh
Portadown
Craigavon
Lurgan
Dromore
Banbridge
Newry
Warrenpoint
Newcastle
Slieve Donard 852m
Kilkeel
Downpatrick
Saintfield
Ards Peninsula
Strangford Lough
Belfast Lough
North Channel
Isle of Man
Ramsey
Snaefell 620m
Kirk Michael
Peel
Douglas
Castletown
Port Erin
Calf of Man

Transverse Mercator Projection

Key
international boundary
national boundary
motorway
main road
railway
main airport
river
canal
lake
towns
built-up area
largest towns
large towns
other towns
land height
above sea level in metres
more than 1000m
500 – 1000m
200 – 500m
100 – 200m
less than 100 metres
land below sea level
highest peaks with heights in metres
NORTH SEA
ENGLAND
UPLANDS
PENNINES
Pitlochry
Aberfeldy
Brechin
Montrose
Milton Ness
Kirriemuir
Forfar
Blairgowrie
Sidlaw Hills
Arbroath
Carnoustie
Dundee
Firth of Tay
Perth
Crieff
Leuchars
St. Andrews
Cupar
Auchterarder
Auchtermuchty
Loch Leven
Glenrothes
Anstruther
Ochil Hills
Kinross
Tillicoultry
Buckhaven
Cowdenbeath
Kirkcaldy
Alloa
Dunfermline
Firth of Forth
North Berwick
Grangemouth
Inverkeithing
Dunbar
Falkirk
Linlithgow
Edinburgh
Haddington
Musselburgh
St. Abb's Head
Bathgate
Livingston
Dalkeith
Lammermuir Hills
Eyemouth
Penicuik
Pentland Hills
Berwick-upon-Tweed
Duns
Wishaw
River Tweed
Holy Island
Lanark
Peebles
Galashiels
Coldstream
Biggar
Melrose
Bamburgh
Kelso
Broad Law 840m
Selkirk
Wooler
The Cheviot 815m
Jedburgh
R. Teviot
Alnwick
Hawick
R. Aln
Ettrick Water
Amble
Daer Reservoir
Peel Fell 602m
River Coquet
Moffat
Cheviot Hills
Ashington
River Esk
Kielder Water
R. North Tyne
R. Wansbeck
Blyth
Langholm
Liddell Water
Cramlington
Lockerbie
River Annan
Whitley Bay
Dumfries
Tynemouth
Newcastle upon Tyne
South Shields
Annan
R. Irthing
Gateshead
Dalbeattie
Brampton
Haltwhistle
Hexham
R. Tyne
Sunderland
Solway Firth
Carlisle
Consett
Washington
Houghton-le-Spring
River Eden
Chester-le-Street
Wigton
Peterlee
Durham
Cross Fell 893m
River Wear
Spennymoor
Hartlepool
Maryport
Bishop Auckland
Billingham
R. Derwent
Skiddaw 931m
Penrith
Redcar
Workington
Cockermouth
Mickle Fell 790m
River Tees
Newton Aycliffe
Stockton-on-Tees
Middlesbrough
Derwent Water
Keswick
Ullswater
Barnard Castle
Guisborough
Whitehaven
Helvellyn 950m
Appleby-in-Westmorland
Brough
Darlington
Thornaby-on-Tees
Whitby
St. Bees Head
R. Tees
Scafell Pike 978m
Lake District
Cleveland Hills
River Esk
Ambleside
Richmond
Seascale
Wast Water
Windermere
River Swale
Northallerton
North York Moors
Scarborough
Coniston Water
Kendal
Leyburn
Vale of York
Pickering
River Lune
Whernside 737m
River Ure
Thirsk
Filey
Vale of Pickering
Ulverston
R. Wharfe
Great Whernside 704m
Malton
Ingleborough 723m
693m Pen-y-Ghent
Ripon
Yorkshire Wolds
Bridlington
Barrow-in-Furness
Carnforth
River Aire
River Nidd
Haxby
Morecambe
Lancaster
Settle
Knaresborough
Great Driffield
Heysham
Ward's Stone 560m
Harrogate
York
3°W
2°W
1°W
56°N
55°N
54°N
E
F
G
H
1
2
3

A
B
C
D
E
1
2
3
4
5°W
4°W
3°W
6°W
54°N
53°N
52°N
IRISH SEA
Isle of Man
Port Erin
Castletown
Calf of Man
Warrenpoint
Kilkeel
Dundalk Bay
Balbriggan
Swords
Dublin
Dún Laoghaire
Bray
Wicklow
Arklow
Cahore Point
St. George's Channel
Barrow-in-Furness
Morecambe
Heysham
Carnforth
Lancaster
560m Ward's Stone
Fleetwood
Thornton
Blackpool
Preston
Lytham St. Anne's
Leyland
Southport
Formby
Skelmersdale
Wigan
Kirkby
St. Helens
Bootle
Wallasey
Liverpool
Birkenhead
Widnes
Runcorn
R. Mersey
River Dee
Ellesmere Port
Winsford
Chester
Nantwich
Wrexham
Ruabon
Chirk
Oswestry
Shrewsbury
The Wrekin
Wenlock Edge
Ludlow
Knighton
Kington
Hay-on-Wye
Black Mountains
Ross-on-Wye
Monmouth
R. Wye
River Severn
Chepstow
Newport
Cwmbran
Pontypool
Abertillery
Ebbw Vale
Abergavenny
Tredegar
Merthyr Tydfil
Mountain Ash
Aberdare
Rhondda
Gelligaer
Pontypridd
Caerphilly
Cardiff
Penarth
Barry
R. Taff
Bridgend
Porthcawl
Maesteg
Port Talbot
Neath
R. Neath
Swansea
Gower
Worms Head
Gorseinon
Pontardulais
Llanelli
Burry Port
Kidwelly
Cross Hands
Ammanford
Llandeilo
R. Tywi
Carmarthen
St. Clears
Carmarthen Bay
Saundersfoot
Tenby
Pembroke Dock
Pembroke
Milford Haven
St. Brides Bay
St. David's Head
Preseli Mountains
Fishguard
Newport
Strumble Head
Cemaes Head
Cardigan
River Teifi
Newcastle Emlyn
Lampeter
Aberaeron
New Quay
Aberystwyth
Cardigan Bay
Llandovery
Brecon
River Usk
886m
Brecon Beacons
Mynydd Eppynt
Builth Wells
Llandrindod Wells
Lake Brianne Reservoir
Claerwen Reservoir
Rhayader
Llanidloes
Newtown
Montgomery
Welshpool
R. Severn
Plynlimon 752m
Machynlleth
Tywyn
Cadair Idris 892m
R. Dyfi
Barmouth
Dolgellau
R. Vyrnwy
Lake Vyrnwy
Bala Lake
Bala
Harlech
Blaenau Ffestiniog
Porthmadog
Pwllheli
Lleyn Peninsula
Bardsey Island
Corwen
R. Dee
Llangollen
Caernarfon Bay
Snowdon 1085m
Betws-y-Coed
Llanrwst
Lake Brenig
Ruthin
Mold
R. Clwyd
Denbigh
Connah's Quay
Flint
Holywell
Rhyl
Prestatyn
Colwyn Bay
Llandudno
Conwy
R. Conwy
Bangor
Bethesda
Caernarfon
Menai Bridge
Llangefni
Anglesey
Holyhead
Holy Island
Carmel Head
Amlwch
WALES
CAMBRIAN MOUNTAINS
Bristol Channel
Weston-super-Mare
Clevedon
Bristol

Transverse Mercator Projection

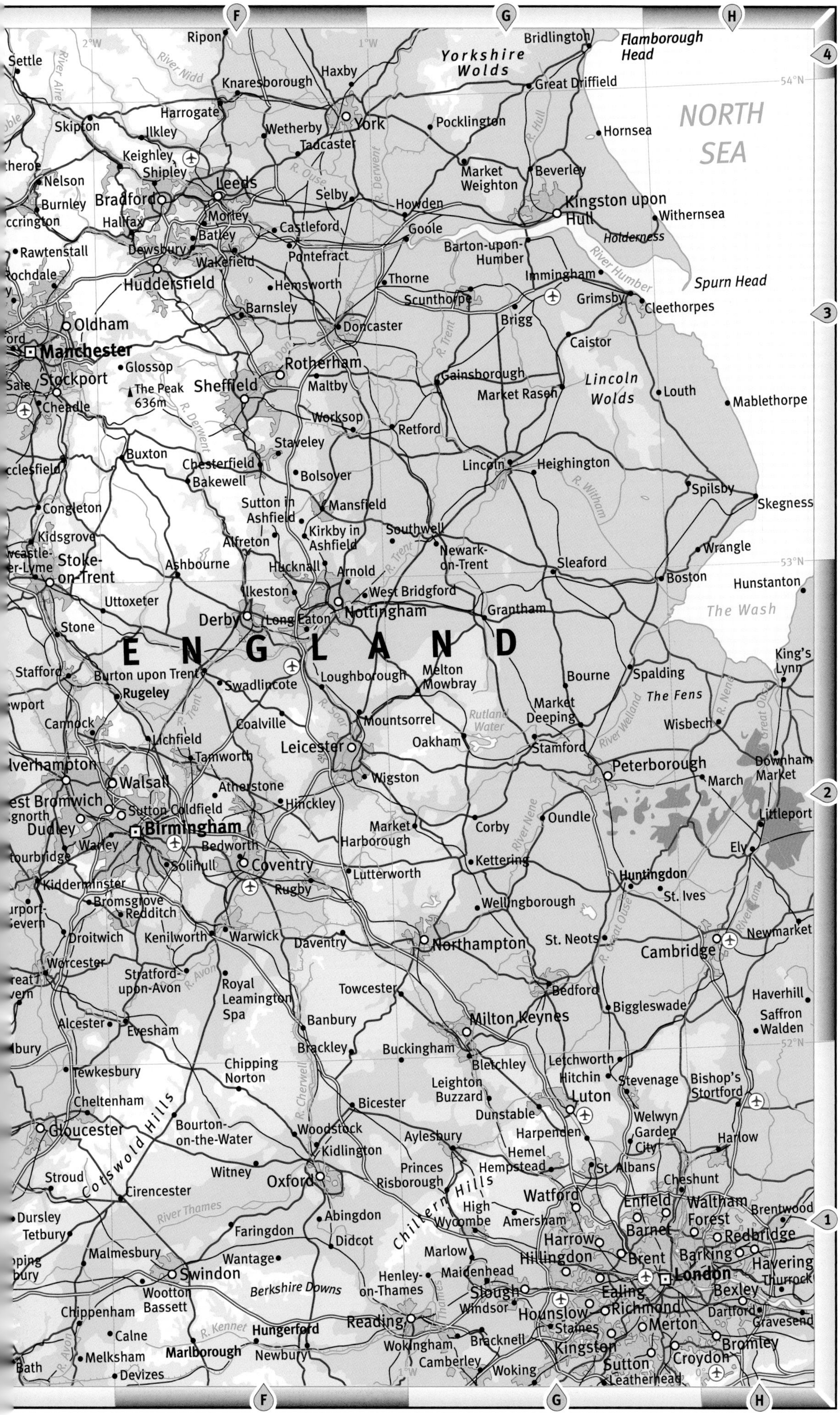

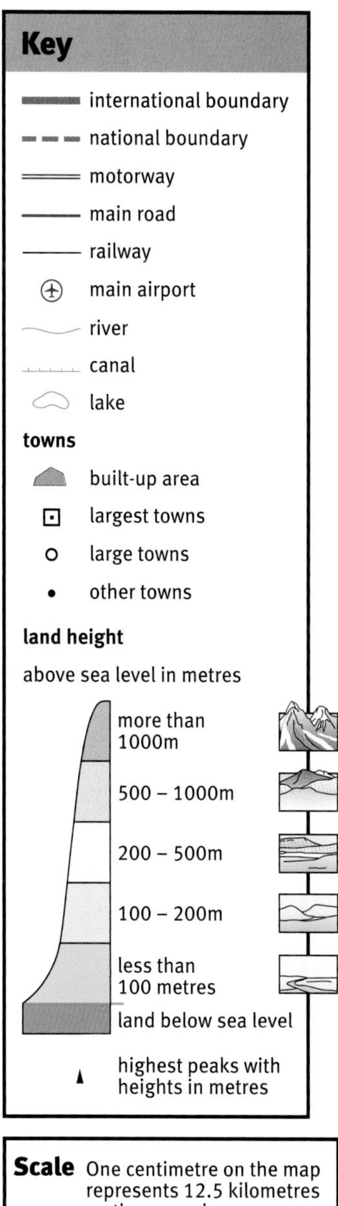
Key
international boundary
national boundary
motorway
main road
railway
main airport
river
canal
lake
towns
built-up area
largest towns
large towns
other towns
land height
above sea level in metres
more than 1000m
500 – 1000m
200 – 500m
100 – 200m
less than 100 metres
land below sea level
highest peaks with heights in metres

Scale One centimetre on the map represents 12.5 kilometres on the ground.

0 12.5 25 37.5km

South East England

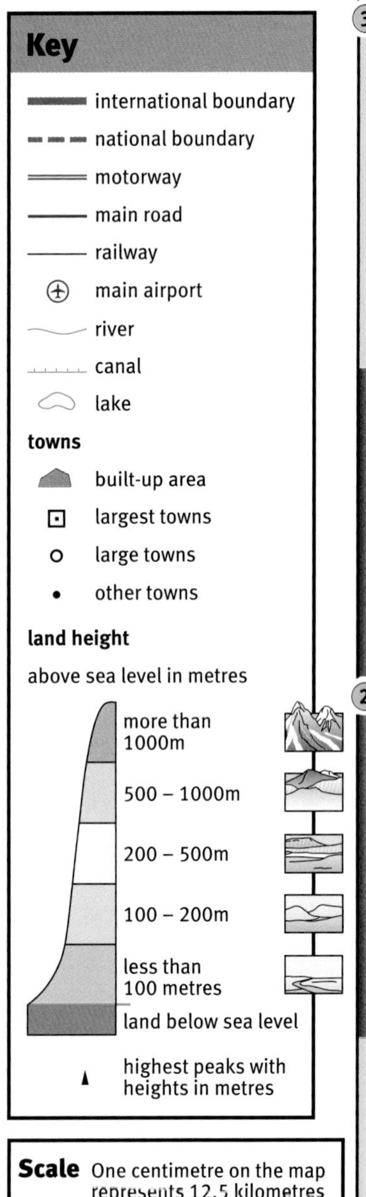

Key
international boundary
national boundary
motorway
main road
railway
main airport
river
canal
lake
towns
built-up area
largest towns
large towns
other towns
land height
above sea level in metres
more than 1000m
500 – 1000m
200 – 500m
100 – 200m
less than 100 metres
land below sea level
highest peaks with heights in metres

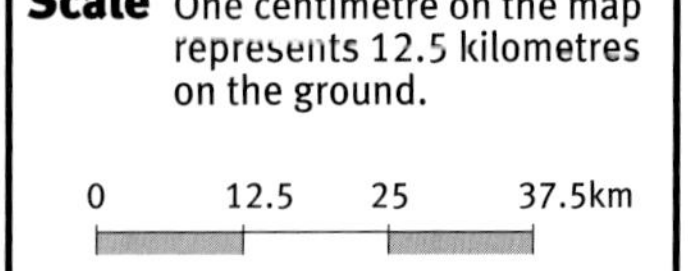

Scale One centimetre on the map represents 12.5 kilometres on the ground.
0
12.5
25
37.5km

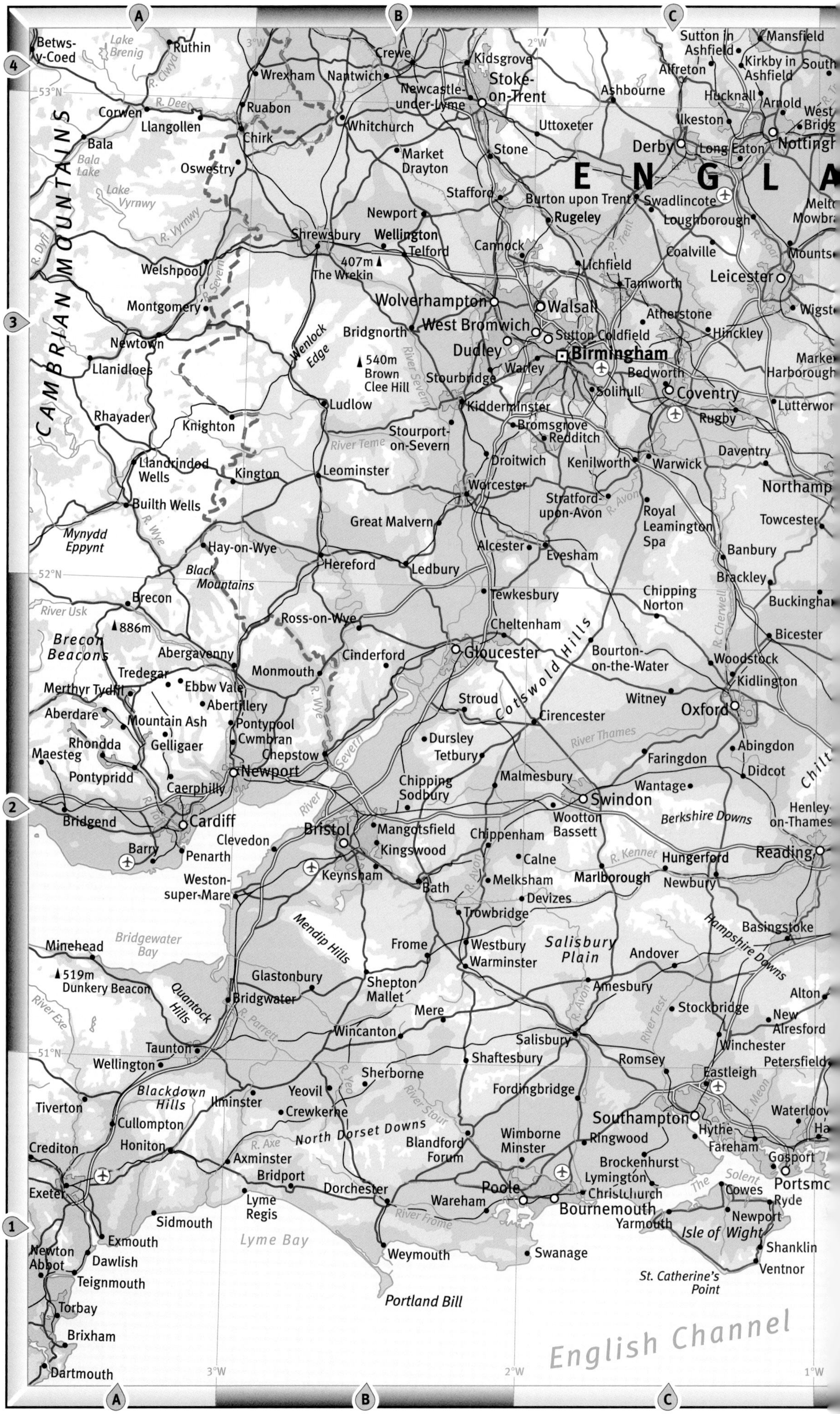

A
B
C
4
3
2
1
53°N
52°N
51°N
3°W
2°W
1°W
Betws-y-Coed
Lake Brenig
Ruthin
R. Clwyd
Wrexham
Nantwich
Crewe
Kidsgrove
Stoke-on-Trent
Newcastle-under-Lyme
Sutton in Ashfield
Mansfield
Kirkby in Ashfield
Alfreton
Ashbourne
Hucknall
Arnold
Corwen
R. Dee
Llangollen
Ruabon
Whitchurch
Uttoxeter
Ilkeston
Nottingh
Bala
Bala Lake
Chirk
Oswestry
Market Drayton
Stone
Derby
Long Eaton
CAMBRIAN MOUNTAINS
Lake Vyrnwy
R. Vyrnwy
Stafford
Burton upon Trent
Swadlincote
E N G L A
Newport
Rugeley
Loughborough
Shrewsbury
Wellington
Telford
Cannock
R. Trent
Coalville
407m
The Wrekin
Lichfield
Tamworth
Leicester
R. Dyfi
Welshpool
R. Severn
Montgomery
Wolverhampton
Walsall
Atherstone
Wenlock Edge
Bridgnorth
West Bromwich
Sutton Coldfield
Hinckley
Newtown
540m Brown Clee Hill
River Severn
Dudley
Birmingham
Llanidloes
Stourbridge
Warley
Bedworth
Solihull
Coventry
Ludlow
Kidderminster
Lutterworth
Rhayader
Knighton
Bromsgrove
Redditch
Rugby
River Teme
Stourport-on-Severn
Daventry
Llandrindod Wells
Kington
Leominster
Droitwich
Kenilworth
Warwick
Worcester
Northamp
Builth Wells
Stratford-upon-Avon
R. Avon
Royal Leamington Spa
R. Wye
Great Malvern
Towcester
Mynydd Eppynt
Hay-on-Wye
Alcester
Evesham
Banbury
Black Mountains
Hereford
Ledbury
Brackley
Tewkesbury
Chipping Norton
Brecon
River Usk
886m
Ross-on-Wye
Cheltenham
Buckingha
Brecon Beacons
Abergavenny
Cinderford
Gloucester
Bourton-on-the-Water
Bicester
Tredegar
Monmouth
Cotswold Hills
R. Cherwell
Woodstock
Merthyr Tydfil
Ebbw Vale
Kidlington
Abertillery
Stroud
Witney
Aberdare
Mountain Ash
Pontypool
Cirencester
Oxford
Rhondda
Gelligaer
Cwmbran
Dursley
River Thames
Abingdon
Maesteg
Chepstow
Tetbury
Faringdon
Pontypridd
Newport
Chipping Sodbury
Malmesbury
Wantage
Didcot
Caerphilly
Swindon
Henley-on-Thames
Bridgend
Cardiff
Bristol
Mangotsfield
Wootton Bassett
Berkshire Downs
Barry
Clevedon
Kingswood
Chippenham
Penarth
Calne
R. Kennet
Hungerford
Reading
Keynsham
Marlborough
Newbury
Weston-super-Mare
Bath
Melksham
Devizes
Trowbridge
Hampshire Downs
Basingstoke
Minehead
Bridgewater Bay
Mendip Hills
Frome
Westbury
Warminster
Salisbury Plain
Andover
519m Dunkery Beacon
Glastonbury
Shepton Mallet
Quantock Hills
Bridgwater
R. Parrett
Amesbury
Alton
River Exe
Mere
Stockbridge
New Alresford
Wincanton
River Test
Taunton
Salisbury
Winchester
Wellington
Shaftesbury
Romsey
Petersfield
Sherborne
R. Yeo
Eastleigh
Blackdown Hills
Yeovil
Fordingbridge
Tiverton
Ilminster
Crewkerne
River Stour
Southampton
Waterlooville
Cullompton
North Dorset Downs
Hythe
Crediton
Honiton
R. Axe
Wimborne Minster
Ringwood
Fareham
Axminster
Blandford Forum
Brockenhurst
Gosport
Bridport
Lymington
The Solent
Cowes
Portsmo
Exeter
Dorchester
Poole
Christchurch
Ryde
Lyme Regis
Wareham
Bournemouth
Newport
River Frome
Yarmouth
Sidmouth
Isle of Wight
Lyme Bay
Exmouth
Weymouth
Swanage
Shanklin
Newton Abbot
Dawlish
Ventnor
Teignmouth
St. Catherine's Point
Torbay
Portland Bill
Brixham
English Channel
Dartmouth

Transverse Mercator Projection

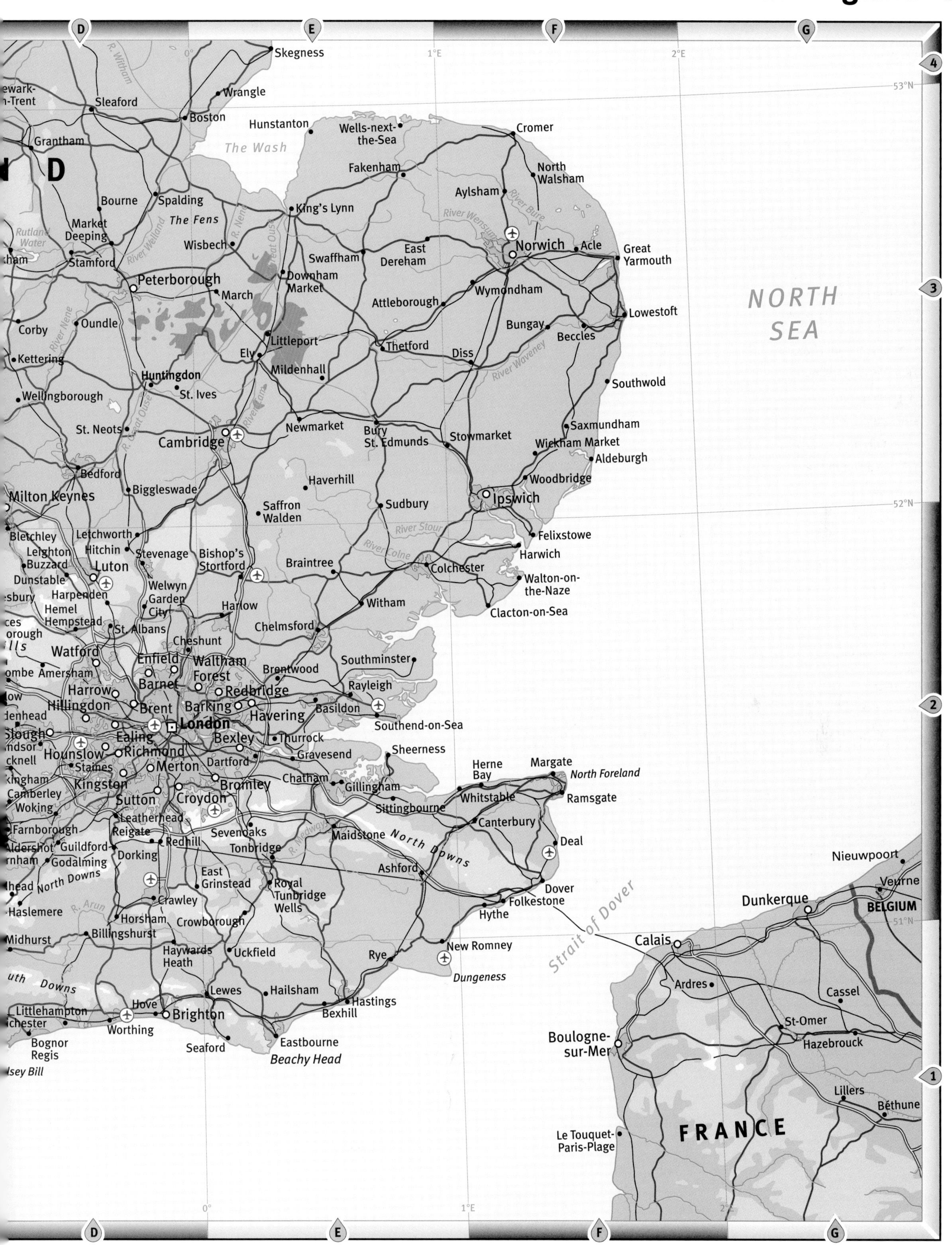
D
E
F
G
4
3
2
1
0°
1°E
2°E
53°N
52°N
51°N
Skegness
Wrangle
Sleaford
Boston
Grantham
Hunstanton
Wells-next-the-Sea
Cromer
The Wash
Fakenham
North Walsham
Aylsham
River Bure
Bourne
Spalding
King's Lynn
River Wensum
Rutland Water
Market Deeping
The Fens
Wisbech
River Welland
R. Nene
Great Ouse
Stamford
Swaffham
East Dereham
Norwich
Acle
Great Yarmouth
Peterborough
Downham Market
March
Attleborough
Wymondham
NORTH SEA
Lowestoft
Corby
Oundle
River Nene
Littleport
Bungay
Beccles
Thetford
Diss
River Waveney
Kettering
Ely
Mildenhall
Huntingdon
St. Ives
Southwold
Wellingborough
River Great Ouse
River Cam
Newmarket
Bury St. Edmunds
Stowmarket
Saxmundham
St. Neots
Cambridge
Wickham Market
Aldeburgh
Bedford
Haverhill
Woodbridge
Milton Keynes
Biggleswade
Ipswich
Saffron Walden
Sudbury
Bletchley
Letchworth
River Stour
Felixstowe
Leighton Buzzard
Hitchin
Stevenage
Bishop's Stortford
River Colne
Harwich
Luton
Braintree
Colchester
Dunstable
Walton-on-the-Naze
Harpenden
Welwyn Garden City
Hemel Hempstead
Harlow
Witham
Clacton-on-Sea
St. Albans
Chelmsford
Cheshunt
Watford
Enfield
Waltham Forest
Southminster
Amersham
Barnet
Brentwood
Harrow
Redbridge
Rayleigh
Hillingdon
Brent
Barking
Havering
Basildon
Southend-on-Sea
London
Ealing
Bexley
Thurrock
Hounslow
Richmond
Gravesend
Sheerness
Staines
Merton
Dartford
Herne Bay
Margate
North Foreland
Kingston
Bromley
Chatham
Gillingham
Camberley
Woking
Sutton
Croydon
Whitstable
Ramsgate
Sittingbourne
Leatherhead
Canterbury
Farnborough
Reigate
Sevenoaks
R. Medway
Maidstone
North Downs
Deal
Guildford
Redhill
Tonbridge
Dorking
Godalming
Ashford
Nieuwpoort
North Downs
East Grinstead
Royal Tunbridge Wells
Dover
Veurne
Crawley
Folkestone
Dunkerque
BELGIUM
Haslemere
R. Arun
Hythe
Strait of Dover
Horsham
Crowborough
Midhurst
Billingshurst
Calais
Haywards Heath
Uckfield
New Romney
Rye
Dungeness
Ardres
Cassel
Lewes
Hailsham
Hove
Hastings
Littlehampton
Brighton
Bexhill
St-Omer
Worthing
Boulogne-sur-Mer
Hazebrouck
Bognor Regis
Seaford
Eastbourne
Beachy Head
Lillers
Béthune
Le Touquet-Paris-Plage
FRANCE

South West England

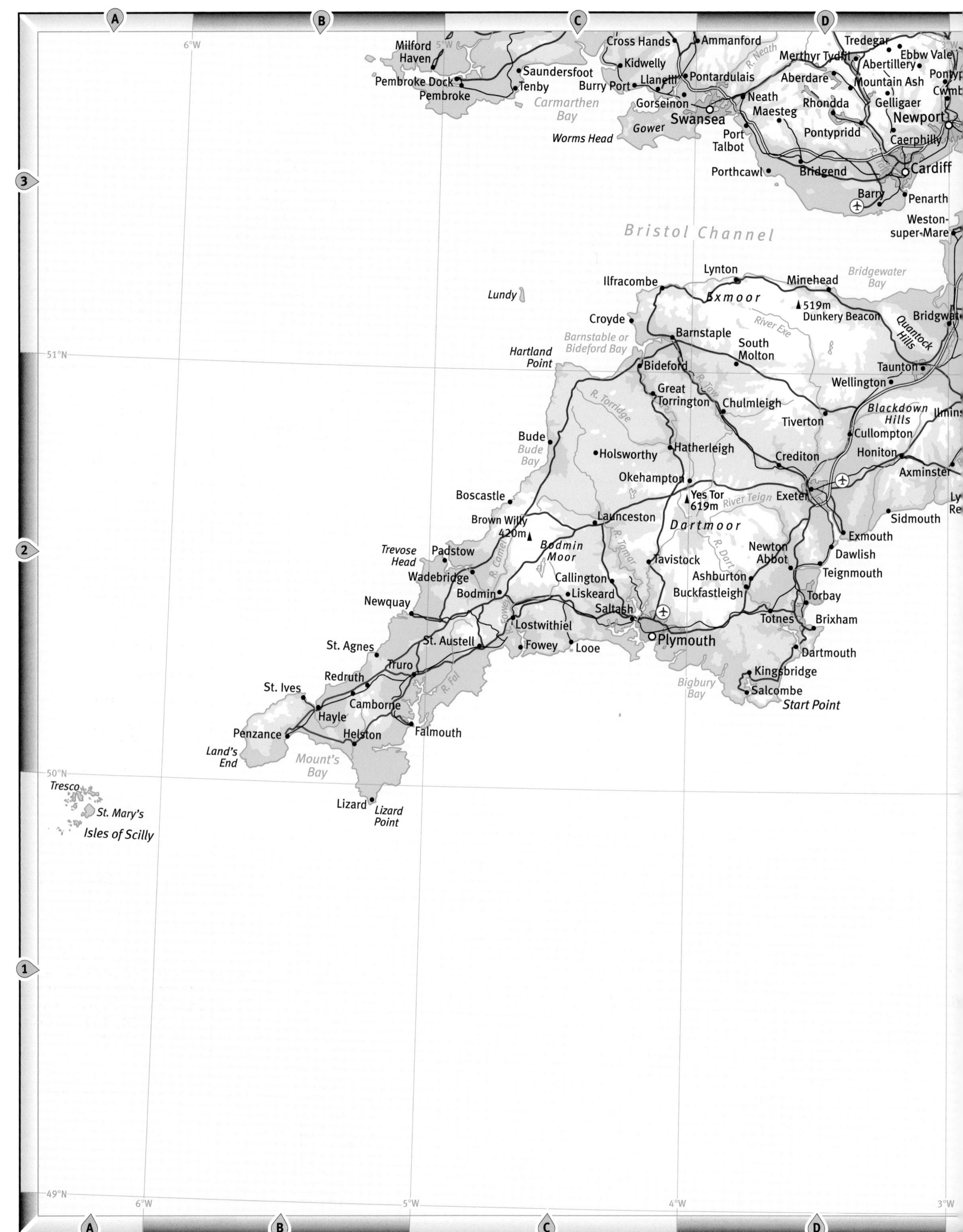

Milford Haven
Pembroke Dock
Pembroke
Saundersfoot
Tenby
Carmarthen Bay
Cross Hands
Ammanford
Kidwelly
Llanelli
Pontardulais
Burry Port
Gorseinon
Swansea
Gower
Worms Head
Port Talbot
Neath
Maesteg
Merthyr Tydfil
Aberdare
Rhondda
Pontypridd
Tredegar
Ebbw Vale
Abertillery
Mountain Ash
Gelligaer
Newport
Caerphilly
Cardiff
Porthcawl
Bridgend
Barry
Penarth
Weston-super-Mare
Bristol Channel
Lundy
Ilfracombe
Lynton
Minehead
Bridgewater Bay
Exmoor
519m Dunkery Beacon
Quantock Hills
Croyde
Barnstaple
River Exe
South Molton
Barnstable or Bideford Bay
Hartland Point
Bideford
Great Torrington
Chulmleigh
R. Torridge
R. Taw
Taunton
Wellington
Blackdown Hills
Tiverton
Cullompton
Honiton
Axminster
Bude
Bude Bay
Holsworthy
Hatherleigh
Crediton
Okehampton
Exeter
Yes Tor 619m
River Teign
Boscastle
Brown Willy 420m
Launceston
Dartmoor
Sidmouth
Exmouth
Trevose Head
Padstow
Bodmin Moor
R. Camel
R. Tamar
R. Dart
Tavistock
Newton Abbot
Dawlish
Teignmouth
Wadebridge
Callington
Ashburton
Bodmin
Liskeard
Buckfastleigh
Torbay
Newquay
Saltash
Lostwithiel
Totnes
Brixham
Plymouth
St. Austell
Fowey
Looe
Dartmouth
St. Agnes
Truro
Redruth
R. Fal
Kingsbridge
Salcombe
Start Point
Bigbury Bay
St. Ives
Camborne
Hayle
Penzance
Helston
Falmouth
Land's End
Mount's Bay
Lizard
Lizard Point
Tresco
St. Mary's
Isles of Scilly
51°N
50°N
49°N
6°W
5°W
4°W
3°W
A
B
C
D
1
2
3

Transverse Mercator Projection

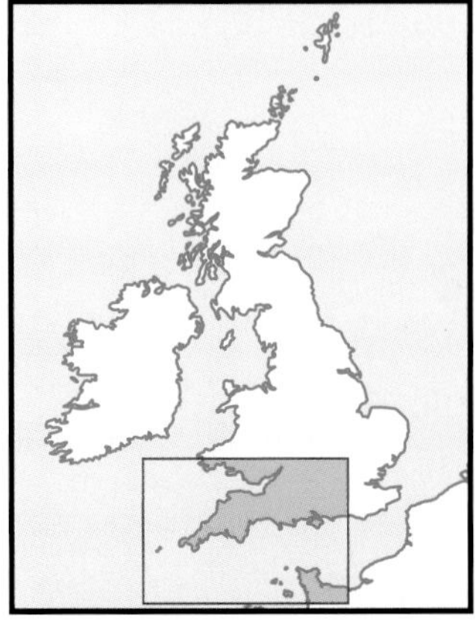

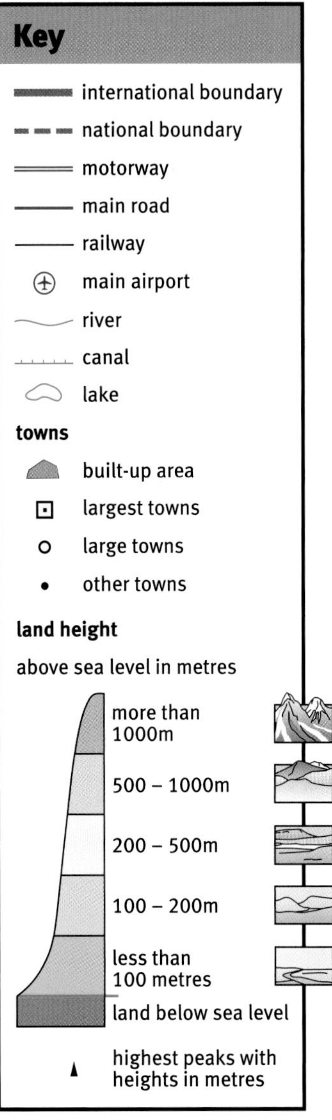
Key
international boundary
national boundary
motorway
main road
railway
main airport
river
canal
lake
towns
built-up area
largest towns
large towns
other towns
land height
above sea level in metres
more than 1000m
500 – 1000m
200 – 500m
100 – 200m
less than 100 metres
land below sea level
highest peaks with heights in metres

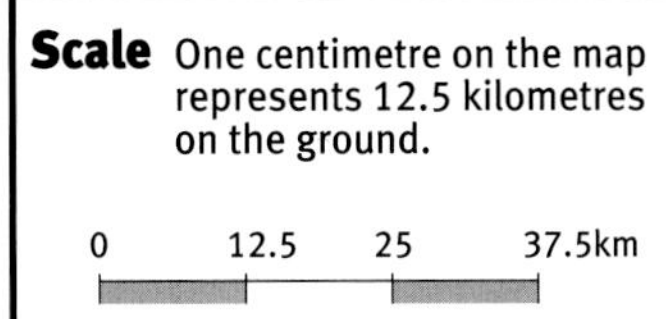
Scale One centimetre on the map represents 12.5 kilometres on the ground.
0
12.5
25
37.5km

Highest mountains
few places in Britain are more than 1000 metres high
Mountains
steep rocky places
Moors and uplands
high windswept places with heather and rough grass
Hills
smooth slopes and gentle valleys
Low land
flat marshy land with wide rivers

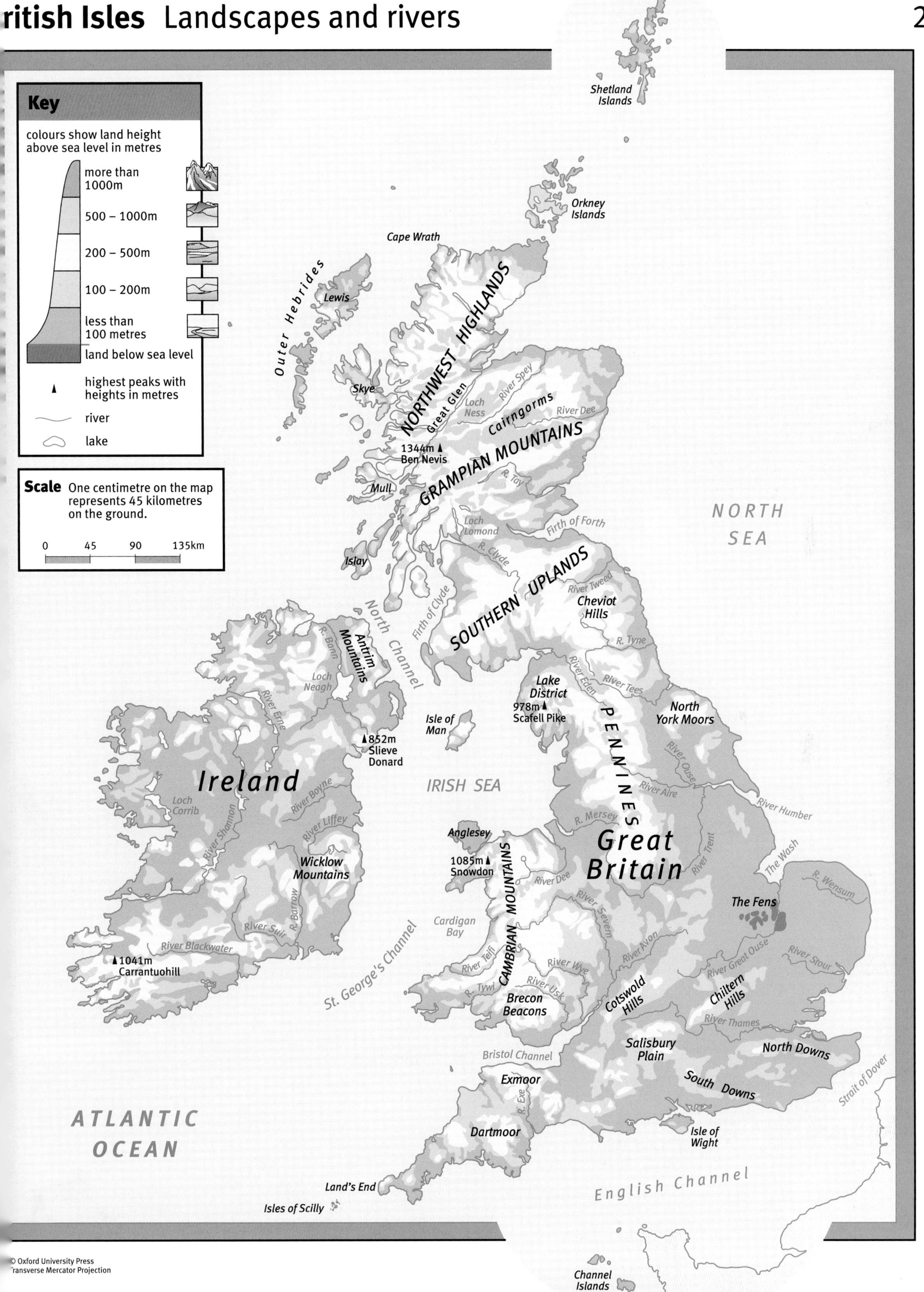
Key
colours show land height above sea level in metres
more than 1000m
500 – 1000m
200 – 500m
100 – 200m
less than 100 metres
land below sea level
highest peaks with heights in metres
river
lake
Scale One centimetre on the map represents 45 kilometres on the ground.
0
45
90
135km
Shetland Islands
Orkney Islands
Cape Wrath
Outer Hebrides
Lewis
Skye
NORTHWEST HIGHLANDS
Great Glen
Loch Ness
River Spey
Cairngorms
River Dee
GRAMPIAN MOUNTAINS
1344m Ben Nevis
Mull
R. Tay
Loch Lomond
Firth of Forth
NORTH SEA
Islay
R. Clyde
SOUTHERN UPLANDS
River Tweed
Cheviot Hills
Firth of Clyde
North Channel
R. Bann
Antrim Mountains
Loch Neagh
R. Tyne
River Eden
River Tees
Lake District
978m Scafell Pike
PENNINES
North York Moors
River Erne
Isle of Man
852m Slieve Donard
River Ouse
Ireland
IRISH SEA
River Aire
River Humber
Loch Corrib
River Boyne
River Liffey
River Shannon
R. Mersey
Anglesey
Great Britain
River Trent
The Wash
R. Wensum
Wicklow Mountains
1085m Snowdon
CAMBRIAN MOUNTAINS
River Dee
River Severn
The Fens
R. Barrow
River Suir
Cardigan Bay
St. George's Channel
River Blackwater
1041m Carrantuohill
River Teifi
R. Tywi
River Wye
River Usk
River Avon
River Great Ouse
River Stour
Brecon Beacons
Cotswold Hills
Chiltern Hills
River Thames
Salisbury Plain
North Downs
Bristol Channel
Exmoor
South Downs
Strait of Dover
ATLANTIC OCEAN
R. Exe
Dartmoor
Isle of Wight
Land's End
Isles of Scilly
English Channel
Channel Islands

Transverse Mercator Projection

British Isles Weather and climate

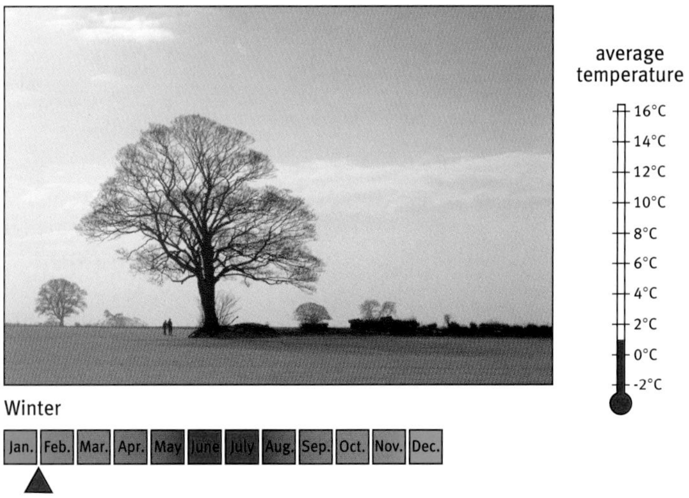

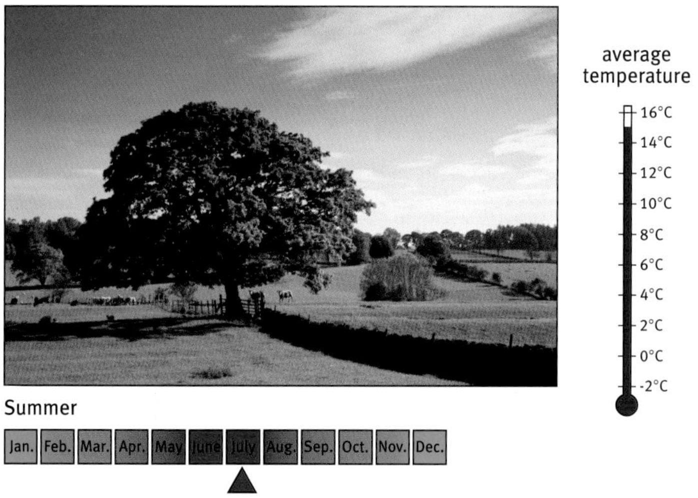

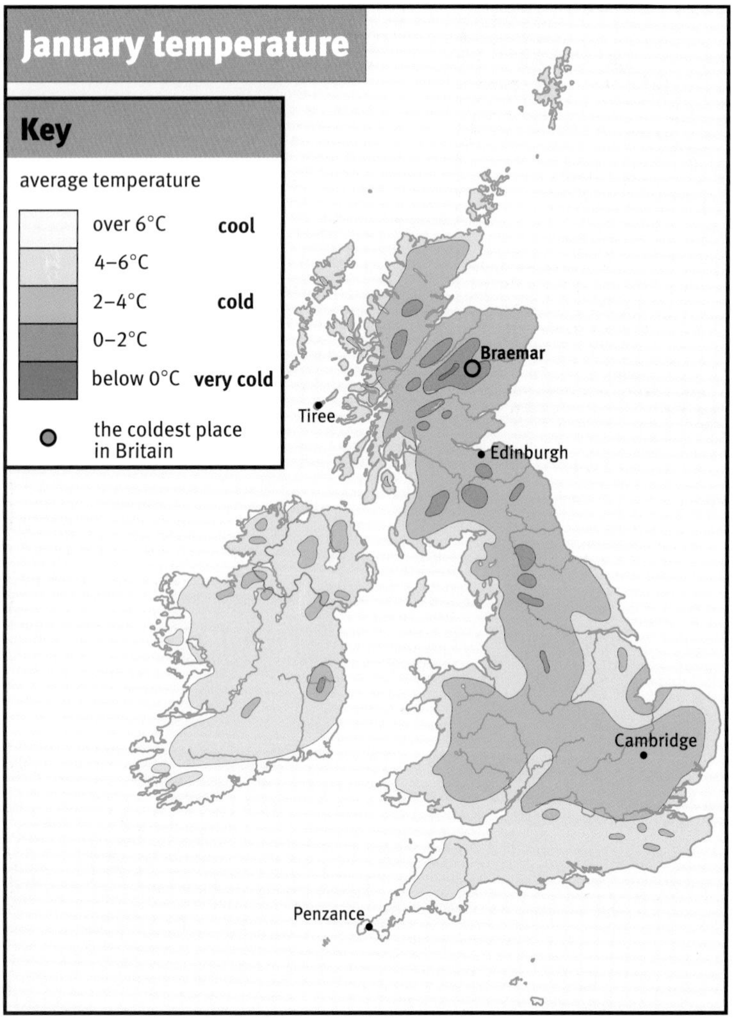

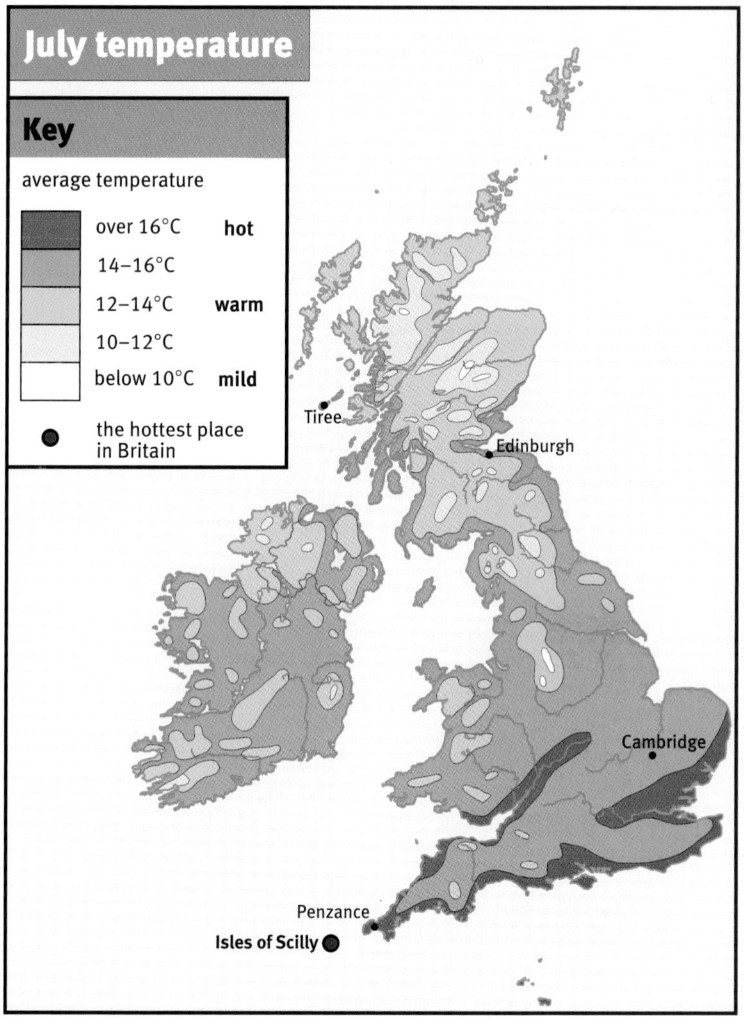

Winter

average temperature

16°C
14°C
12°C
10°C
8°C
6°C
4°C
2°C
0°C
-2°C

Jan. Feb. Mar. Apr. May June July Aug. Sep. Oct. Nov. Dec.

Summer

average temperature

16°C
14°C
12°C
10°C
8°C
6°C
4°C
2°C
0°C
-2°C

Jan. Feb. Mar. Apr. May June July Aug. Sep. Oct. Nov. Dec.

January temperature

Key

average temperature

	over 6°C	**cool**
	4–6°C	
	2–4°C	**cold**
	0–2°C	
	below 0°C	**very cold**

the coldest place in Britain

Braemar
Tiree
Edinburgh
Cambridge
Penzance

July temperature

Key

average temperature

	over 16°C	**hot**
	14–16°C	
	12–14°C	**warm**
	10–12°C	
	below 10°C	**mild**

the hottest place in Britain

Tiree
Edinburgh
Cambridge
Penzance
Isles of Scilly

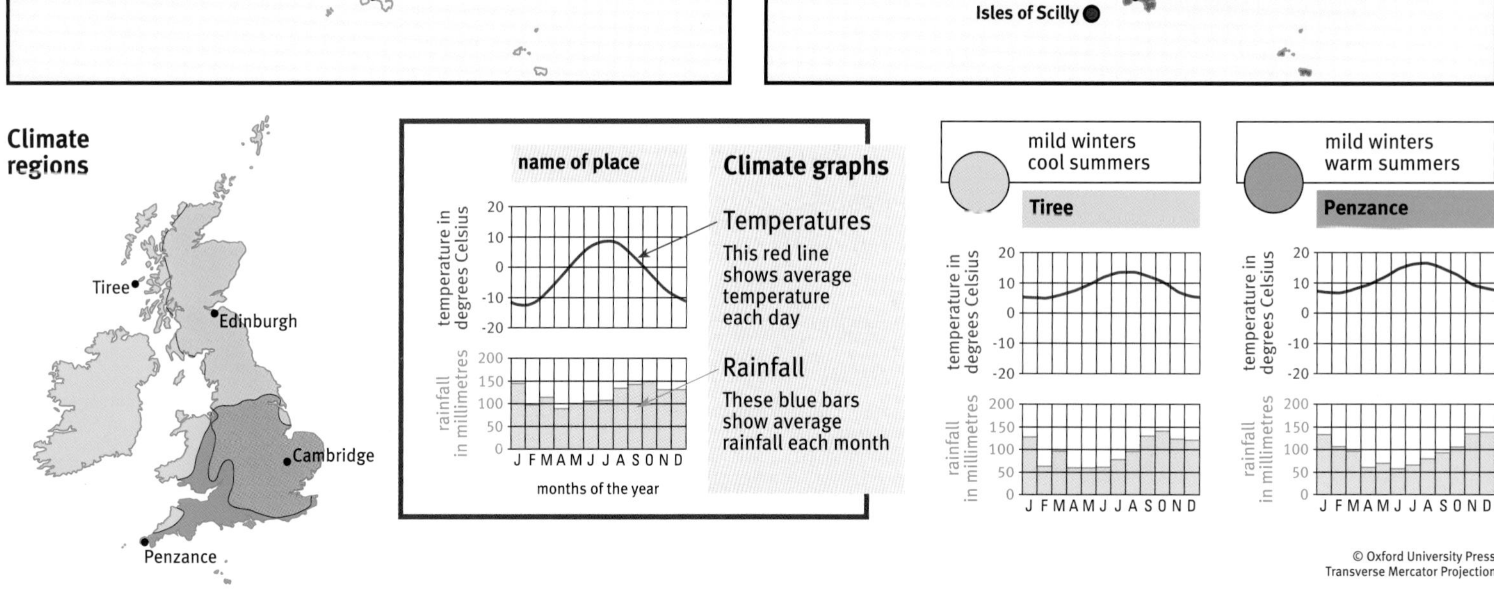

Climate regions
Tiree
Edinburgh
Cambridge
Penzance
name of place
Climate graphs
temperature in degrees Celsius
20
10
0
-10
-20
Temperatures
This red line shows average temperature each day
rainfall in millimetres
200
150
100
50
0
Rainfall
These blue bars show average rainfall each month
J F M A M J J A S O N D
months of the year
mild winters cool summers
Tiree
mild winters warm summers
Penzance

Transverse Mercator Projection

Jan.
Feb.
Mar.
Apr.
May
June
July
Aug.
Sep.
Oct.
Nov.
Dec.

average rainfall
very wet
2400mm
2200mm
quite wet
2000mm
1800mm
1600mm
wet
1400mm
1200mm
1000mm
quite dry
800mm
600mm
very dry
400mm
200mm
Wet winds from the west rise and cool to give rain and snow. Mountains are the wettest places in the British Isles.
West is wetter
East is drier

Annual rainfall

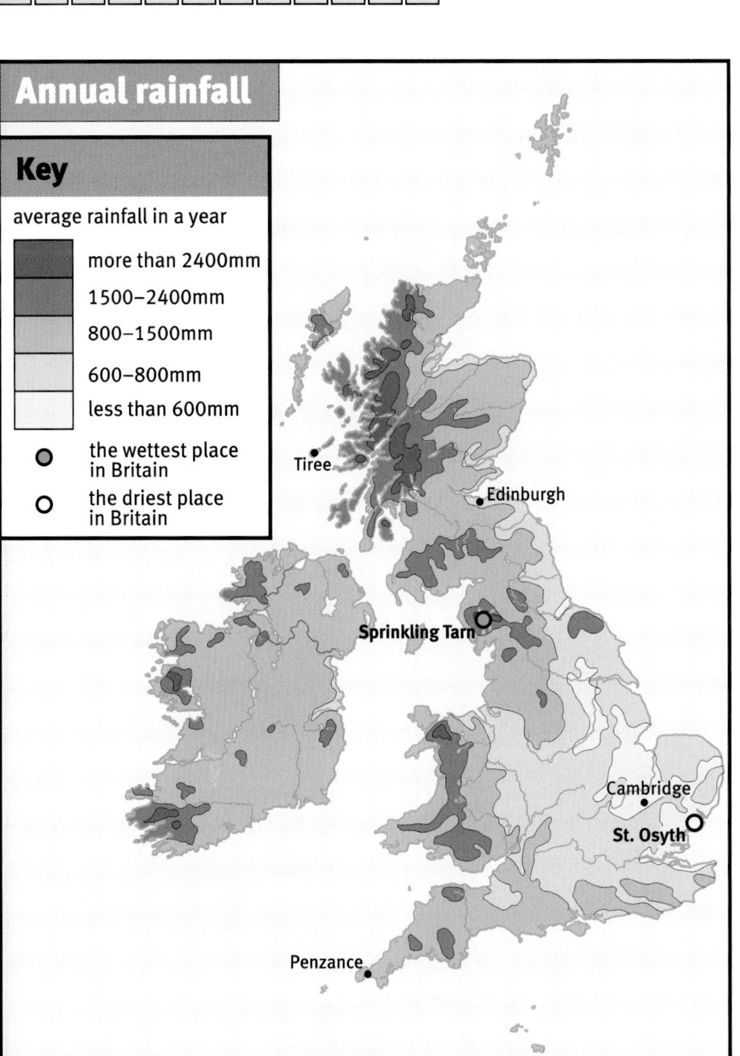
Key
average rainfall in a year
more than 2400mm
1500–2400mm
800–1500mm
600–800mm
less than 600mm
the wettest place in Britain
the driest place in Britain
Tiree
Edinburgh
Sprinkling Tarn
Cambridge
St. Osyth
Penzance

Water supply

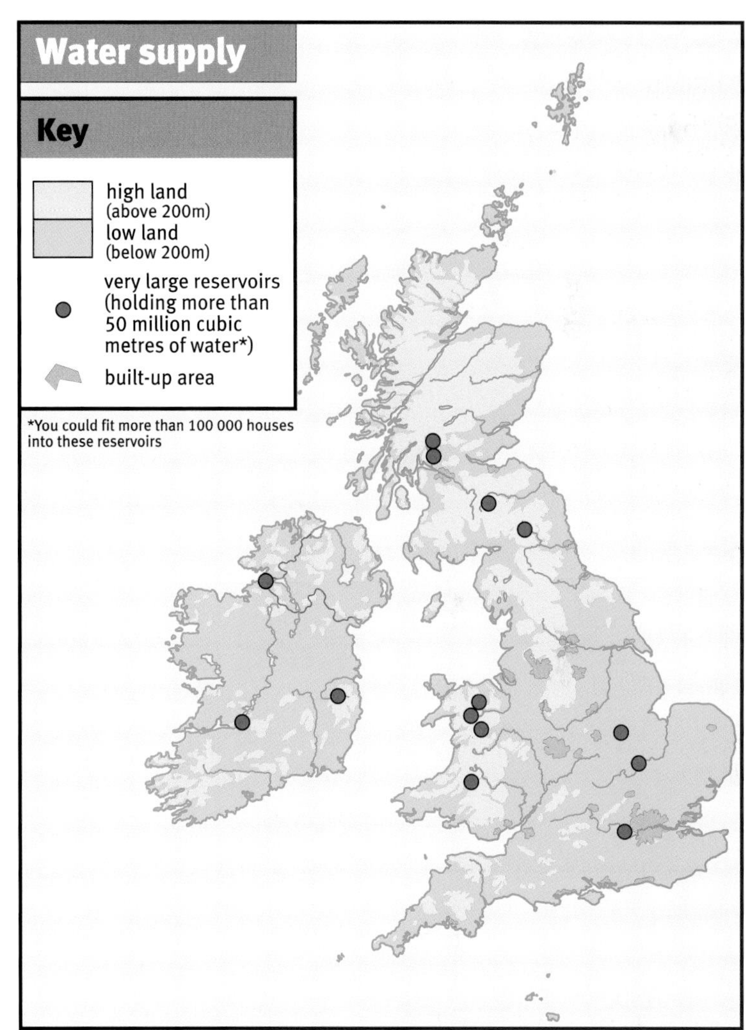
Key
high land (above 200m)
low land (below 200m)
very large reservoirs (holding more than 50 million cubic metres of water*)
built-up area
*You could fit more than 100 000 houses into these reservoirs

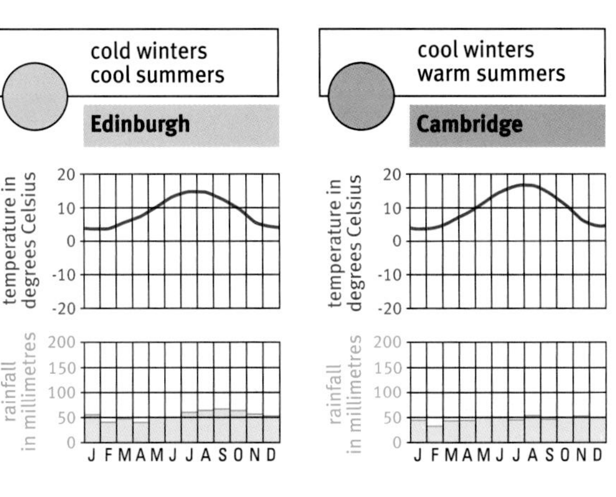
cold winters
cool summers
Edinburgh
cool winters
warm summers
Cambridge
temperature in degrees Celsius
20
10
0
-10
-20
rainfall in millimetres
200
150
100
50
0
J F M A M J J A S O N D

The water cycle

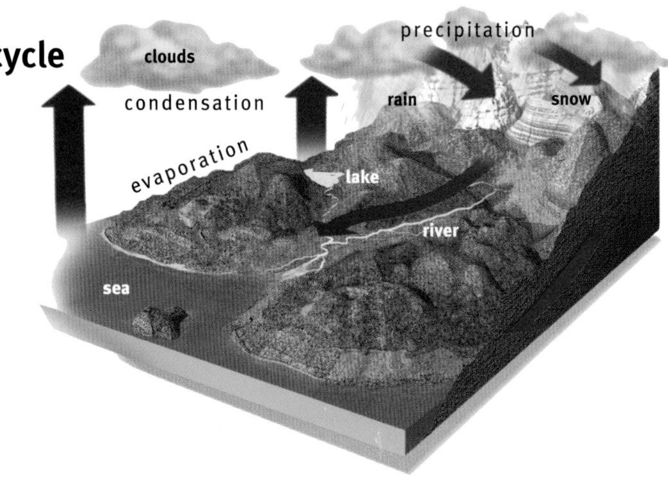
clouds
condensation
precipitation
rain
snow
evaporation
lake
river
sea

Transverse Mercator Projection

United Kingdom People and settlements

Cities and towns

People live in settlements of different sizes

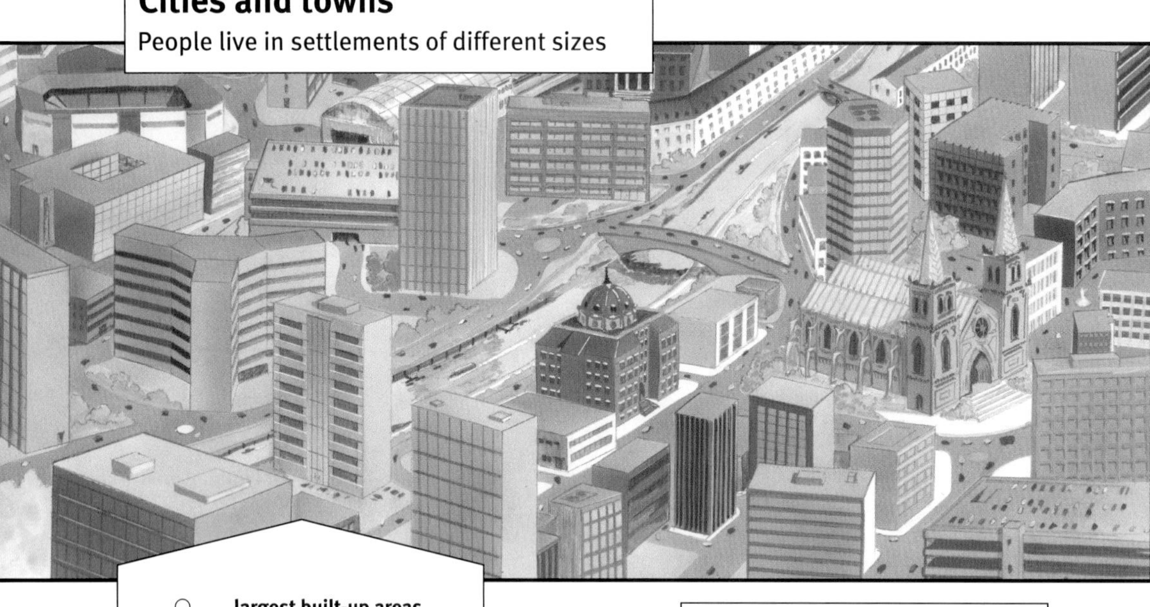

○ **largest built-up areas**
over 400 000 people

◉ **largest towns**
100 000 – 400 000 people

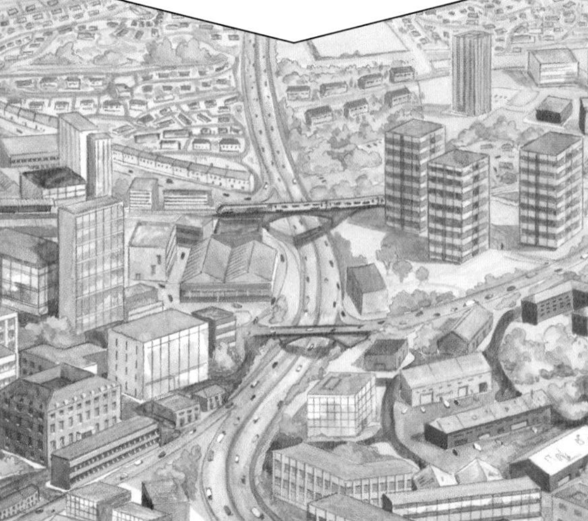

• **large towns**
25 000 – 100 000

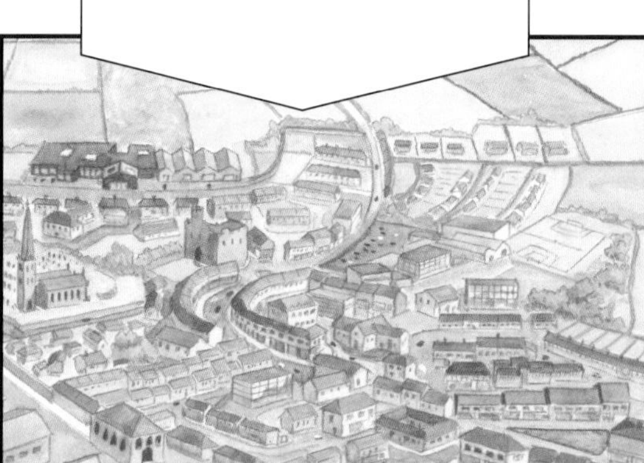

small towns and villages
under 25 000 people
(not shown on the map)

Population density

The number of people that live in an area

very crowded
over 250 people living in a square kilometre

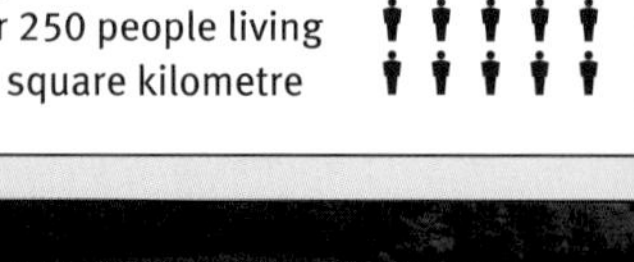

quite crowded
50 – 250 people living in a square kilometre

quite empty
under 50 people living in a square kilometre

Where people live

If there were 100 people in the United Kingdom, this is where they would live:

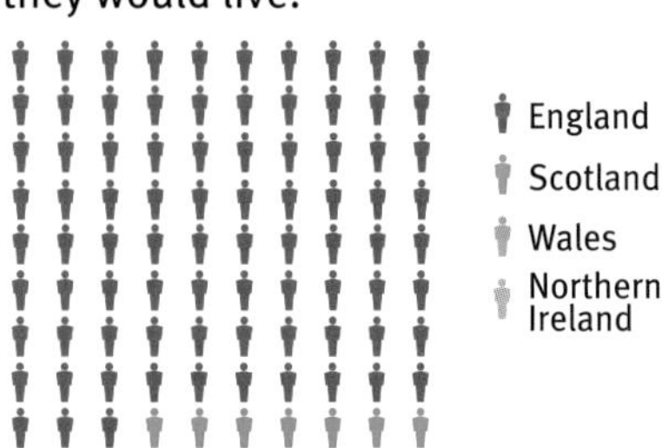

England
Scotland
Wales
Northern Ireland

Population pyramid

If there were 100 people in the United Kingdom, this is how old they would be:

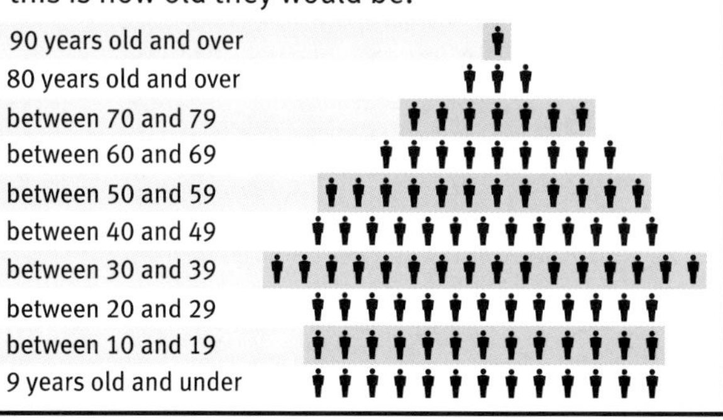

90 years old and over
80 years old and over
between 70 and 79
between 60 and 69
between 50 and 59
between 40 and 49
between 30 and 39
between 20 and 29
between 10 and 19
9 years old and under

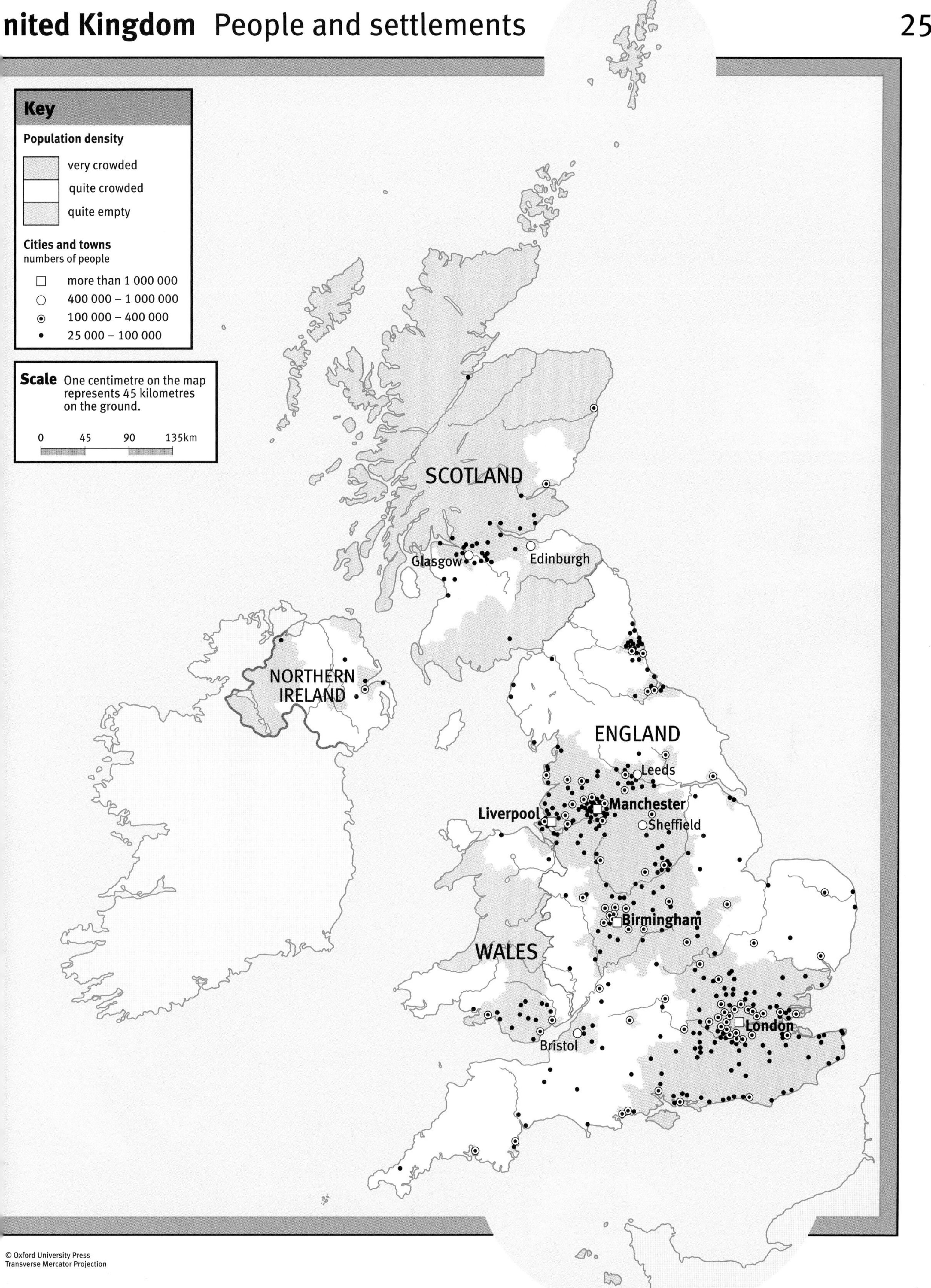
Key
Population density
very crowded
quite crowded
quite empty
Cities and towns
numbers of people
more than 1 000 000
400 000 – 1 000 000
100 000 – 400 000
25 000 – 100 000
Scale One centimetre on the map represents 45 kilometres on the ground.
0
45
90
135km
SCOTLAND
Glasgow
Edinburgh
NORTHERN IRELAND
ENGLAND
Leeds
Liverpool
Manchester
Sheffield
Birmingham
WALES
Bristol
London

Transverse Mercator Projection

United Kingdom Air and sea connections

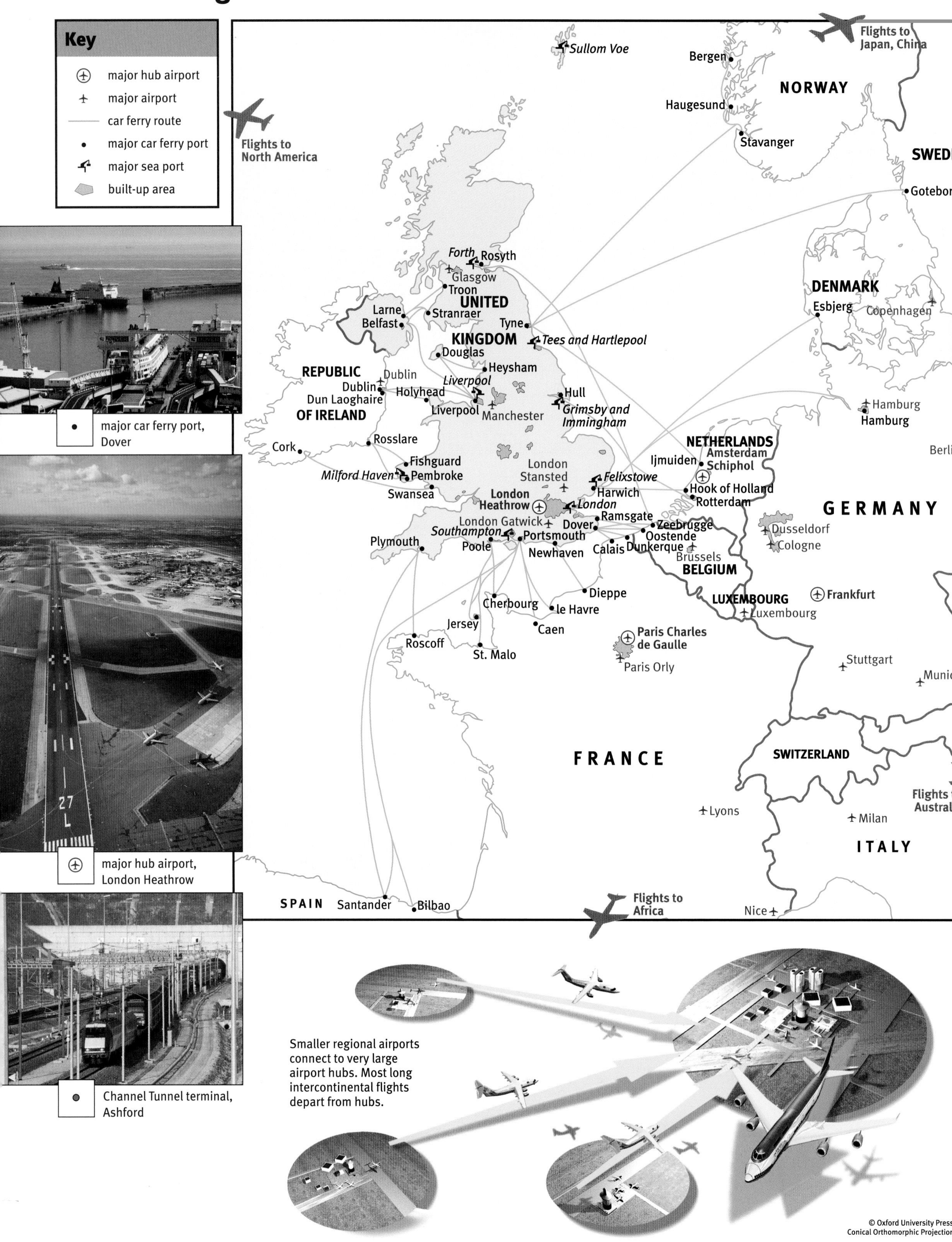

Key
major hub airport
major airport
car ferry route
major car ferry port
major sea port
built-up area
Flights to North America
Flights to Japan, China
Flights to Africa
Flights to Australia
Sullom Voe
Bergen
Haugesund
Stavanger
NORWAY
SWEDEN
Goteborg
DENMARK
Esbjerg
Copenhagen
Forth
Rosyth
Glasgow
Troon
UNITED KINGDOM
Larne
Belfast
Stranraer
Tyne
Tees and Hartlepool
Douglas
Heysham
REPUBLIC OF IRELAND
Dublin
Dun Laoghaire
Holyhead
Liverpool
Manchester
Hull
Grimsby and Immingham
Hamburg
Cork
Rosslare
Fishguard
Milford Haven
Pembroke
Swansea
London Stansted
Felixstowe
Harwich
NETHERLANDS
Ijmuiden
Amsterdam Schiphol
Hook of Holland
Rotterdam
Berlin
London Heathrow
London
Ramsgate
GERMANY
London Gatwick
Dover
Zeebrugge
Oostende
Dusseldorf
Cologne
Plymouth
Southampton
Poole
Portsmouth
Newhaven
Calais
Dunkerque
Brussels
BELGIUM
Dieppe
Cherbourg
le Havre
LUXEMBOURG
Luxembourg
Frankfurt
Jersey
Caen
Roscoff
St. Malo
Paris Charles de Gaulle
Paris Orly
Stuttgart
Munich
FRANCE
SWITZERLAND
Lyons
Milan
ITALY
SPAIN
Santander
Bilbao
Nice

major car ferry port, Dover

major hub airport, London Heathrow

Channel Tunnel terminal, Ashford

Smaller regional airports connect to very large airport hubs. Most long intercontinental flights depart from hubs.

Conical Orthomorphic Projection

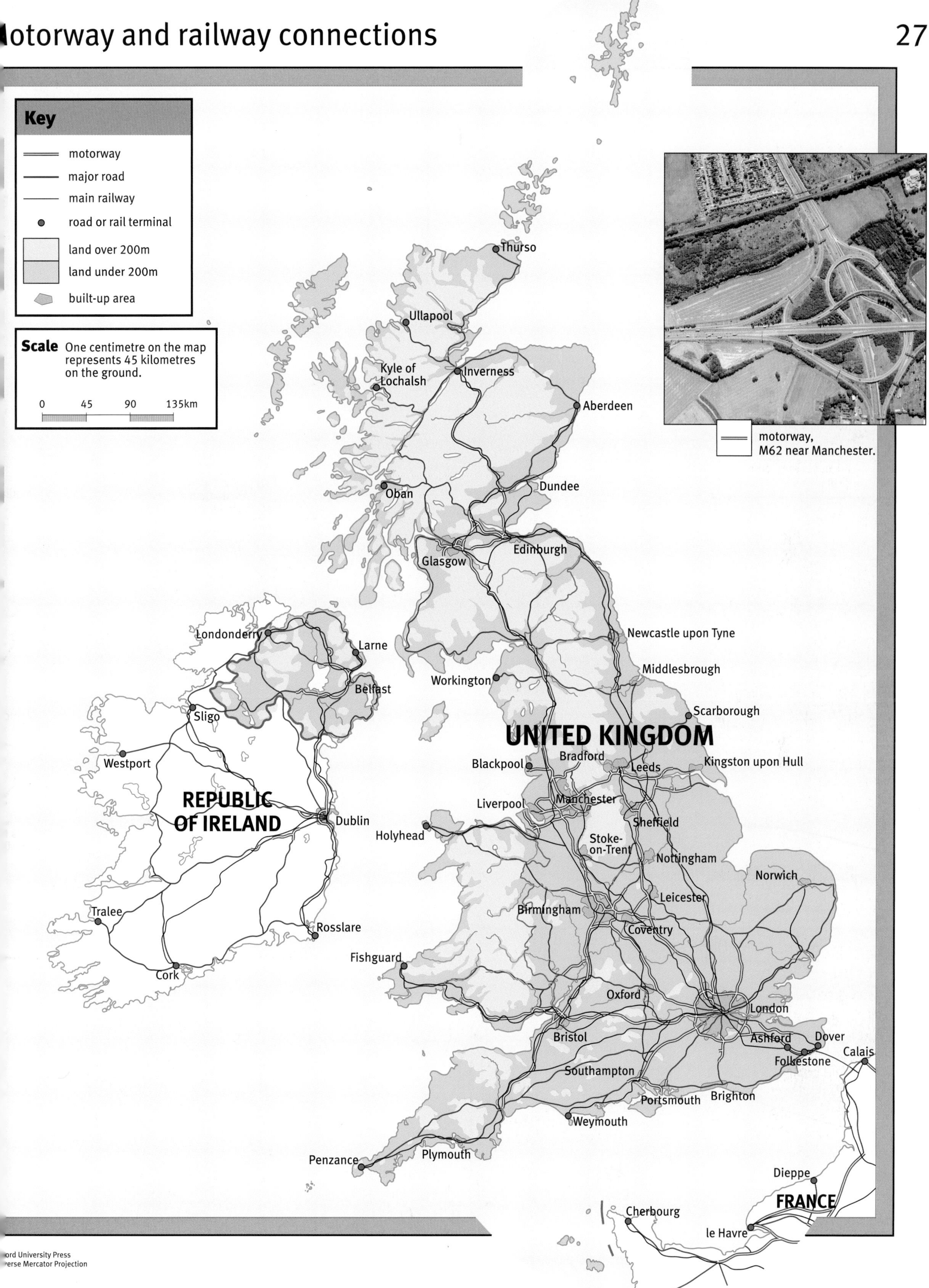

Key
motorway
major road
main railway
road or rail terminal
land over 200m
land under 200m
built-up area
Scale One centimetre on the map represents 45 kilometres on the ground.
0
45
90
135km
motorway, M62 near Manchester.
Thurso
Ullapool
Kyle of Lochalsh
Inverness
Aberdeen
Oban
Dundee
Edinburgh
Glasgow
Newcastle upon Tyne
Middlesbrough
Londonderry
Larne
Belfast
Workington
Sligo
Scarborough
UNITED KINGDOM
Westport
Blackpool
Bradford
Leeds
Kingston upon Hull
REPUBLIC OF IRELAND
Liverpool
Manchester
Sheffield
Dublin
Holyhead
Stoke-on-Trent
Nottingham
Norwich
Leicester
Birmingham
Coventry
Tralee
Rosslare
Fishguard
Cork
Oxford
London
Bristol
Ashford
Dover
Folkestone
Calais
Southampton
Portsmouth
Brighton
Weymouth
Penzance
Plymouth
Dieppe
FRANCE
Cherbourg
le Havre

verse Mercator Projection

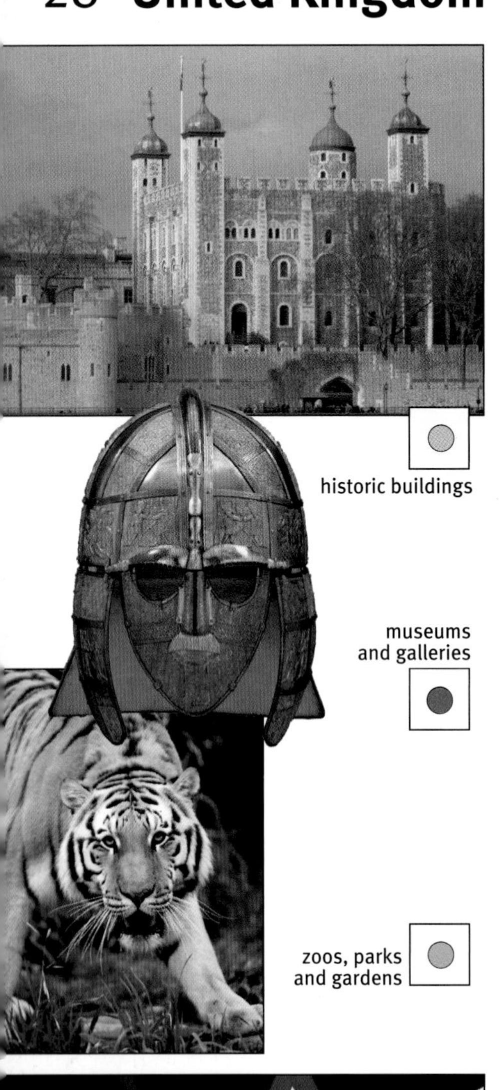

historic buildings

museums and galleries

zoos, parks and gardens

theme parks and piers

Top UK tourist attractions

Key

Symbol **colour** shows the type of tourist attraction
- historic buildings
- museums and galleries
- zoos, parks and gardens
- theme parks and piers

Symbol **size** shows how popular the attraction is
- over 4 million visitors each year
- 2–4 million visitors each year
- 1–2 million visitors each year
- built-up area

Drumpellier Country Park
Edinburgh Castle
Kelvingrove Art Gallery and Museum
Strathclyde Country Park
Windermere Lake Cruises
Flamingoland Theme Park and Zoo, Kirby Misperton
Blackpool Pleasure Beach
York Minster
Pleasureland Theme Park Southport
Upper Derwent Reservoirs
Chester Zoo
Alton Towers
Drayton Manor Family Theme Park, Tamworth
Pleasure Beach, Great Yarmouth
Fairlands Valley Park
Ashton Court Estate
Legoland, Windsor
Kew Gardens
Canterbury Cathedral
Eastbourne Pier
Eden Project

Inner London
Madam Tussaud's
British Museum
National Gallery
National Portrait Gallery
London Eye
Science Museum
Tower of London
Natural History Museum
Tate Modern
Tate Britain
Westminster Abbey
Victoria & Albert Museum

Holidays in the UK and abroad

Number of holidays taken by people who live in the UK

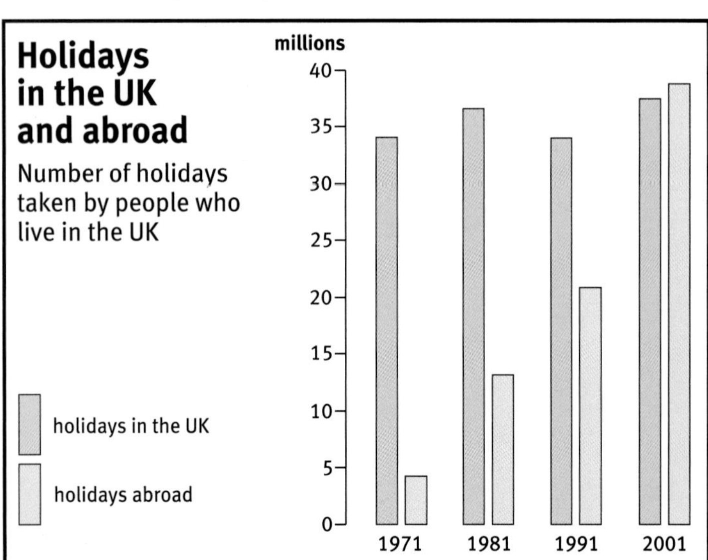
millions
40
35
30
25
20
15
10
5
0
1971
1981
1991
2001
holidays in the UK
holidays abroad

Holidays abroad

Canada
USA
each symbol stands for 1 million British tourists

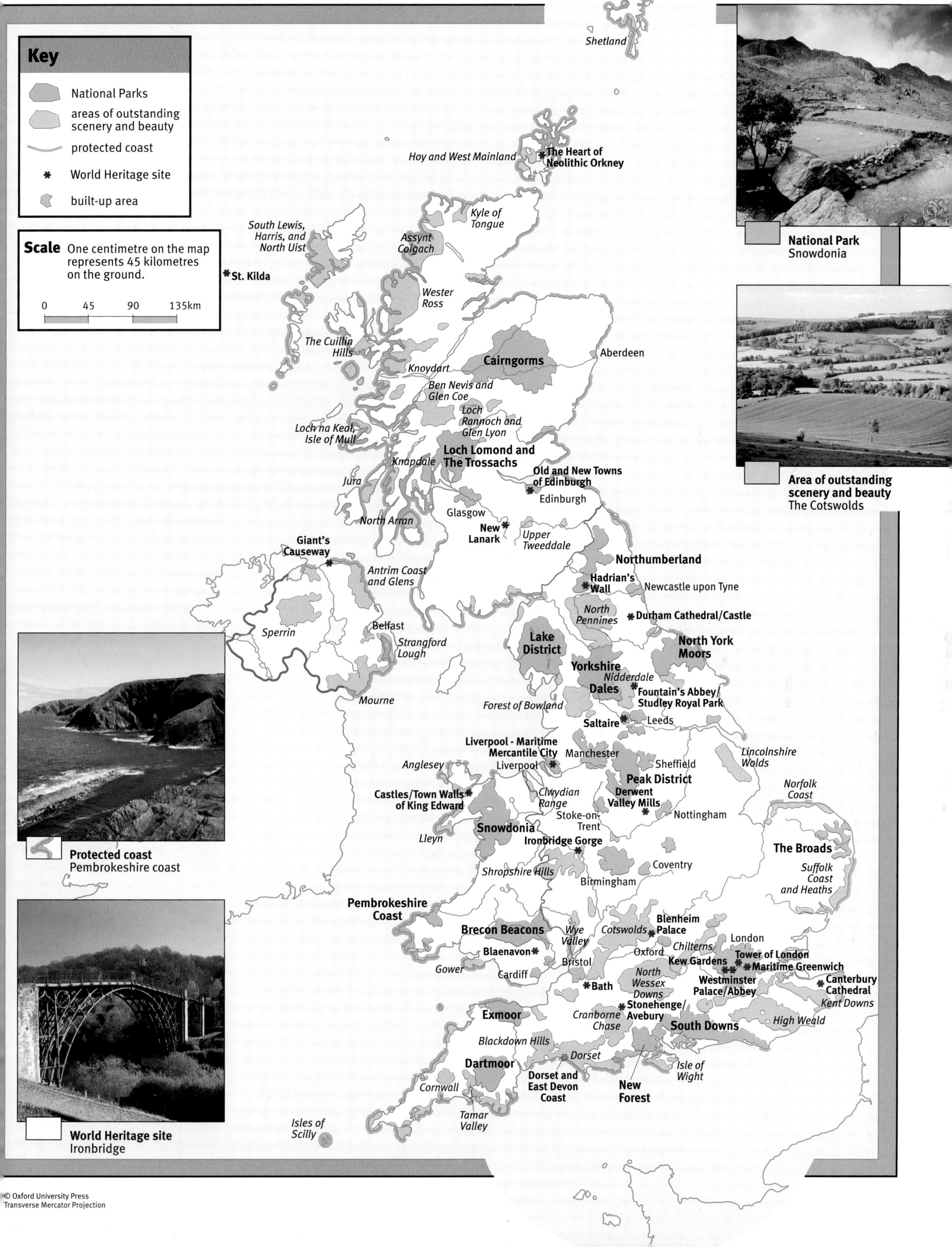

Key
National Parks
areas of outstanding scenery and beauty
protected coast
World Heritage site
built-up area
Scale One centimetre on the map represents 45 kilometres on the ground.
0 45 90 135km
Shetland
Hoy and West Mainland
The Heart of Neolithic Orkney
Kyle of Tongue
South Lewis, Harris, and North Uist
Assynt Coigach
St. Kilda
Wester Ross
The Cuillin Hills
Knoydart
Cairngorms
Aberdeen
Ben Nevis and Glen Coe
Loch Rannoch and Glen Lyon
Loch na Keal, Isle of Mull
Loch Lomond and The Trossachs
Knapdale
Jura
Old and New Towns of Edinburgh
Edinburgh
Glasgow
North Arran
New Lanark
Upper Tweeddale
Giant's Causeway
Antrim Coast and Glens
Northumberland
Hadrian's Wall
Newcastle upon Tyne
North Pennines
Durham Cathedral/Castle
Sperrin
Belfast
Strangford Lough
Lake District
North York Moors
Yorkshire Dales
Nidderdale
Fountain's Abbey/ Studley Royal Park
Mourne
Forest of Bowland
Saltaire
Leeds
Liverpool - Maritime Mercantile City
Manchester
Liverpool
Lincolnshire Wolds
Anglesey
Sheffield
Peak District
Castles/Town Walls of King Edward
Clwydian Range
Derwent Valley Mills
Norfolk Coast
Stoke-on-Trent
Nottingham
Snowdonia
Lleyn
Ironbridge Gorge
The Broads
Coventry
Shropshire Hills
Birmingham
Suffolk Coast and Heaths
Pembrokeshire Coast
Brecon Beacons
Wye Valley
Cotswolds
Blenheim Palace
London
Blaenavon
Oxford
Chilterns
Tower of London
Kew Gardens
Maritime Greenwich
Gower
Bristol
Cardiff
Bath
North Wessex Downs
Westminster Palace/Abbey
Canterbury Cathedral
Kent Downs
Exmoor
Cranborne Chase
Stonehenge/ Avebury
South Downs
High Weald
Blackdown Hills
Dorset
Dartmoor
Dorset and East Devon Coast
Isle of Wight
New Forest
Cornwall
Tamar Valley
Isles of Scilly

National Park
Snowdonia

Area of outstanding scenery and beauty
The Cotswolds

Protected coast
Pembrokeshire coast

World Heritage site
Ironbridge

Transverse Mercator Projection

Europe Landscapes and rivers

Arctic Circle
GREENLAND SEA
Prime Meridian
Iceland
1491m Mount Hekla
Lofoten Islands
Kola Peninsula
WHITE SEA
Lappland
Scandinavia
URAL MOUNTAINS
River Ob
R. Pechora
River North Dvina
Faroe Islands
Shetland Islands
Gulf of Bothnia
Lake Onega
Lake Ladoga
ATLANTIC OCEAN
Orkney Islands
Lake Vänern
Lake Peipus
Rybinsk Reservoir
NORTH SEA
Gotland
Lake Vättern
BALTIC SEA
Ireland
Great Britain
Jylland
Central Russian Uplands
River Volga
Bornholm
Friesian Islands
River Elbe
North European Plain
River Dnieper
R. Thames
English Channel
R. Rhine
River Oder
R. Vistula
River Don
River Seine
River Donets
R. Dniester
CARPATHIANS
CASPIAN SEA
Bay of Biscay
River Loire
Jura
Cape Finisterre
4807m Mont Blanc
ALPS
Hungarian Basin
SEA OF AZOV
Cantabrian Mts.
Massif Central
R. Rhône
2548m
CAUCASUS
River Ebro
River Po
Pyrénées
River Duero
R. Tagus
Dinaric Alps
BLACK SEA
5642m Mt. Elbrus
River Danube
5123m Mt. Ararat
Corsica
APPENNINES
ADRIATIC SEA
Balearic Islands
Menorca
Mallorca
Ibiza
Cape St. Vincent
Sardinia
Pindus Mountains
2917m Mt. Olympus
Anatolian Plateau
Lake Van
Str. of Gibraltar
TYRRHENIAN SEA
AEGEAN SEA
Taurus Mountains
MEDITERRANEAN SEA
Mt. Etna 3323m
IONIAN SEA
Sicily
Peloponnese
Rhodes
Malta
Crete
Cyprus
Tropic of Cancer
20°W
0°
20°E
40°E
60°E
60°N
40°N
A B C D E F
1 2 3
Key
land height in metres above sea level
more than 2000m
1000 – 2000m
500 – 1000m
200 – 500m
less than 200 metres
land below sea level
highest peaks with heights in metres
lake
river
Scale One centimetre on the map represents 240 kilometres on the ground.
0 240 480 720km

Conical Orthomorphic Projection

ATLANTIC OCEAN
ICELAND
Reykjavik
NORWAY
SWEDEN
FINLAND
RUSSIAN FEDERATION (RUSSIA)
Oslo
Stockholm
Helsinki
St. Petersburg
Tallinn
ESTONIA
LATVIA
Riga
LITHUANIA
Vilnius
KALININGRAD (Russia)
Minsk
BELARUS
Moscow
Nizhniy-Novgorod
NORTH SEA
BALTIC SEA
Göteborg
DENMARK
Copenhagen
UNITED KINGDOM
Edinburgh
Belfast
REPUBLIC OF IRELAND
Dublin
Manchester
Birmingham
London
NETHERLANDS
Amsterdam
Rotterdam
BELGIUM
Brussels
LUXEMBOURG
Luxembourg
Hamburg
Berlin
GERMANY
Düsseldorf
POLAND
Warsaw
Krakow
Prague
CZECH REP.
SLOVAKIA
Kiev
UKRAINE
Kharkov
Donets'k
Volgograd
Rostov-on-Don
Paris
FRANCE
Munich
Vienna
Bratislava
AUSTRIA
Bern
LIECHTENSTEIN
SWITZERLAND
Bordeaux
Lyons
Budapest
HUNGARY
MOLDOVA
Chisinau
Odessa
Ljubljana
SLOVENIA
Zagreb
CROATIA
Milan
ROMANIA
Bucharest
BLACK SEA
GEORGIA
T'bilisi
Oporto
PORTUGAL
Lisbon
SPAIN
Madrid
ANDORRA
Marseilles
MONACO
SAN MARINO
BOSNIA-HERZEGOVINA
Sarajevo
Belgrade
SERBIA AND MONTENEGRO
BULGARIA
Sofia
Barcelona
Valencia
Seville
Gibraltar (UK)
ITALY
Rome
Naples
Skopje
FYRO MACEDONIA
Tiranë
ALBANIA
Istanbul
Ankara
TURKEY
GREECE
Izmir
Athens
Adana
Ceuta (Sp.)
Melilla (Sp.)
MOROCCO
MEDITERRANEAN SEA
Valletta
MALTA
Nicosia
CYPRUS
SYRIA
LEBANON
ISRAEL
IRAQ
JORDAN
TUNISIA
SAUDI ARABIA
LIBYA
EGYPT
Arctic Circle
Prime Meridian
Tropic of Cancer
20°W
0°
20°E
40°E
60°E
60°N
40°N
N
A
B
C
D
E
F
1
2
3
Key
colours show countries
ITALY country names are labelled like this
capital cities
other important cities

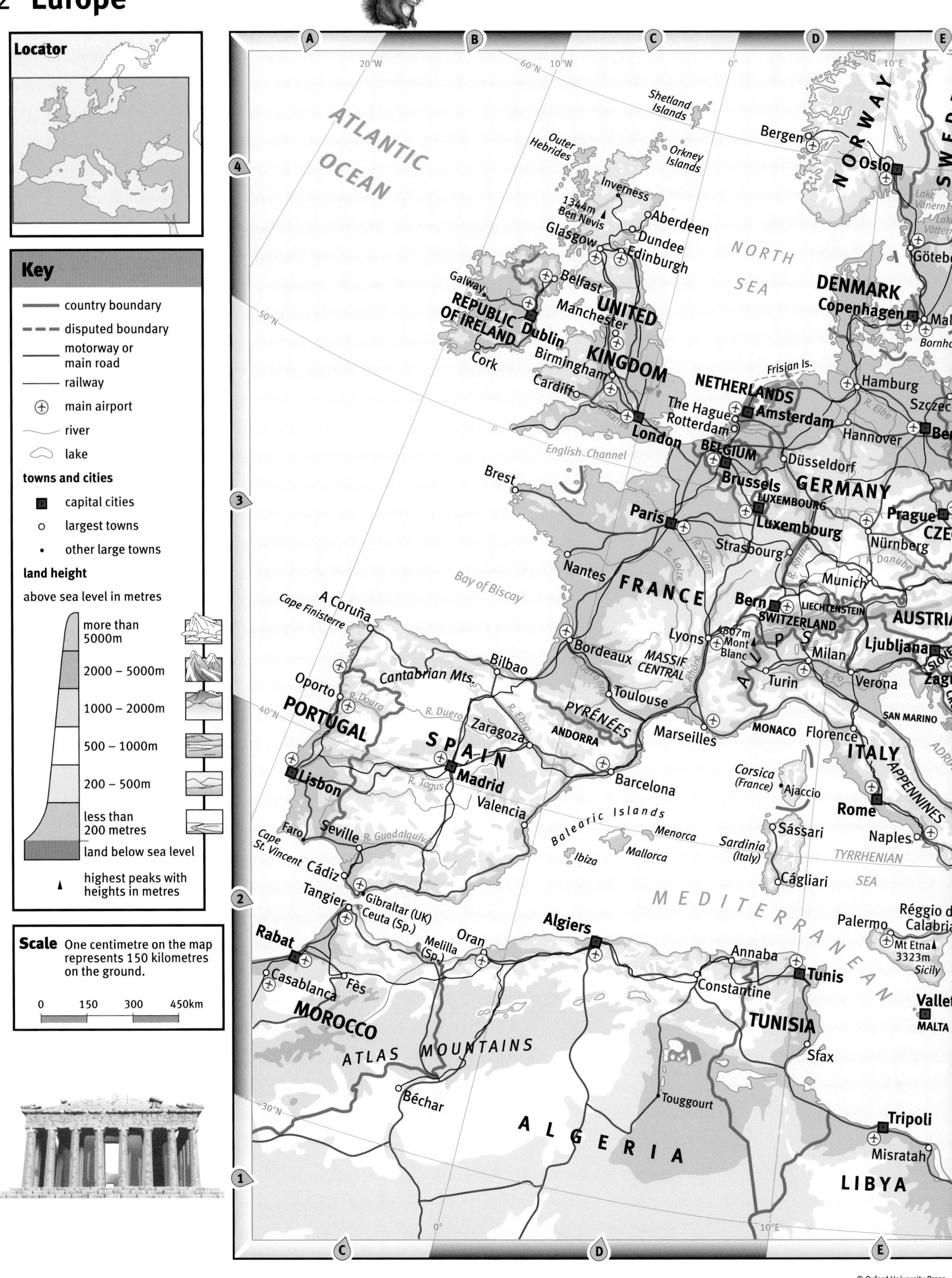
Locator
Key
country boundary
disputed boundary
motorway or main road
railway
main airport
river
lake
towns and cities
capital cities
largest towns
other large towns
land height
above sea level in metres
more than 5000m
2000 – 5000m
1000 – 2000m
500 – 1000m
200 – 500m
less than 200 metres
land below sea level
highest peaks with heights in metres
Scale One centimetre on the map represents 150 kilometres on the ground.
0
150
300
450km
A
B
C
D
E
4
3
2
1
20°W
10°W
0°
10°E
60°N
50°N
40°N
30°N
ATLANTIC OCEAN
Shetland Islands
Orkney Islands
Outer Hebrides
Inverness
1344m Ben Nevis
Aberdeen
Dundee
Glasgow
Edinburgh
NORTH SEA
Belfast
Galway
REPUBLIC OF IRELAND
Dublin
Cork
UNITED KINGDOM
Manchester
Birmingham
Cardiff
London
English Channel
Bergen
Oslo
NORWAY
SWEDEN
Lake Vänern
Lake Vättern
Göteborg
DENMARK
Copenhagen
Malmö
Bornholm
Frisian Is.
NETHERLANDS
Amsterdam
The Hague
Rotterdam
BELGIUM
Brussels
LUXEMBOURG
Luxembourg
Hamburg
R. Elbe
Szczecin
Berlin
Hannover
Düsseldorf
GERMANY
Prague
CZECH REPUBLIC
Nürnberg
R. Danube
Munich
Brest
Paris
R. Seine
R. Loire
Strasbourg
R. Rhine
Nantes
FRANCE
Bay of Biscay
Bern
SWITZERLAND
LIECHTENSTEIN
AUSTRIA
Lyons
4807m Mont Blanc
ALPS
Milan
Ljubljana
SLOVENIA
Zagreb
CROATIA
Bordeaux
MASSIF CENTRAL
R. Garonne
R. Rhône
Turin
R. Po
Verona
Toulouse
PYRÉNÉES
ANDORRA
Marseilles
MONACO
SAN MARINO
Florence
ITALY
APPENNINES
ADRIATIC
A Coruña
Cape Finisterre
Bilbao
Cantabrian Mts.
Oporto
R. Douro
R. Duero
PORTUGAL
SPAIN
R. Ebro
Zaragoza
Madrid
R. Tagus
Lisbon
Barcelona
Valencia
Corsica (France)
Ajaccio
Rome
Balearic Islands
Menorca
Mallorca
Ibiza
Sássari
Sardinia (Italy)
Naples
TYRRHENIAN SEA
Cágliari
Faro
Seville
R. Guadalquivir
Cape St. Vincent
Cádiz
Tangier
Gibraltar (UK)
Ceuta (Sp.)
Melilla (Sp.)
Oran
Algiers
MEDITERRANEAN
Palermo
Réggio di Calabria
Mt Etna 3323m
Sicily
Rabat
Casablanca
Fès
Annaba
Tunis
Constantine
Valletta
MALTA
MOROCCO
ATLAS MOUNTAINS
TUNISIA
Sfax
Béchar
Touggourt
ALGERIA
Tripoli
Misratah
LIBYA

Conical Orthomorphic Projection

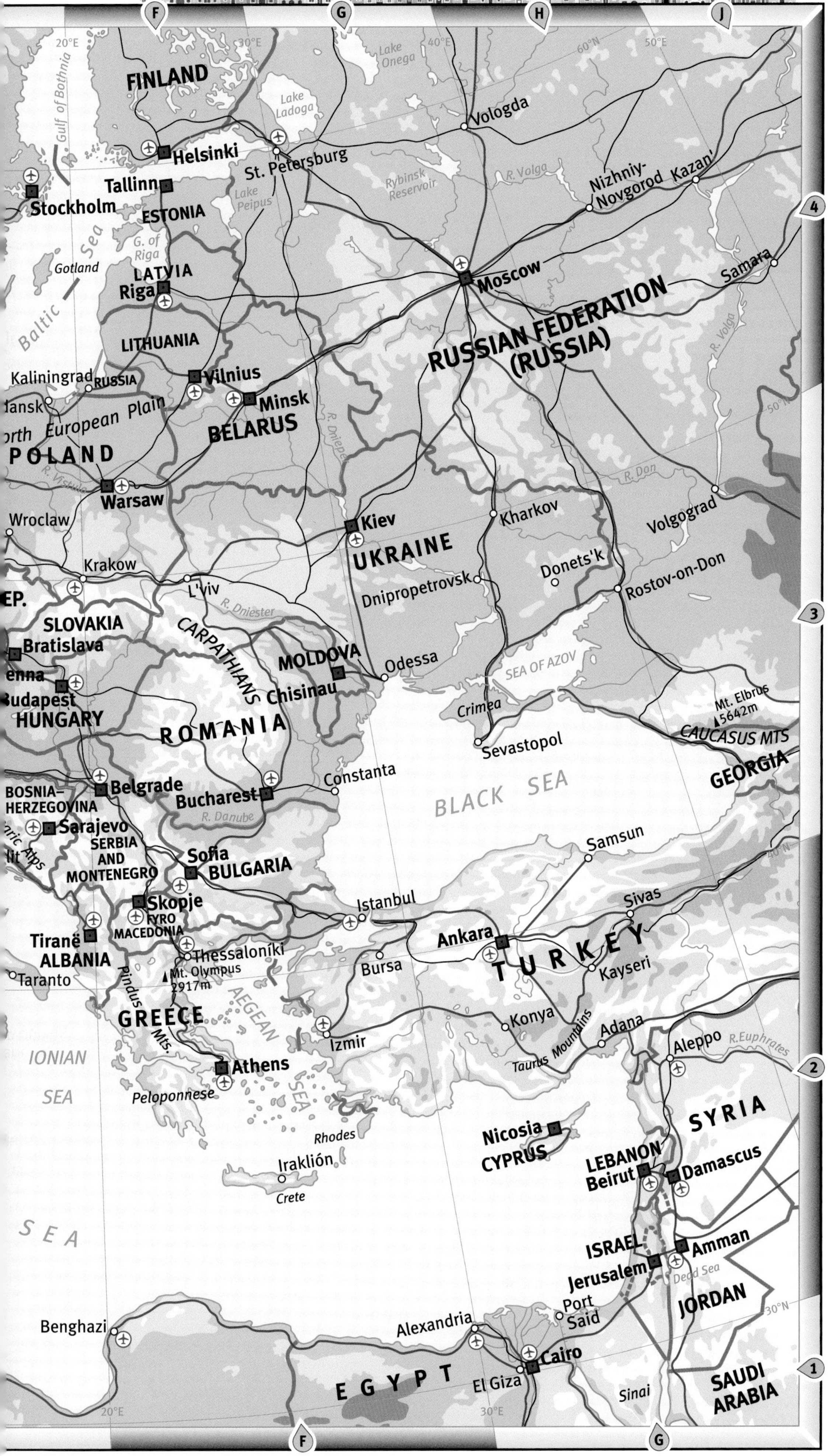

F G H J

FINLAND
Helsinki
Tallinn
ESTONIA
Stockholm
Gulf of Bothnia
Lake Ladoga
Lake Onega
St. Petersburg
Lake Peipus
Vologda
Rybinsk Reservoir
R. Volga
Nizhniy-Novgorod
Kazan'
G. of Riga
LATVIA
Riga
Gotland
Baltic Sea
Moscow
Samara
RUSSIAN FEDERATION (RUSSIA)
LITHUANIA
Kaliningrad
RUSSIA
Vilnius
Minsk
Gdansk
North European Plain
BELARUS
POLAND
R. Vistula
R. Dnieper
Warsaw
R. Don
Wroclaw
Kiev
Kharkov
Volgograd
UKRAINE
Krakow
Donets'k
Dnipropetrovsk
Rostov-on-Don
L'viv
R. Dniester
CZECH REP.
SLOVAKIA
Bratislava
CARPATHIANS
MOLDOVA
Odessa
SEA OF AZOV
Vienna
Budapest
HUNGARY
Chisinau
Crimea
Mt. Elbrus 5642m
ROMANIA
Sevastopol
CAUCASUS MTS
GEORGIA
BOSNIA-HERZEGOVINA
Belgrade
Bucharest
Constanta
BLACK SEA
Sarajevo
R. Danube
Dinaric Alps
SERBIA AND MONTENEGRO
Sofia
BULGARIA
Samsun
Skopje
FYRO MACEDONIA
Istanbul
Sivas
Tiranë
ALBANIA
Ankara
Thessaloníki
Bursa
TURKEY
Kayseri
Taranto
Mt. Olympus 2917m
Pindus Mts.
GREECE
AEGEAN SEA
Konya
Taurus Mountains
Adana
Izmir
Aleppo
R. Euphrates
IONIAN SEA
Athens
Peloponnese
SYRIA
Rhodes
Nicosia
CYPRUS
LEBANON
Beirut
Damascus
Iraklión
Crete
SEA
ISRAEL
Amman
Jerusalem
Dead Sea
JORDAN
Port Said
Benghazi
Alexandria
Cairo
El Giza
EGYPT
Sinai
SAUDI ARABIA
20°E 30°E 40°E 50°E 60°N 50°N 40°N 30°N
1 2 3 4
F G

Bridges over the River Seine in Paris

Bridges over the the River Vltava in Prague

ARCTIC OCEAN
North Pole
Prime Meridian
BARENTS SEA
Bering Strait
BERING SEA
Arctic Circle
R. Kolyma
Kamchatka
Central Siberian Plateau
River Lena
Yenisey River
River Ob
Siberian Lowland
URAL MOUNTAINS
Lake Ladoga
Lake Onega
River Volga
Angara River
Lake Baykal
SEA OF OKHOTSK
Sakhalin
Kuril Islands
Hokkaido
River Amur (Heilong Jiang)
BLACK SEA
CAUCASUS
Mt. Elbrus 5642m
Anatolian Plateau
Mt. Ararat 5123m
MEDITERRANEAN SEA
Caspian Sea
Aral Sea
Kazakh Upland
River Irtysh
Lake Balkhash
ALTAI MOUNTAINS
Gobi Desert
SEA OF JAPAN
Honshu
Mt. Fuji 3776m
Dead Sea
R. Euphrates
R. Tigris
Elburz Mts.
ZAGROS MTS.
Qullai Garmo 7495m
TIEN SHAN
Turpan Depression −154m
Tarim Basin
Hindu Kush
KUNLUN SHAN
8611m K2
RED SEA
Arabian Peninsula
The Gulf
Plateau of Tibet
Huang He
YELLOW SEA
Kyushu
EAST CHINA SEA
Ryukyu Islands
Tropic of Cancer
River Indus
HIMALAYA
Mt. Everest 8848m
Chang Jiang (Yangtze R.)
Thar Desert
Brahmaputra
River Ganges
Taiwan
PACIFIC OCEAN
Gulf of Aden
ARABIAN SEA
Socotra
Mouths of the Ganges
Irrawaddy R.
Salween R.
Mekong River
Luzon
SOUTH CHINA SEA
Laccadive Islands
Deccan
Bay of Bengal
Mindoro
Mindanao
Andaman Islands
ANDAMAN SEA
Gulf of Thailand
4094m Mt. Kinabalu
Nicobar Islands
CELEBES SEA
Maldive Archipelago
Malay Peninsula
New Guinea
Equator
Sumatra
Borneo
Sulawesi
INDIAN OCEAN
JAVA SEA
ARAFURA SEA
Java
Bali
Timor
TIMOR SEA
Tropic of Capricorn
N
60°N
20°W
40°W
80°W
120°W
80°N
160°W
180°
40°N
20°E
160°E
20°N
40°E
60°E
80°E
100°E
120°E
0°
20°S
Key
land height in metres above sea level
more than 5000m
2000 – 5000m
1000 – 2000m
500 – 1000m
200 – 500m
less than 200 metres
land below sea level
highest peaks with heights in metres
lake
river
Scale One centimetre on the map represents 550 kilometres on the ground.
0 550 1100 1650km
A B C D E F G H J
1 2 3 4 5
B C D E

Zenithal Equal Area Projection

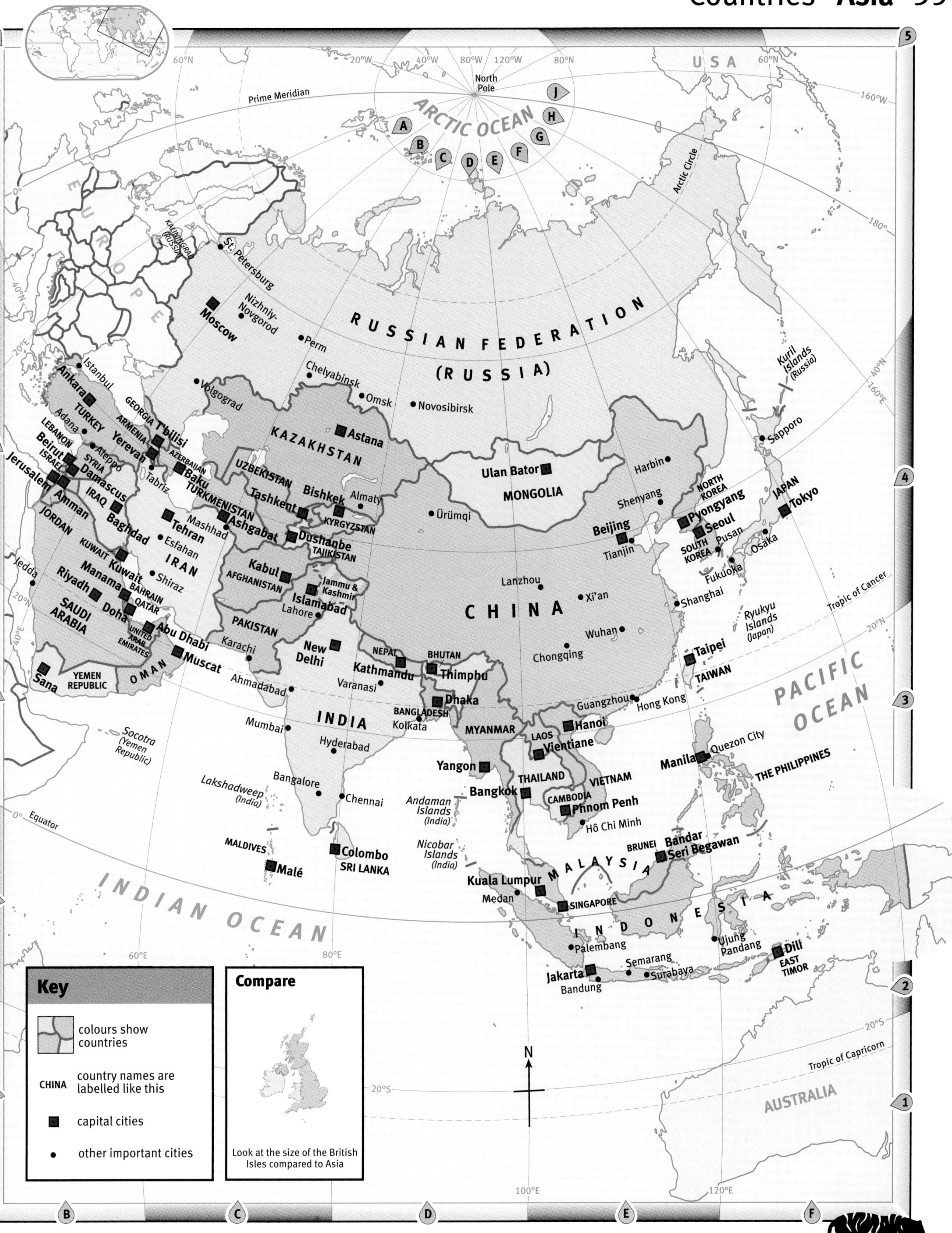

ARCTIC OCEAN
North Pole
Prime Meridian
RUSSIAN FEDERATION
(RUSSIA)
EUROPE
KALININGRAD (RUSSIA)
St. Petersburg
Moscow
Nizhniy-Novgorod
Perm
Chelyabinsk
Omsk
Novosibirsk
Volgograd
Istanbul
Ankara
TURKEY
Adana
GEORGIA
T'bilisi
ARMENIA
Yerevan
AZERBAIJAN
Baku
LEBANON
Beirut
SYRIA
Aleppo
ISRAEL
Damascus
Jerusalem
Amman
JORDAN
IRAQ
Baghdad
Tabriz
Tehran
IRAN
Esfahan
Shiraz
Mashhad
TURKMENISTAN
Ashgabat
UZBEKISTAN
Tashkent
KAZAKHSTAN
Astana
Bishkek
KYRGYZSTAN
Almaty
Dushanbe
TAJIKISTAN
Kabul
AFGHANISTAN
Islamabad
Jammu & Kashmir
Lahore
PAKISTAN
Karachi
KUWAIT
Kuwait
BAHRAIN
Manama
QATAR
Doha
Riyadh
SAUDI ARABIA
Jedda
UNITED ARAB EMIRATES
Abu Dhabi
Muscat
OMAN
YEMEN REPUBLIC
Sana
Socotra (Yemen Republic)
Ürümqi
Ulan Bator
MONGOLIA
Harbin
Shenyang
Beijing
Tianjin
CHINA
Lanzhou
Xi'an
Shanghai
Wuhan
Chongqing
Guangzhou
Hong Kong
NORTH KOREA
Pyongyang
Seoul
SOUTH KOREA
Pusan
Fukuoka
Osaka
JAPAN
Tokyo
Sapporo
Kuril Islands (Russia)
Ryukyu Islands (Japan)
Taipei
TAIWAN
New Delhi
NEPAL
Kathmandu
BHUTAN
Thimphu
Varanasi
Ahmadabad
Dhaka
BANGLADESH
Kolkata
INDIA
Mumbai
Hyderabad
Bangalore
Chennai
Lakshadweep (India)
MALDIVES
Malé
Colombo
SRI LANKA
Andaman Islands (India)
Nicobar Islands (India)
MYANMAR
Yangon
LAOS
Vientiane
Hanoi
THAILAND
Bangkok
VIETNAM
CAMBODIA
Phnom Penh
Hô Chi Minh
Manila
Quezon City
THE PHILIPPINES
BRUNEI
Bandar Seri Begawan
MALAYSIA
Kuala Lumpur
Medan
SINGAPORE
INDONESIA
Palembang
Ujung Pandang
Dili
EAST TIMOR
Jakarta
Bandung
Semarang
Surabaya
PACIFIC OCEAN
INDIAN OCEAN
USA
AUSTRALIA
Arctic Circle
Tropic of Cancer
Equator
Tropic of Capricorn
60°N
40°N
20°N
0°
20°S
60°E
80°E
100°E
120°E
160°E
160°W
180°
20°W
40°W
80°W
120°W
80°N
20°E
A
B
C
D
E
F
G
H
J
1
2
3
4
5
N
Key
colours show countries
CHINA country names are labelled like this
capital cities
other important cities
Compare
Look at the size of the British Isles compared to Asia

India, Pakistan and Bangladesh

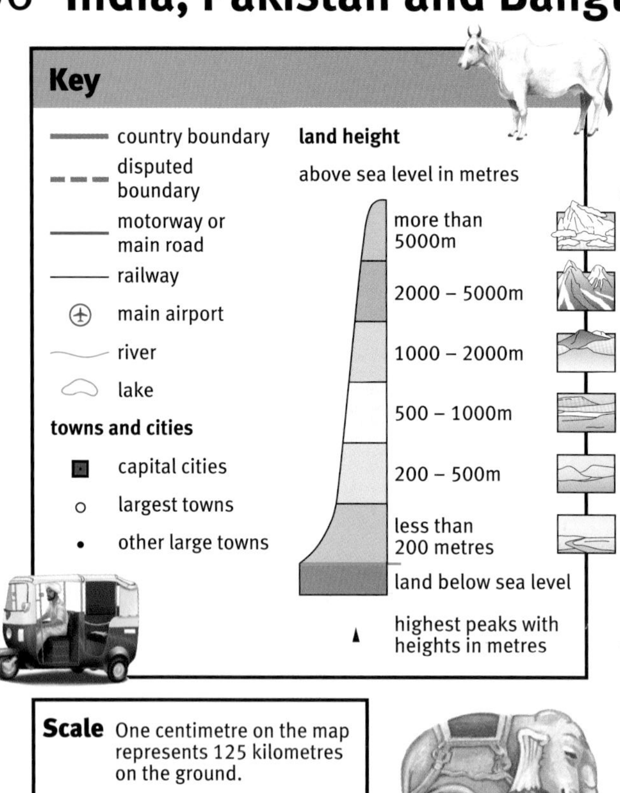
Key
country boundary
disputed boundary
motorway or main road
railway
main airport
river
lake
towns and cities
capital cities
largest towns
other large towns
land height
above sea level in metres
more than 5000m
2000 – 5000m
1000 – 2000m
500 – 1000m
200 – 500m
less than 200 metres
land below sea level
highest peaks with heights in metres
Scale
One centimetre on the map represents 125 kilometres on the ground.
0
125
250
375km

Traffic jam in Rajasthan

Rush hour in Jaipur

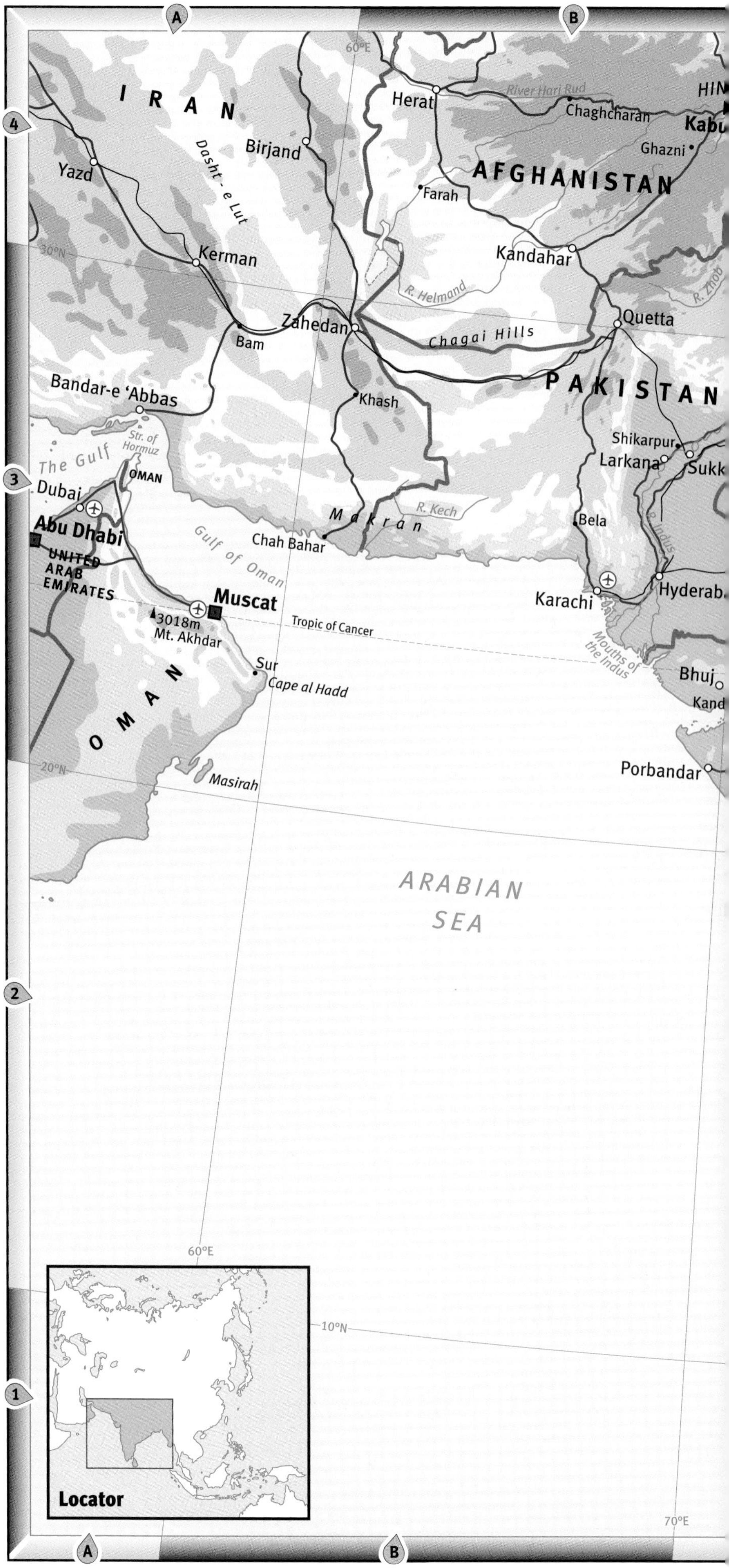

A B
4
3
2
1
60°E
30°N
20°N
10°N
70°E
IRAN
Yazd
Birjand
Dasht-e Lut
Kerman
Bam
Zahedan
Khash
Bandar-e 'Abbas
Herat
River Hari Rud
Chaghcharan
Kabu
HIN
Ghazni
AFGHANISTAN
Farah
Kandahar
R. Helmand
R. Zhob
Quetta
Chagai Hills
PAKISTAN
Shikarpur
Larkana
Sukk
Bela
R. Indus
Karachi
Hyderab
Mouths of the Indus
Bhuj
Kand
Porbandar
Makran
R. Kech
Chah Bahar
Str. of Hormuz
The Gulf
OMAN
Dubai
Abu Dhabi
UNITED ARAB EMIRATES
Gulf of Oman
Muscat
3018m Mt. Akhdar
Tropic of Cancer
Sur
Cape al Hadd
OMAN
Masirah
ARABIAN SEA
Locator

Conical Orthomorphic Projection

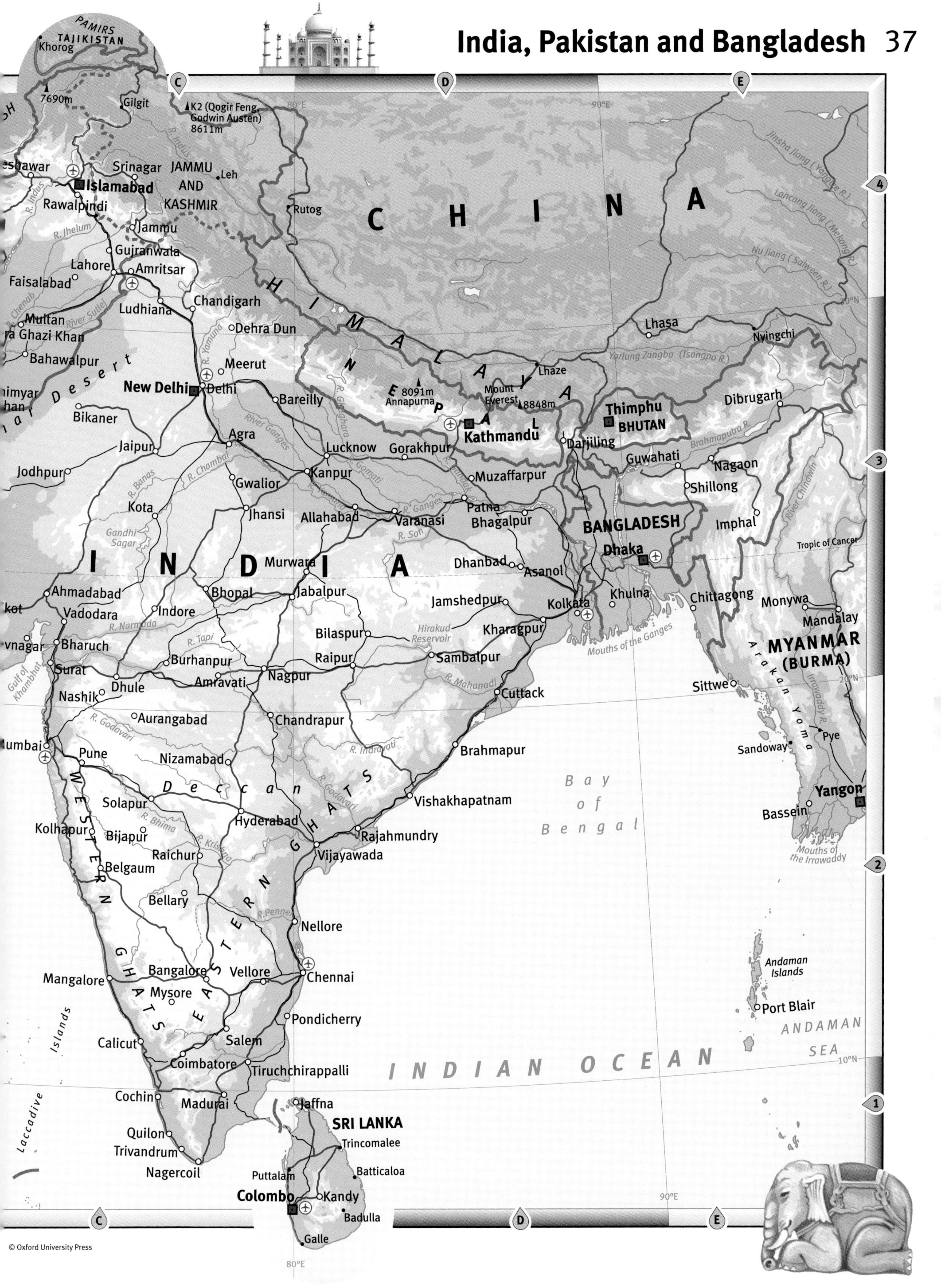

PAMIRS
TAJIKISTAN
Khorog
7690m
Gilgit
K2 (Qogir Feng, Godwin Austen) 8611m
Srinagar
JAMMU AND KASHMIR
Leh
Islamabad
Rawalpindi
Jammu
Gujranwala
Lahore
Amritsar
Faisalabad
Multan
Ghazi Khan
Bahawalpur
Ludhiana
Chandigarh
Dehra Dun
Meerut
New Delhi
Delhi
Bikaner
Jaipur
Jodhpur
Agra
Bareilly
Lucknow
Gorakhpur
Kanpur
Gwalior
Kota
Jhansi
Allahabad
Varanasi
Patna
Bhagalpur
Muzaffarpur
Gandhi Sagar
Thar Desert
R. Indus
R. Jhelum
R. Chenab
River Sutlej
R. Yamuna
River Ganges
R. Chambal
R. Banas
R. Ghaghara
R. Gomati
R. Gandak
R. Son
C H I N A
Rutog
H I M A L A Y A
N E P A L
8091m Annapurna
Mount Everest 8848m
Kathmandu
Lhaze
Lhasa
Nyingchi
Yarlung Zangbo (Tsangpo R.)
Jinsha Jiang (Yangtze R.)
Lancang Jiang (Mekong R.)
Nu Jiang (Salween R.)
Thimphu
BHUTAN
Darjiling
Dibrugarh
Brahmaputra R.
Guwahati
Nagaon
Shillong
Imphal
River Chindwin
BANGLADESH
Dhaka
Tropic of Cancer
I N D I A
Murwara
Dhanbad
Asanol
Ahmadabad
Bhopal
Jabalpur
Jamshedpur
Kolkata
Khulna
Chittagong
Monywa
Mandalay
Vadodara
Indore
R. Narmada
Bharuch
Bilaspur
Hirakud Reservoir
Kharagpur
Mouths of the Ganges
MYANMAR (BURMA)
R. Tapi
Burhanpur
Surat
Raipur
Sambalpur
Gulf of Khambhat
Amravati
Nagpur
Dhule
Nashik
R. Mahanadi
Cuttack
Sittwe
Arakan Yoma
Irrawaddy R.
Aurangabad
Chandrapur
R. Godavari
Mumbai
Pune
Nizamabad
R. Indravati
Brahmapur
Pye
Sandoway
D e c c a n
Solapur
Hyderabad
Vishakhapatnam
B a y o f B e n g a l
Yangon
Bassein
Kolhapur
Bijapur
R. Bhima
R. Krishna
Rajahmundry
Vijayawada
Mouths of the Irrawaddy
Raichur
Belgaum
W E S T E R N G H A T S
E A S T E R N G H A T S
Bellary
R. Penner
Nellore
Andaman Islands
Bangalore
Vellore
Chennai
Mangalore
Mysore
Port Blair
Pondicherry
ANDAMAN SEA
Laccadive Islands
Calicut
Salem
Coimbatore
Tiruchchirappalli
I N D I A N O C E A N
Cochin
Madurai
Jaffna
SRI LANKA
Quilon
Trivandrum
Nagercoil
Trincomalee
Puttalam
Batticaloa
Colombo
Kandy
Badulla
Galle
80°E
90°E
20°N
10°N
C
D
E
1
2
3
4

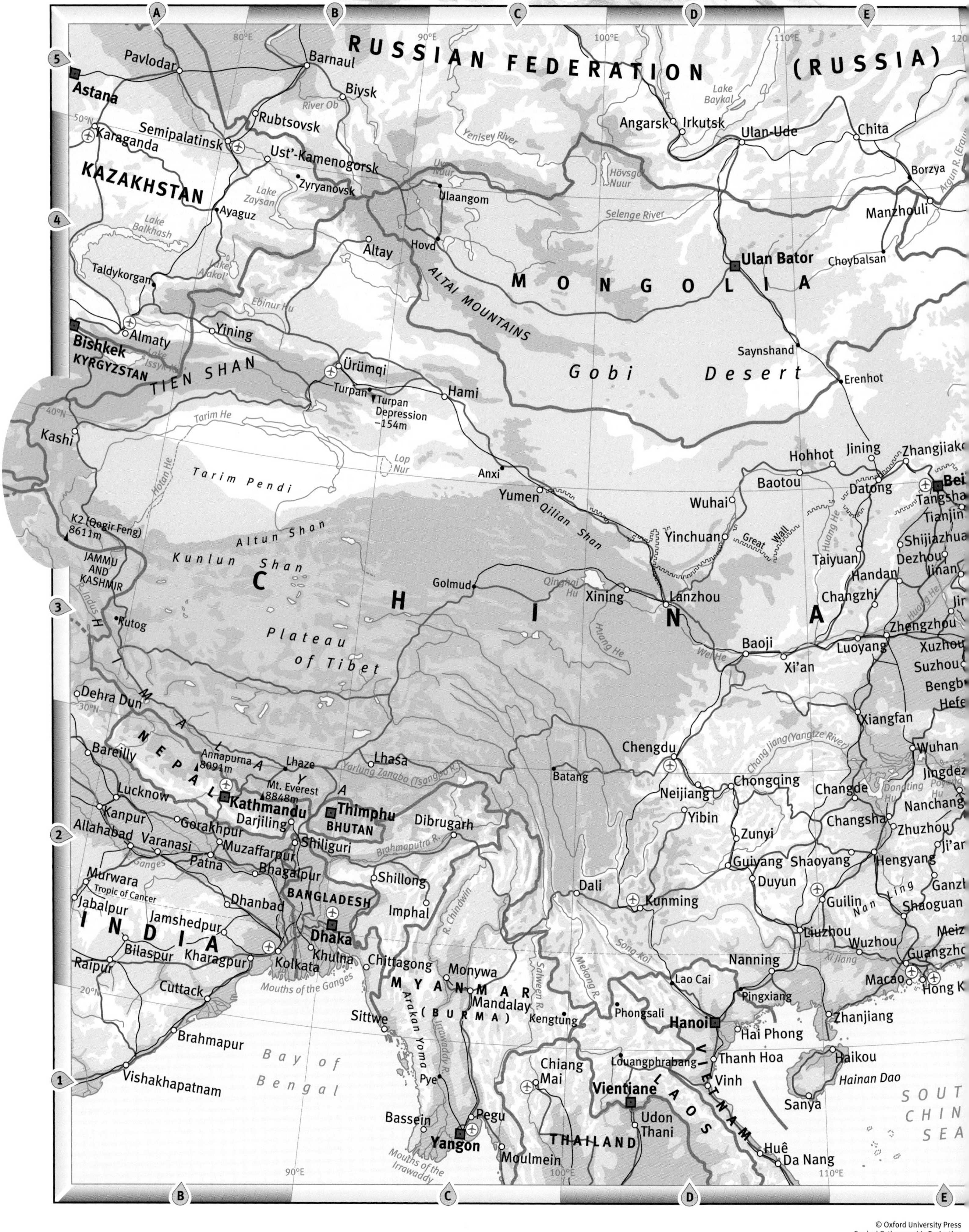

China and Japan

A
B
C
D
E
80°E
90°E
100°E
110°E
120
5
Pavlodar
Barnaul
RUSSIAN FEDERATION (RUSSIA)
Astana
Biysk
River Ob
Lake Baykal
Angarsk
Irkutsk
Ulan-Ude
Chita
50°N
Rubtsovsk
Semipalatinsk
Karaganda
Yenisey River
Ust'-Kamenogorsk
KAZAKHSTAN
Uvs Nuur
Hövsgöl Nuur
Borzya
Argun R. (Erguna)
Zyryanovsk
Ulaangom
Lake Zaysan
Ayaguz
Selenge River
Manzhouli
4
Lake Balkhash
Altay
Hovd
Ulan Bator
Choybalsan
Taldykorgan
Lake Alakol'
ALTAI MOUNTAINS
MONGOLIA
Ebinur Hu
Almaty
Yining
Bishkek
Lake Issyk-Kul
KYRGYZSTAN
Saynshand
TIEN SHAN
Ürümqi
Gobi Desert
Turpan
Turpan Depression −154m
Hami
Erenhot
40°N
Tarim He
Kashi
Lop Nur
Hohhot
Jining
Zhangjiakou
Hotan He
Tarim Pendi
Anxi
Baotou
Datong
Beijing
Yumen
Wuhai
Tangshan
Tianjin
K2 (Qogir Feng) 8611m
Qilian Shan
Yinchuan
Great Wall
Huang He
Shijiazhuang
Altun Shan
Kunlun Shan
Taiyuan
Dezhou
JAMMU AND KASHMIR
Jinan
CHINA
Golmud
Qinghai Hu
Xining
Lanzhou
Handan
Changzhi
3
R. Indus
Rutog
Huang He
Plateau of Tibet
Zhengzhou
Wei He
Baoji
Luoyang
Xuzhou
Xi'an
Suzhou
HIMALAYA
Bengbu
Dehra Dun
Hefei
30°N
Xiangfan
NEPAL
Chengdu
Wuhan
Bareilly
Annapurna 8091m
Lhaze
Lhasa
Chang Jiang (Yangtze River)
Jingdezhen
Yarlung Zangbo (Tsangpo R.)
Batang
Chongqing
Dongting Hu
Poyang Hu
Lucknow
Mt. Everest 8848m
Neijiang
Changde
Nanchang
Kathmandu
Thimphu
Kanpur
Gorakhpur
Darjiling
BHUTAN
Dibrugarh
Yibin
Changsha
Zhuzhou
2
Allahabad
Varanasi
Shiliguri
Zunyi
Ji'an
Muzaffarpur
Brahmaputra R.
Ganges
Patna
Bhagalpur
Guiyang
Shaoyang
Hengyang
Murwara
Shillong
Duyun
Tropic of Cancer
BANGLADESH
Dali
Ganzhou
Jabalpur
Dhanbad
Kunming
Guilin
Nan Ling
Shaoguan
INDIA
Jamshedpur
Imphal
R. Chindwin
Dhaka
Liuzhou
Meizhou
Bilaspur
Kharagpur
Kolkata
Song Koi
Wuzhou
Raipur
Khulna
Chittagong
Salween R.
Mekong R.
Nanning
Xi Jiang
Guangzhou
Monywa
Mouths of the Ganges
Lao Cai
Macao
Hong Kong
Cuttack
MYANMAR (BURMA)
20°N
Mandalay
Pingxiang
Arakan Yoma
Phongsali
Sittwe
Kengtung
Hanoi
Zhanjiang
Irrawaddy R.
Hai Phong
Brahmapur
Bay of Bengal
Louangphrabang
Thanh Hoa
Haikou
Chiang Mai
VIETNAM
1
Vishakhapatnam
Pye
Vinh
Hainan Dao
Vientiane
LAOS
SOUTH CHINA SEA
Sanya
Udon Thani
Bassein
Pegu
Yangon
THAILAND
Moulmein
Huê
Da Nang
Mouths of the Irrawaddy
90°E
100°E
110°E
B
C
D
E

Conical Orthomorphic Projection

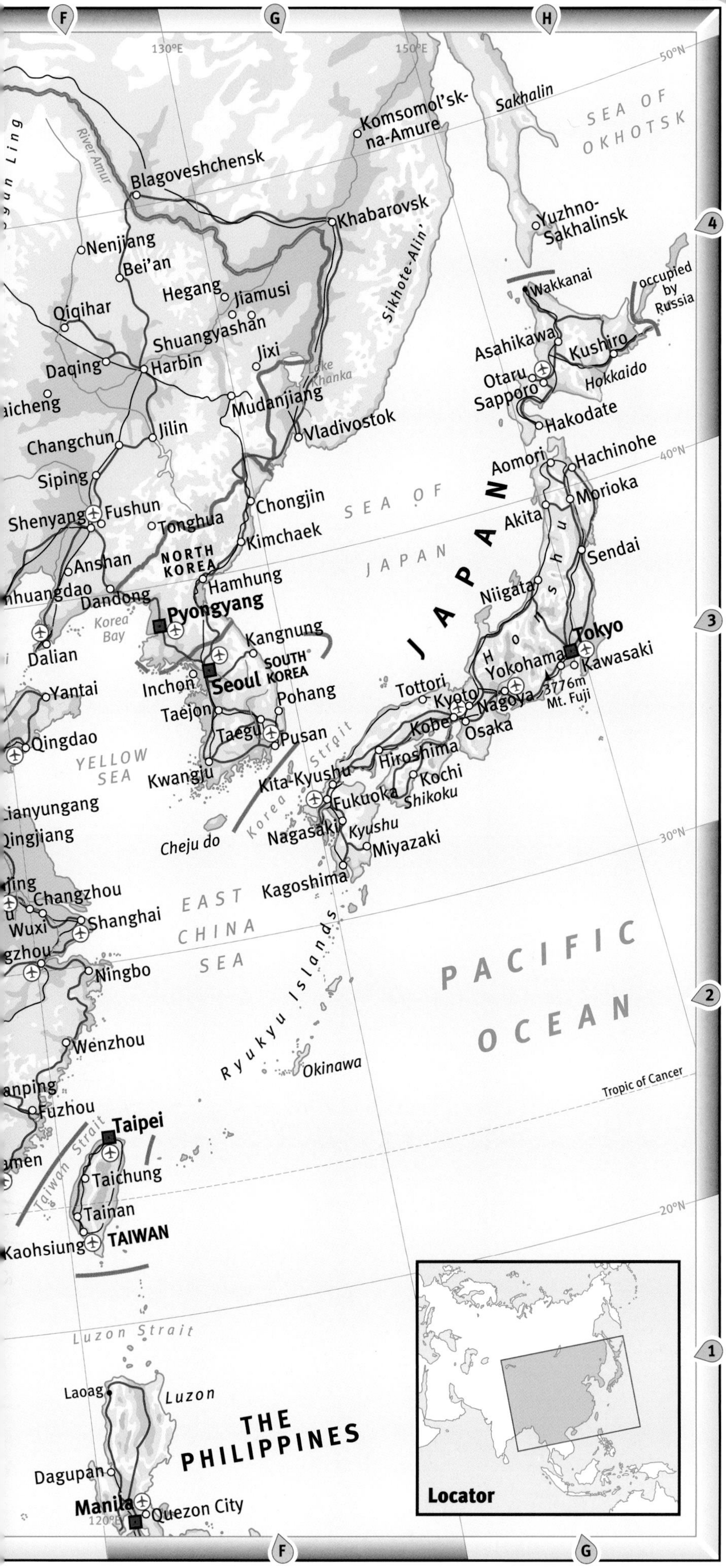

F G H

130°E 150°E 50°N 40°N 30°N 20°N 120°E

Sea of Okhotsk · Sakhalin · Komsomol'sk-na-Amure · River Amur · Blagoveshchensk · Khabarovsk · Yuzhno-Sakhalinsk · Sikhote-Alin' · Nenjiang · Bei'an · Hegang · Jiamusi · Qiqihar · Shuangyashan · Daqing · Harbin · Jixi · Lake Khanka · Mudanjiang · Vladivostok · Changchun · Jilin · Siping · Shenyang · Fushun · Tonghua · Chongjin · Kimchaek · Anshan · NORTH KOREA · Hamhung · Dandong · Pyongyang · Korea Bay · Dalian · Kangnung · Seoul · SOUTH KOREA · Inchon · Yantai · Taejon · Pohang · Taegu · Pusan · Qingdao · YELLOW SEA · Kwangju · Korea Strait · Cheju do · Lianyungang · Qingjiang · Changzhou · Shanghai · Wuxi · Ningbo · EAST CHINA SEA · Wenzhou · Fuzhou · Taipei · Taiwan Strait · Taichung · Tainan · TAIWAN · Kaohsiung · Luzon Strait · Laoag · Luzon · THE PHILIPPINES · Dagupan · Manila · Quezon City

SEA OF JAPAN · JAPAN · Wakkanai · occupied by Russia · Asahikawa · Kushiro · Otaru · Sapporo · Hokkaido · Hakodate · Aomori · Hachinohe · Morioka · Akita · Sendai · Honshu · Niigata · Tokyo · Yokohama · Kawasaki · 3776m Mt. Fuji · Tottori · Kyoto · Nagoya · Kobe · Osaka · Hiroshima · Kochi · Shikoku · Kita-Kyushu · Fukuoka · Nagasaki · Kyushu · Miyazaki · Kagoshima · Ryukyu Islands · Okinawa · PACIFIC OCEAN · Tropic of Cancer

4 3 2 1

Locator

F G

Mt. Fuji is Japan's highest peak

茂昌眼鏡公司
AOCHANG

Shopping in Shanghai, China

Key

- country boundary
- disputed boundary
- motorway or main road
- railway
- main airport
- river
- lake

towns and cities

- capital cities
- largest towns
- other large towns

land height

above sea level in metres

- more than 5000m
- 2000 – 5000m
- 1000 – 2000m
- 500 – 1000m
- 200 – 500m
- less than 200 metres
- land below sea level
- highest peaks with heights in metres

Scale One centimetre on the map represents 180 kilometres on the ground.

0 180 360 540km

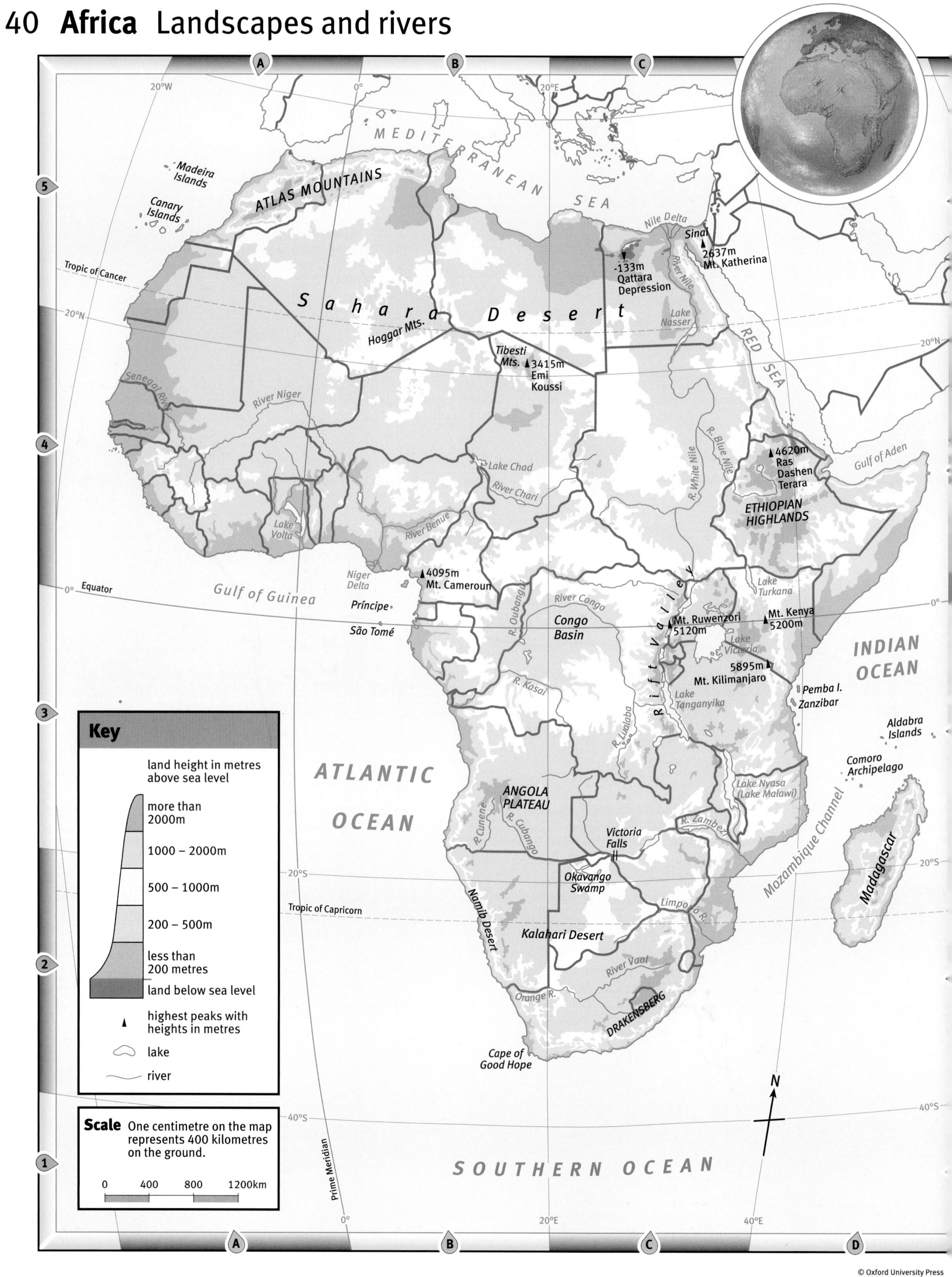

A
B
C
D
5
4
3
2
1
20°W
0°
20°E
40°E
20°N
0°
20°S
40°S
MEDITERRANEAN SEA
Madeira Islands
Canary Islands
ATLAS MOUNTAINS
Tropic of Cancer
Sahara Desert
Hoggar Mts.
Nile Delta
Sinai
2637m Mt. Katherina
-133m Qattara Depression
River Nile
Lake Nasser
RED SEA
Tibesti Mts.
3415m Emi Koussi
Senegal River
River Niger
Lake Chad
River Chari
R. Blue Nile
R. White Nile
4620m Ras Dashen Terara
ETHIOPIAN HIGHLANDS
Gulf of Aden
Lake Volta
River Benue
Niger Delta
4095m Mt. Cameroun
Equator
Gulf of Guinea
Príncipe
São Tomé
R. Oubangui
River Congo
Congo Basin
Lake Turkana
Mt. Ruwenzori 5120m
Mt. Kenya 5200m
Rift Valley
Lake Victoria
5895m
Mt. Kilimanjaro
INDIAN OCEAN
Pemba I.
Zanzibar
R. Kasai
R. Lualaba
Lake Tanganyika
Aldabra Islands
Comoro Archipelago
ATLANTIC OCEAN
ANGOLA PLATEAU
R. Cunene
R. Cubango
Lake Nyasa (Lake Malawi)
R. Zambezi
Mozambique Channel
Victoria Falls
Madagascar
Okavango Swamp
Namib Desert
Tropic of Capricorn
Limpopo R.
Kalahari Desert
River Vaal
Orange R.
DRAKENSBERG
Cape of Good Hope
N
SOUTHERN OCEAN
Prime Meridian
Key
land height in metres above sea level
more than 2000m
1000 – 2000m
500 – 1000m
200 – 500m
less than 200 metres
land below sea level
highest peaks with heights in metres
lake
river
Scale One centimetre on the map represents 400 kilometres on the ground.
0 400 800 1200km

Zenithal Equal Area Projection

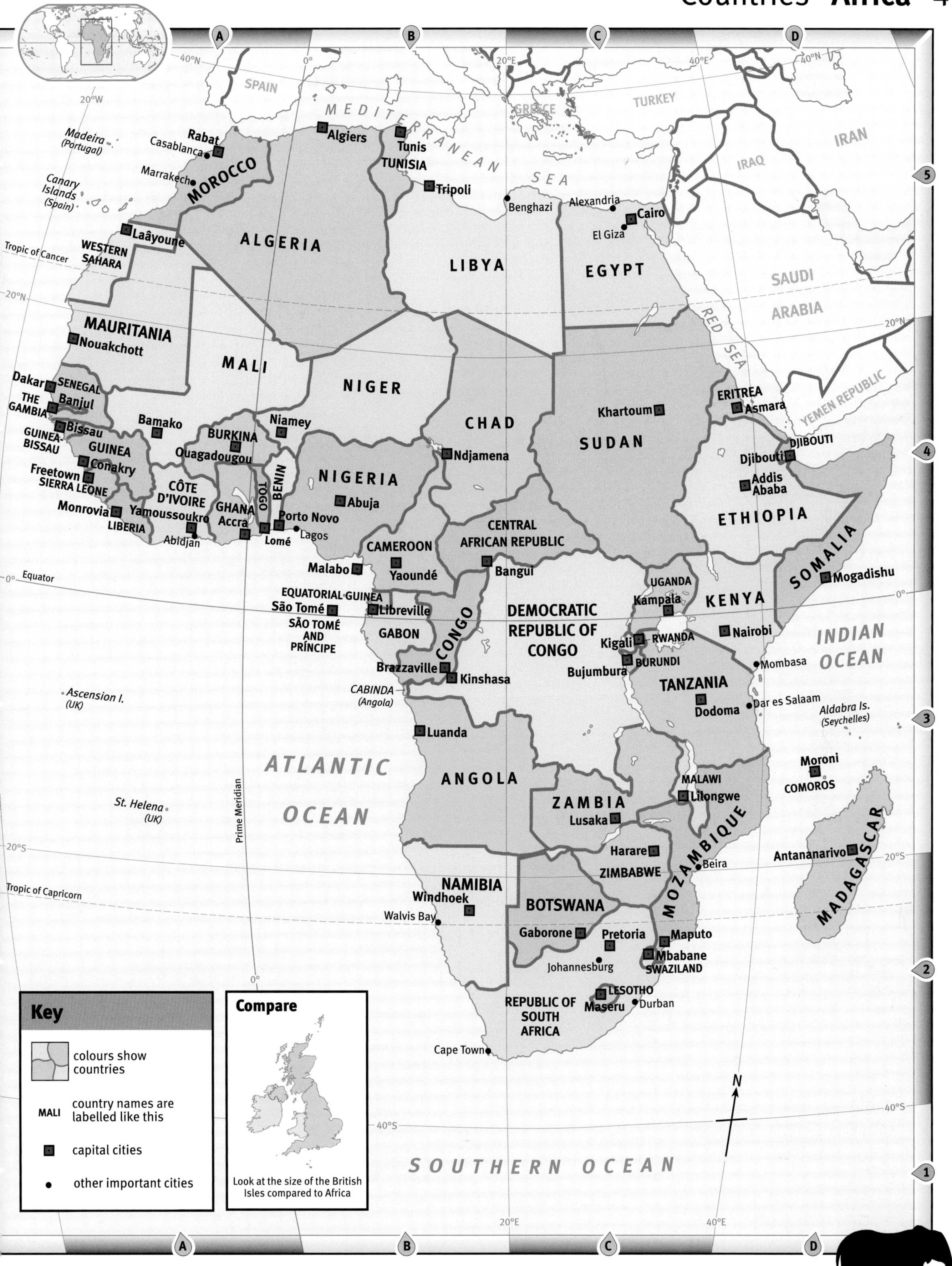
A
B
C
D
SPAIN
MEDITERRANEAN SEA
GREECE
TURKEY
IRAN
IRAQ
SAUDI ARABIA
RED SEA
YEMEN REPUBLIC
Madeira (Portugal)
Canary Islands (Spain)
Rabat
Casablanca
Marrakech
MOROCCO
Algiers
Tunis
TUNISIA
Tripoli
Benghazi
Alexandria
Cairo
El Giza
Laâyoune
WESTERN SAHARA
ALGERIA
LIBYA
EGYPT
Tropic of Cancer
MAURITANIA
Nouakchott
MALI
NIGER
CHAD
SUDAN
Khartoum
ERITREA
Asmara
DJIBOUTI
Djibouti
Addis Ababa
ETHIOPIA
SOMALIA
Mogadishu
Dakar
SENEGAL
THE GAMBIA
Banjul
GUINEA-BISSAU
Bissau
GUINEA
Conakry
Freetown
SIERRA LEONE
Monrovia
LIBERIA
Bamako
BURKINA
Ouagadougou
Niamey
CÔTE D'IVOIRE
Yamoussoukro
Abidjan
GHANA
Accra
TOGO
Lomé
BENIN
Porto Novo
Lagos
NIGERIA
Abuja
Ndjamena
CAMEROON
Yaoundé
Malabo
CENTRAL AFRICAN REPUBLIC
Bangui
EQUATORIAL GUINEA
São Tomé
SÃO TOMÉ AND PRÍNCIPE
Libreville
GABON
CONGO
Brazzaville
Kinshasa
DEMOCRATIC REPUBLIC OF CONGO
UGANDA
Kampala
KENYA
Nairobi
Kigali
RWANDA
BURUNDI
Bujumbura
Mombasa
TANZANIA
Dodoma
Dar es Salaam
INDIAN OCEAN
Equator
CABINDA (Angola)
Ascension I. (UK)
Luanda
ATLANTIC OCEAN
ANGOLA
Aldabra Is. (Seychelles)
Moroni
COMOROS
MALAWI
Lilongwe
ZAMBIA
Lusaka
MOZAMBIQUE
St. Helena (UK)
Prime Meridian
Harare
ZIMBABWE
Beira
Antananarivo
MADAGASCAR
Tropic of Capricorn
NAMIBIA
Windhoek
Walvis Bay
BOTSWANA
Gaborone
Pretoria
Johannesburg
Maputo
Mbabane
SWAZILAND
LESOTHO
Maseru
Durban
REPUBLIC OF SOUTH AFRICA
Cape Town
N
SOUTHERN OCEAN
Key
colours show countries
MALI country names are labelled like this
capital cities
other important cities
Compare
Look at the size of the British Isles compared to Africa
40°N
20°N
0°
20°S
40°S
20°W
0°
20°E
40°E
1
2
3
4
5

Egypt

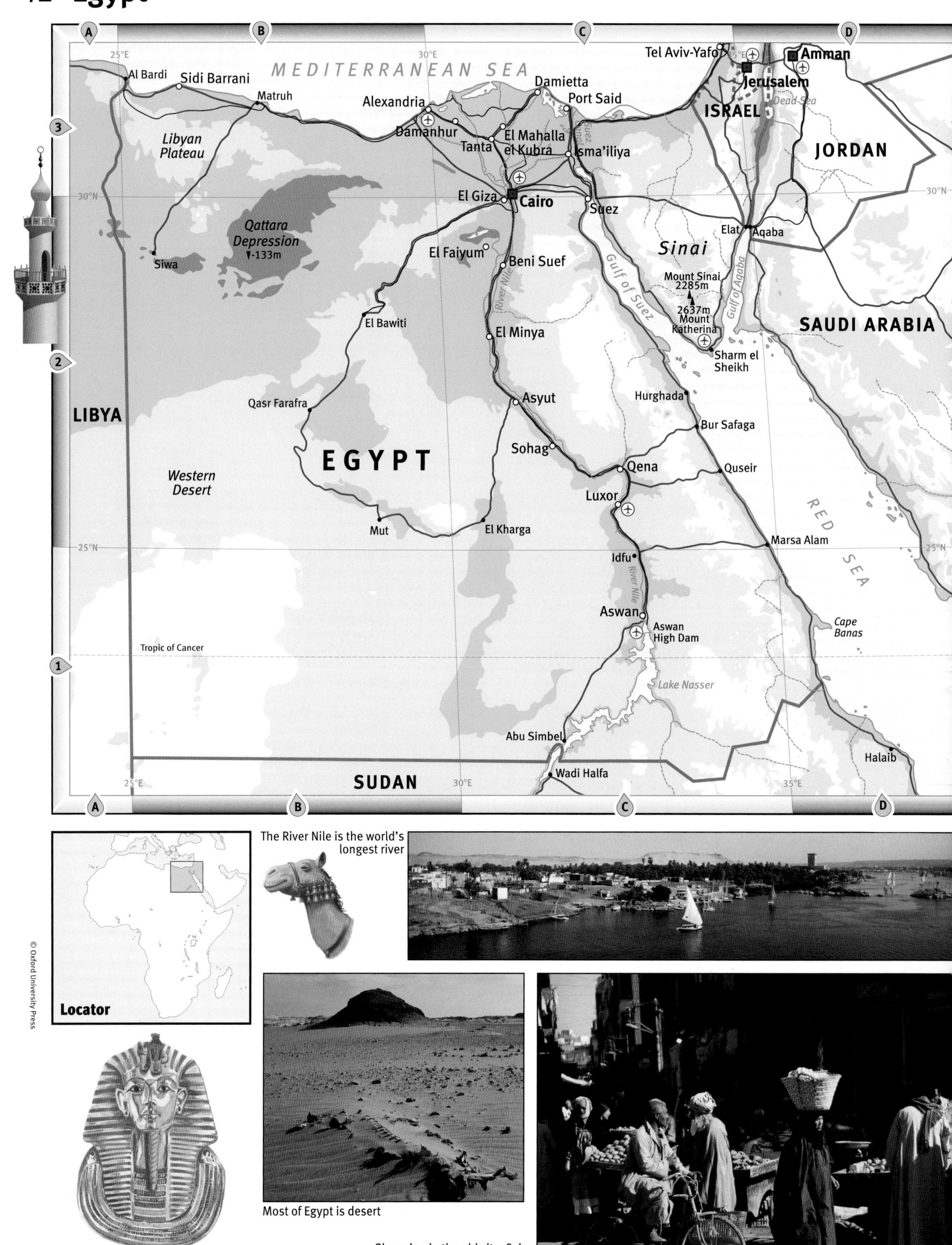
A
B
C
D
3
2
1
25°E
30°E
35°E
30°N
25°N
MEDITERRANEAN SEA
Al Bardi
Sidi Barrani
Matruh
Alexandria
Damietta
Port Said
Tel Aviv-Yafo
Amman
Jerusalem
ISRAEL
Dead Sea
JORDAN
Libyan Plateau
Damanhur
Tanta
El Mahalla el Kubra
Isma'iliya
Suez Canal
El Giza
Cairo
Suez
Qattara Depression
-133m
Siwa
El Faiyum
Beni Suef
Elat
Aqaba
Sinai
Gulf of Suez
Mount Sinai 2285m
2637m Mount Katherina
Gulf of Aqaba
SAUDI ARABIA
El Bawiti
El Minya
River Nile
Sharm el Sheikh
LIBYA
Hurghada
Asyut
Qasr Farafra
Bur Safaga
Sohag
EGYPT
Qena
Quseir
Western Desert
Luxor
RED SEA
Mut
El Kharga
Marsa Alam
Idfu
River Nile
Aswan
Aswan High Dam
Cape Banas
Tropic of Cancer
Lake Nasser
Abu Simbel
Halaib
Wadi Halfa
SUDAN
Locator

The River Nile is the world's longest river

Most of Egypt is desert

Shopping in the old city, Cairo

Key

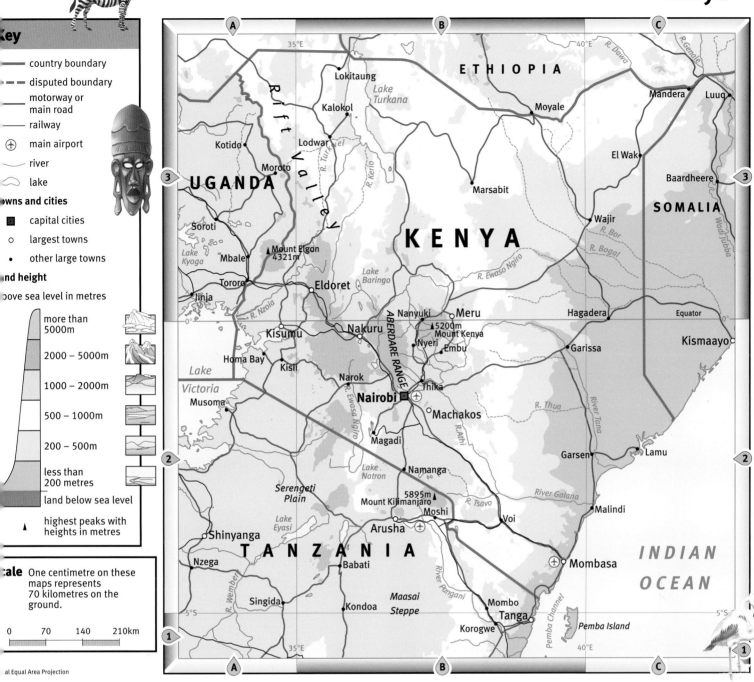

- country boundary
- disputed boundary
- motorway or main road
- railway
- main airport
- river
- lake

Towns and cities

- capital cities
- largest towns
- other large towns

Land height

above sea level in metres

- more than 5000m
- 2000 – 5000m
- 1000 – 2000m
- 500 – 1000m
- 200 – 500m
- less than 200 metres
- land below sea level
- highest peaks with heights in metres

ETHIOPIA
UGANDA
KENYA
SOMALIA
TANZANIA
INDIAN OCEAN
Lokitaung
Lake Turkana
Kalokol
Lodwar
Kotido
Moroto
Rift Valley
Moyale
Mandera
Luuq
El Wak
Marsabit
Baardheere
Wajir
Soroti
Mbale
Mount Elgon 4321m
Lake Kyoga
Tororo
Jinja
Eldoret
Lake Baringo
Kisumu
Nakuru
Nanyuki
Meru
5200m Mount Kenya
Nyeri
Embu
Hagadera
Garissa
Kismaayo
Equator
Homa Bay
Kisii
Lake Victoria
Narok
ABERDARE RANGE
Thika
Nairobi
Machakos
Musoma
Magadi
Garsen
Lamu
Namanga
Lake Natron
Serengeti Plain
5895m Mount Kilimanjaro
Moshi
Arusha
Voi
Malindi
Lake Eyasi
Shinyanga
Mombasa
Nzega
Babati
Singida
Kondoa
Maasai Steppe
Mombo
Tanga
Korogwe
Pemba Channel
Pemba Island
R. Turkwel
R. Kerio
R. Dawa
R. Genale
R. Bor
R. Bogal
R. Ewaso Ngiro
R. Nzoia
R. Ewasa Ngiro
R. Thua
River Tana
R. Athi
River Galana
R. Tsavo
River Pangani
R. Wembere
Wadi Jubba
35°E
40°E
0°
5°S

Scale One centimetre on these maps represents 70 kilometres on the ground.

0 70 140 210km

Lambert Azimuthal Equal Area Projection

The Maasai people herd cattle in central Kenya

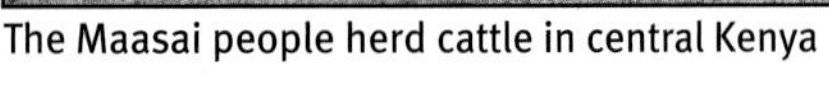

Kilimanjaro is Africa's highest mountain

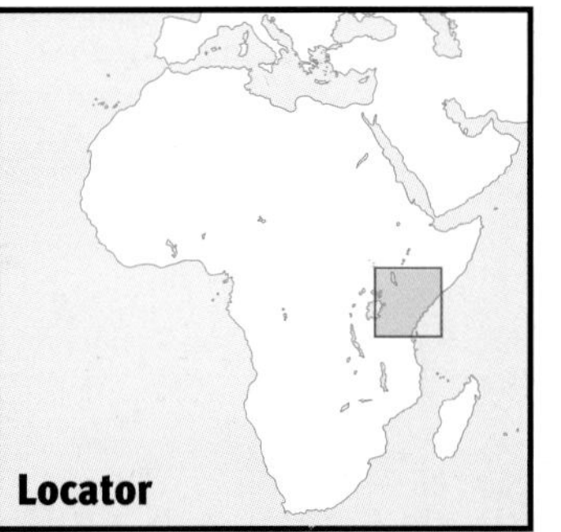
Locator

From Mombasa to Nairobi by road takes about 8 hours

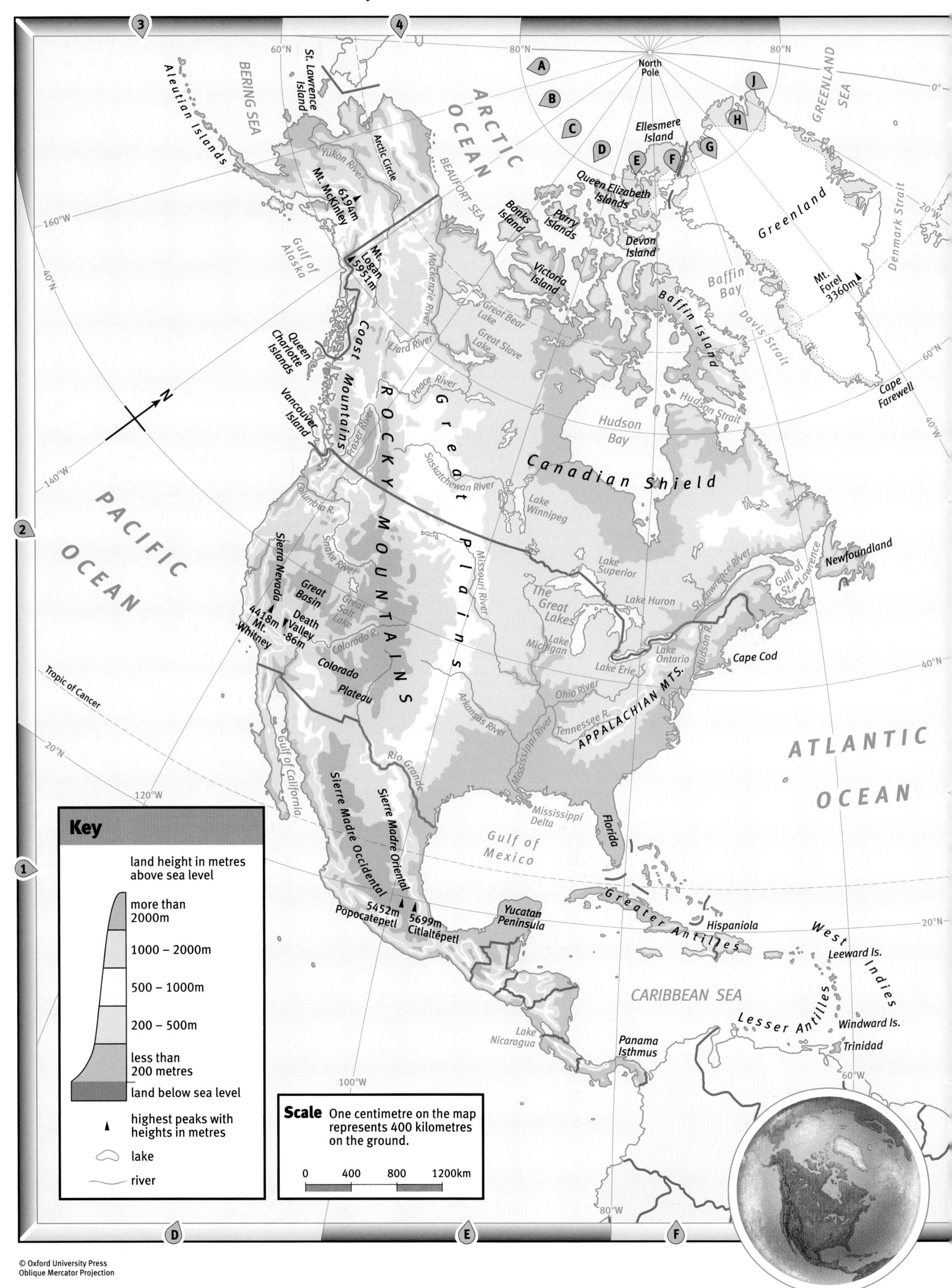

ARCTIC OCEAN
North Pole
BERING SEA
Aleutian Islands
St. Lawrence Island
Yukon River
Arctic Circle
Mt. McKinley 6194m
BEAUFORT SEA
Gulf of Alaska
Mt. Logan 5951m
Mackenzie River
Banks Island
Parry Islands
Queen Elizabeth Islands
Ellesmere Island
Devon Island
Victoria Island
Greenland
GREENLAND SEA
Denmark Strait
Mt. Forel 3360m
Baffin Bay
Baffin Island
Davis Strait
Cape Farewell
Great Bear Lake
Great Slave Lake
Liard River
Peace River
Queen Charlotte Islands
Coast Mountains
Vancouver Island
Fraser River
ROCKY MOUNTAINS
Great Plains
Hudson Strait
Hudson Bay
Canadian Shield
Saskatchewan River
Lake Winnipeg
PACIFIC OCEAN
Columbia R.
Snake River
Sierra Nevada
Great Basin
Great Salt Lake
Death Valley -86m
4418m Mt. Whitney
Missouri River
Lake Superior
The Great Lakes
Lake Huron
Lake Michigan
Lake Ontario
Lake Erie
St. Lawrence River
Gulf of St. Lawrence
Newfoundland
Hudson R.
Cape Cod
Colorado R.
Colorado Plateau
Ohio River
Tennessee R.
APPALACHIAN MTS.
Arkansas River
Mississippi River
Rio Grande
Tropic of Cancer
Gulf of California
Sierre Madre Occidental
Sierre Madre Oriental
Mississippi Delta
Gulf of Mexico
Florida
ATLANTIC OCEAN
5452m Popocatepetl
5699m Citlaltépetl
Yucatan Peninsula
Greater Antilles
Hispaniola
West Indies
Leeward Is.
Windward Is.
CARIBBEAN SEA
Lesser Antilles
Trinidad
Lake Nicaragua
Panama Isthmus
60°N
80°N
160°W
140°W
120°W
100°W
80°W
60°W
40°N
20°N
0°
20°W
40°W
Key
land height in metres above sea level
more than 2000m
1000 – 2000m
500 – 1000m
200 – 500m
less than 200 metres
land below sea level
highest peaks with heights in metres
lake
river
Scale One centimetre on the map represents 400 kilometres on the ground.
0
400
800
1200km

Oblique Mercator Projection

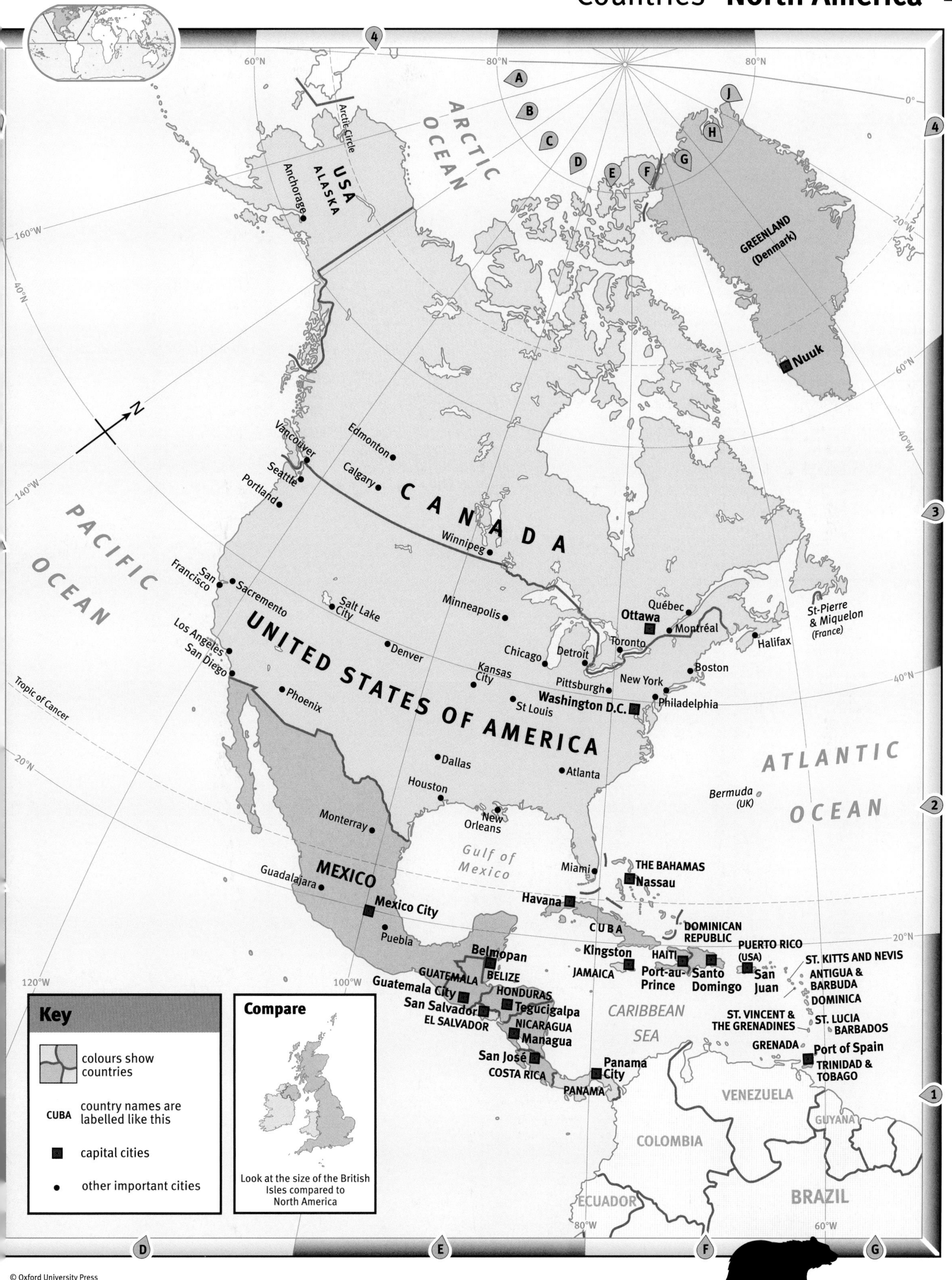
ARCTIC OCEAN
PACIFIC OCEAN
ATLANTIC OCEAN
Gulf of Mexico
CARIBBEAN SEA
USA ALASKA
Anchorage
Arctic Circle
GREENLAND (Denmark)
Nuuk
CANADA
Edmonton
Vancouver
Calgary
Seattle
Portland
Winnipeg
Ottawa
Québec
Montréal
Toronto
Halifax
St-Pierre & Miquelon (France)
UNITED STATES OF AMERICA
San Francisco
Sacremento
Salt Lake City
Minneapolis
Los Angeles
San Diego
Denver
Chicago
Detroit
Boston
Kansas City
Pittsburgh
New York
Philadelphia
Washington D.C.
St Louis
Phoenix
Dallas
Atlanta
Houston
New Orleans
Bermuda (UK)
Monterray
MEXICO
Guadalajara
Mexico City
Puebla
Miami
THE BAHAMAS
Nassau
Havana
CUBA
DOMINICAN REPUBLIC
PUERTO RICO (USA)
Kingston
JAMAICA
HAITI
Port-au-Prince
Santo Domingo
San Juan
ST. KITTS AND NEVIS
ANTIGUA & BARBUDA
DOMINICA
ST. LUCIA
BARBADOS
ST. VINCENT & THE GRENADINES
GRENADA
Port of Spain
TRINIDAD & TOBAGO
Belmopan
BELIZE
GUATEMALA
Guatemala City
HONDURAS
Tegucigalpa
San Salvador
EL SALVADOR
NICARAGUA
Managua
San José
COSTA RICA
Panama City
PANAMA
VENEZUELA
GUYANA
COLOMBIA
ECUADOR
BRAZIL
Tropic of Cancer
60°N
80°N
40°N
20°N
0°
20°W
40°W
60°W
80°W
100°W
120°W
140°W
160°W
N
A
B
C
D
E
F
G
H
J
1
2
3
4
Key
colours show countries
CUBA country names are labelled like this
capital cities
other important cities
Compare
Look at the size of the British Isles compared to North America

United States of America

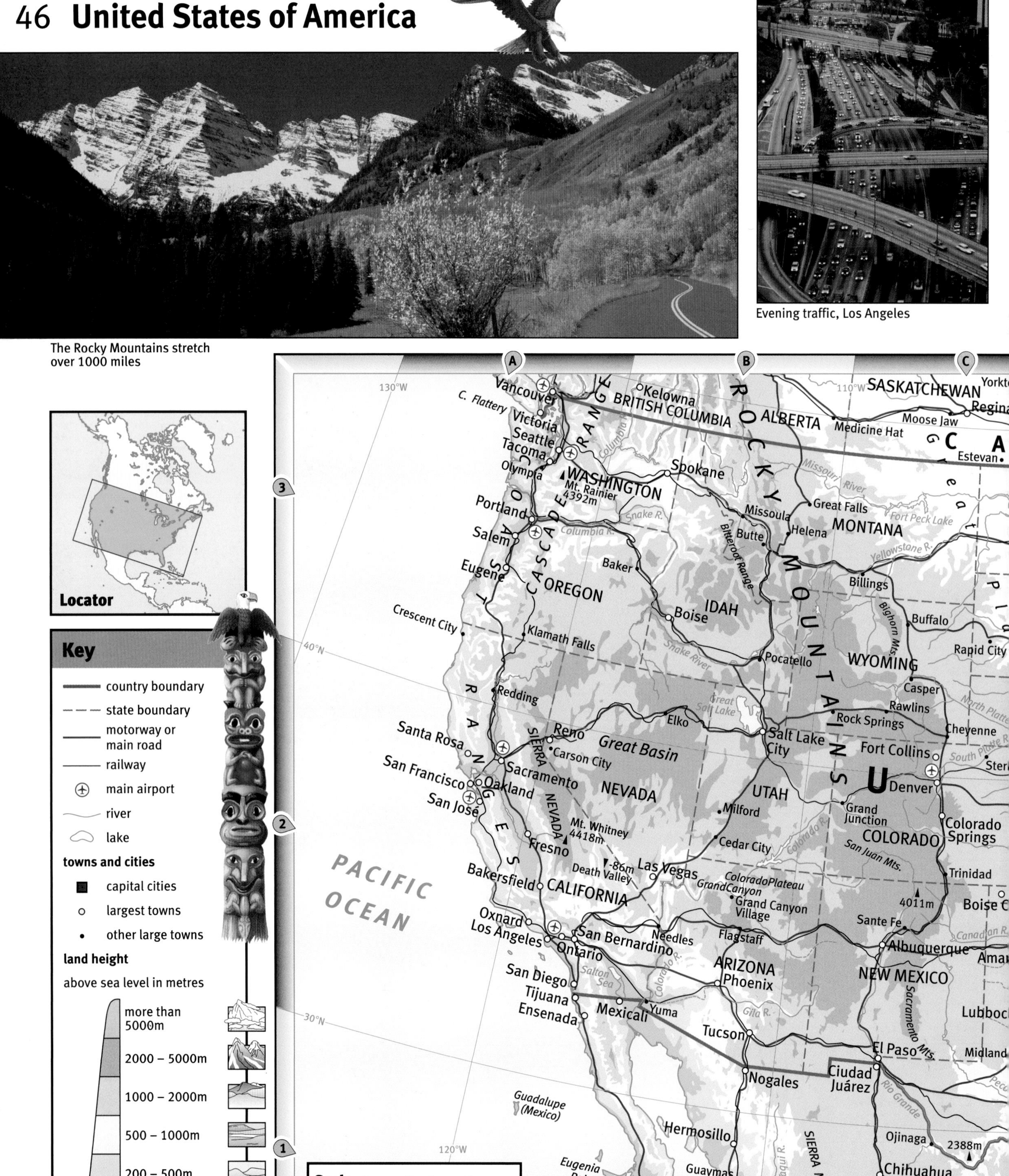

A
B
C
3
2
1
130°W
110°W
120°W
40°N
30°N
SASKATCHEWAN
Yorkt
Regina
Moose Jaw
Medicine Hat
ALBERTA
BRITISH COLUMBIA
Kelowna
Vancouver
C. Flattery
Victoria
Seattle
Tacoma
Olympia
WASHINGTON
Mt. Rainier
4392m
Spokane
Missouri River
Great Falls
Estevan
CA
Fort Peck Lake
Great
Missoula
Butte
Helena
MONTANA
Portland
Salem
Snake R.
Columbia R.
Bitterroot Range
Yellowstone R.
Eugene
Baker
Billings
OREGON
CASCADE RANGE
COAST RANGES
ROCKY MOUNTAINS
Crescent City
Klamath Falls
Boise
IDAHO
Bighorn Mts.
Buffalo
Rapid City
Pocatello
Snake River
WYOMING
Casper
Redding
Great Salt Lake
Rawlins
North Platte
Elko
Rock Springs
Cheyenne
Santa Rosa
Reno
Great Basin
Salt Lake City
Fort Collins
South Platte R.
Carson City
San Francisco
Sacramento
SIERRA NEVADA
Denver
Oakland
NEVADA
UTAH
San José
Milford
Grand Junction
Mt. Whitney
4418m
Colorado Springs
Fresno
Cedar City
Colorado R.
COLORADO
San Juan Mts.
PACIFIC OCEAN
Death Valley
-86m
Las Vegas
Trinidad
Bakersfield
CALIFORNIA
Colorado Plateau
Grand Canyon
Grand Canyon Village
4011m
Oxnard
Los Angeles
Sante Fe
Canadian R.
San Bernardino
Needles
Flagstaff
Ontario
Albuquerque
Salton Sea
ARIZONA
NEW MEXICO
San Diego
Phoenix
Sacramento Mts.
Tijuana
Mexicali
Yuma
Ensenada
Lubboc
Gila R.
Tucson
El Paso
Midland
Nogales
Ciudad Juárez
Rio Grande
Guadalupe (Mexico)
Hermosillo
Ojinaga
2388m
Eugenia Point
Guaymas
Yaqui R.
SIERRA MADRE OCCIDENTAL
Chihuahua
Santa Rosalia
Gulf of California
Ciudad Obregon
MEXICO
Monclo
Hidalgo del Parral
Los Mochis
Scale One centimetre on the map represents 150 kilometres on the ground.
0 150 300 450km
Locator
Key
country boundary
state boundary
motorway or main road
railway
main airport
river
lake
towns and cities
capital cities
largest towns
other large towns
land height
above sea level in metres
more than 5000m
2000 – 5000m
1000 – 2000m
500 – 1000m
200 – 500m
less than 200 metres
land below sea level
highest peaks with heights in metres

Evening traffic, Los Angeles

The Rocky Mountains stretch over 1000 miles

Conical Orthomorphic Projection

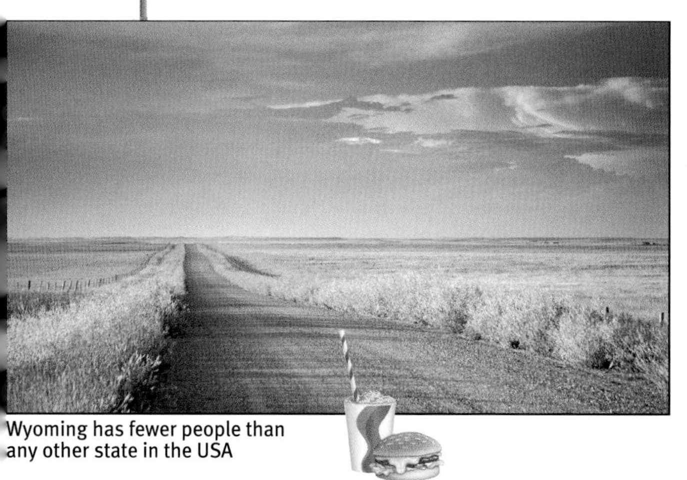
Wyoming has fewer people than any other state in the USA

Manhattan skyline, New York City

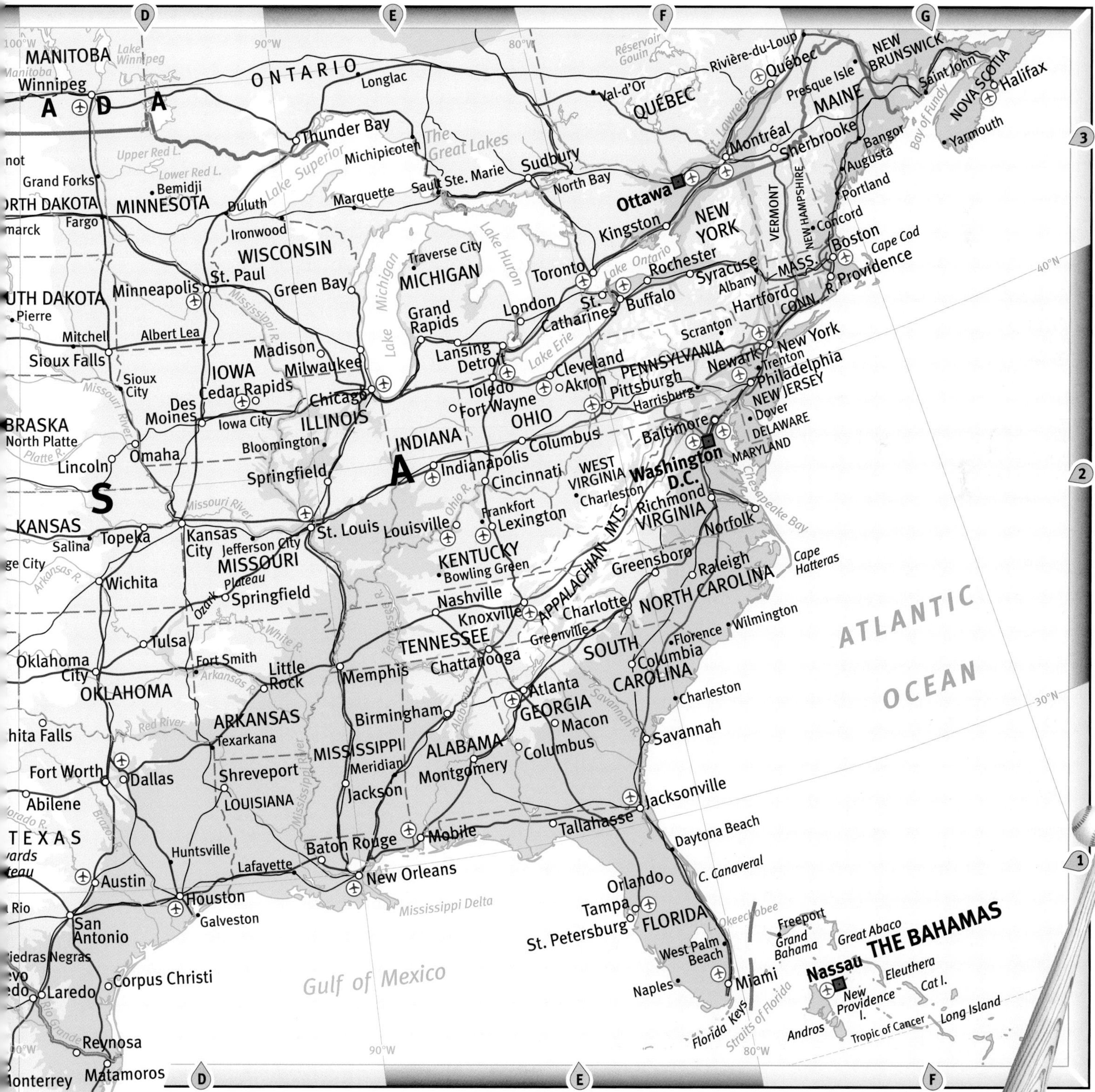

D E F G

100°W 90°W 80°W

MANITOBA
Lake Winnipeg
Manitoba
Winnipeg
ONTARIO
Longlac
A D A
Thunder Bay
Michipicoten
The Great Lakes
Upper Red L.
Lower Red L.
Lake Superior
Sudbury
North Bay
Sault Ste. Marie
Marquette
Grand Forks
Bemidji
MINNESOTA
Duluth
ORTH DAKOTA
Fargo
marck
Ironwood
WISCONSIN
Traverse City
Lake Huron
Lake Michigan
MICHIGAN
St. Paul
Minneapolis
Green Bay
UTH DAKOTA
Pierre
Mitchell
Albert Lea
Sioux Falls
Madison
Milwaukee
Grand Rapids
Lansing
Detroit
London
Toronto
Lake Ontario
St. Catharines
Buffalo
Rochester
Syracuse
Albany
Kingston
Ottawa
Réservoir Gouin
Val-d'Or
QUÉBEC
Rivière-du-Loup
Québec
St. Lawrence
Montréal
Sherbrooke
NEW YORK
VERMONT
NEW HAMPSHIRE
Concord
MAINE
Presque Isle
Bangor
Augusta
Portland
NEW BRUNSWICK
Saint John
Bay of Fundy
NOVA SCOTIA
Halifax
Yarmouth
Boston
Cape Cod
MASS.
Providence
R.I.
CONN.
Hartford
Scranton
New York
Newark
Trenton
Philadelphia
NEW JERSEY
Dover
DELAWARE
MARYLAND
Baltimore
Washington D.C.
Harrisburg
PENNSYLVANIA
Pittsburgh
Cleveland
Akron
Lake Erie
Toledo
Fort Wayne
OHIO
Columbus
IOWA
Cedar Rapids
Sioux City
Missouri River
Des Moines
Iowa City
Chicago
ILLINOIS
INDIANA
Indianapolis
Cincinnati
Bloomington
BRASKA
North Platte
Platte R.
Lincoln
Omaha
Springfield
S
A
WEST VIRGINIA
Charleston
Richmond
VIRGINIA
Norfolk
Chesapeake Bay
Frankfort
Lexington
Louisville
Ohio R.
KENTUCKY
Bowling Green
St. Louis
Missouri River
Mississippi R.
KANSAS
Salina
Topeka
Kansas City
Jefferson City
MISSOURI
ge City
Arkansas R.
Wichita
Ozark Plateau
Springfield
APPALACHIAN MTS.
Greensboro
Raleigh
NORTH CAROLINA
Cape Hatteras
Nashville
Knoxville
Charlotte
Tennessee R.
TENNESSEE
Tulsa
White R.
Greenville
SOUTH CAROLINA
Florence
Wilmington
Columbia
ATLANTIC OCEAN
Oklahoma City
OKLAHOMA
Fort Smith
Arkansas R.
Little Rock
Memphis
Chattanooga
Atlanta
GEORGIA
Charleston
Macon
Savannah R.
Alabama R.
Birmingham
ARKANSAS
Red River
Texarkana
hita Falls
Mississippi River
MISSISSIPPI
ALABAMA
Columbus
Savannah
Meridian
Montgomery
Fort Worth
Dallas
Shreveport
LOUISIANA
Jackson
Jacksonville
Abilene
orado R.
Brazos R.
TEXAS
vards teau
Huntsville
Baton Rouge
Mobile
Tallahasse
Daytona Beach
Lafayette
New Orleans
C. Canaveral
Austin
Houston
Orlando
Rio
San Antonio
Galveston
Mississippi Delta
Tampa
St. Petersburg
FLORIDA
L. Okeechobee
Freeport
Grand Bahama
Great Abaco
THE BAHAMAS
iedras Negras
evo redo
Laredo
Corpus Christi
Gulf of Mexico
West Palm Beach
Naples
Miami
Nassau
Eleuthera
New Providence I.
Cat I.
Rio Grande
Reynosa
Florida Keys
Straits of Florida
Andros
Tropic of Cancer
Long Island
Monterrey
Matamoros

40°N 30°N

3 2 1

D E F

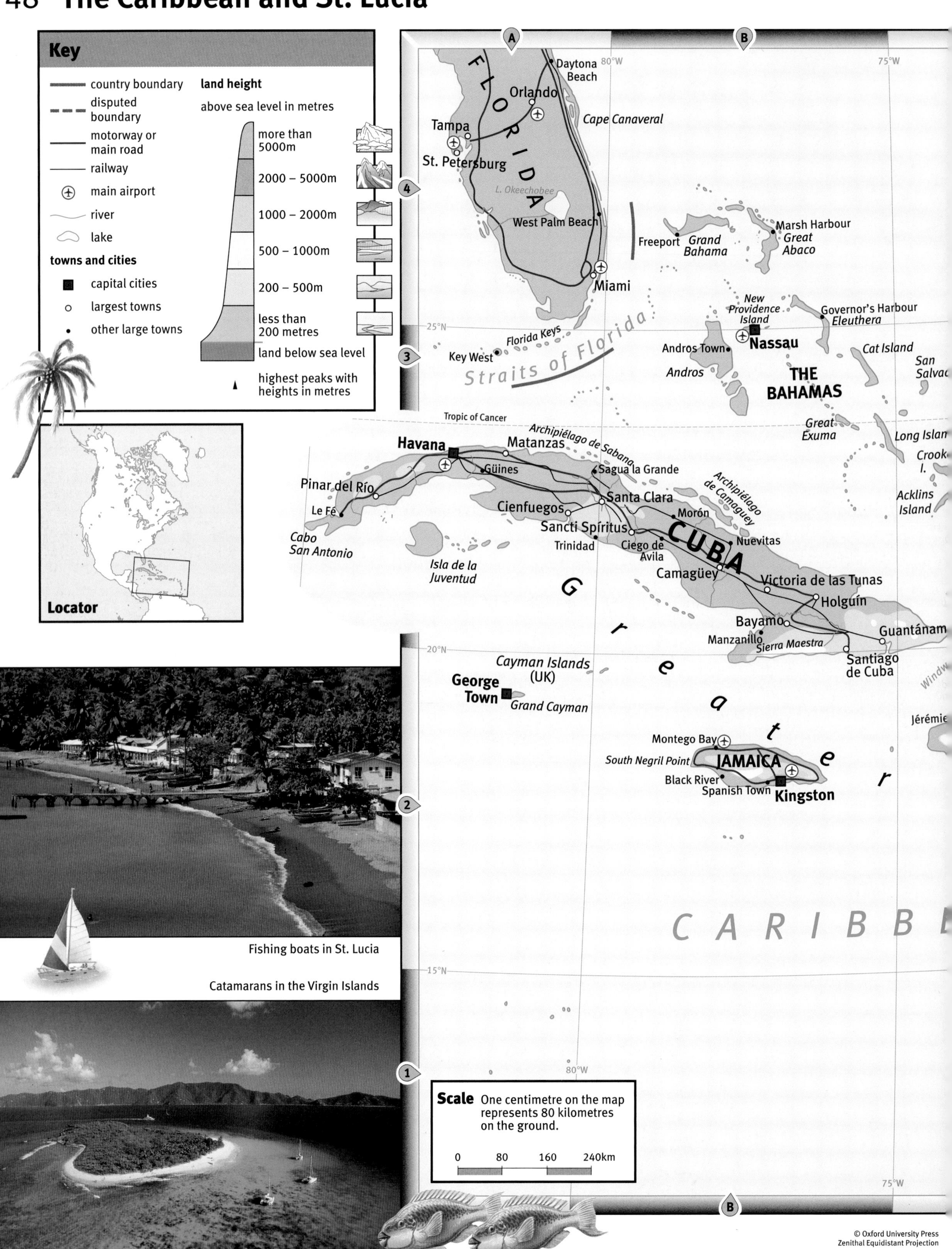
Key
country boundary
disputed boundary
motorway or main road
railway
main airport
river
lake
towns and cities
capital cities
largest towns
other large towns
land height
above sea level in metres
more than 5000m
2000 – 5000m
1000 – 2000m
500 – 1000m
200 – 500m
less than 200 metres
land below sea level
highest peaks with heights in metres
Locator
A
B
4
3
2
1
80°W
75°W
25°N
20°N
15°N
Tropic of Cancer
FLORIDA
Daytona Beach
Orlando
Cape Canaveral
Tampa
St. Petersburg
L. Okeechobee
West Palm Beach
Miami
Florida Keys
Key West
Straits of Florida
Freeport
Grand Bahama
Marsh Harbour
Great Abaco
New Providence Island
Nassau
Governor's Harbour
Eleuthera
Andros Town
Andros
Cat Island
San Salvac
THE BAHAMAS
Great Exuma
Long Islan
Crook I.
Acklins Island
Havana
Matanzas
Archipiélago de Sabana
Güines
Sagua la Grande
Pinar del Río
Le Fé
Cienfuegos
Santa Clara
Archipiélago de Camagüey
Morón
Sancti Spíritus
Trinidad
Ciego de Avila
CUBA
Nuevitas
Cabo San Antonio
Isla de la Juventud
Camagüey
Victoria de las Tunas
Holguín
Bayamo
Manzanillo
Sierra Maestra
Guantánam
Santiago de Cuba
Greater
Cayman Islands (UK)
George Town
Grand Cayman
Windw
Jérémie
Montego Bay
South Negril Point
JAMAICA
Black River
Spanish Town
Kingston
CARIBB
Scale One centimetre on the map represents 80 kilometres on the ground.
0
80
160
240km
© Oxford University Press
Zenithal Equidistant Projection

Fishing boats in St. Lucia

Catamarans in the Virgin Islands

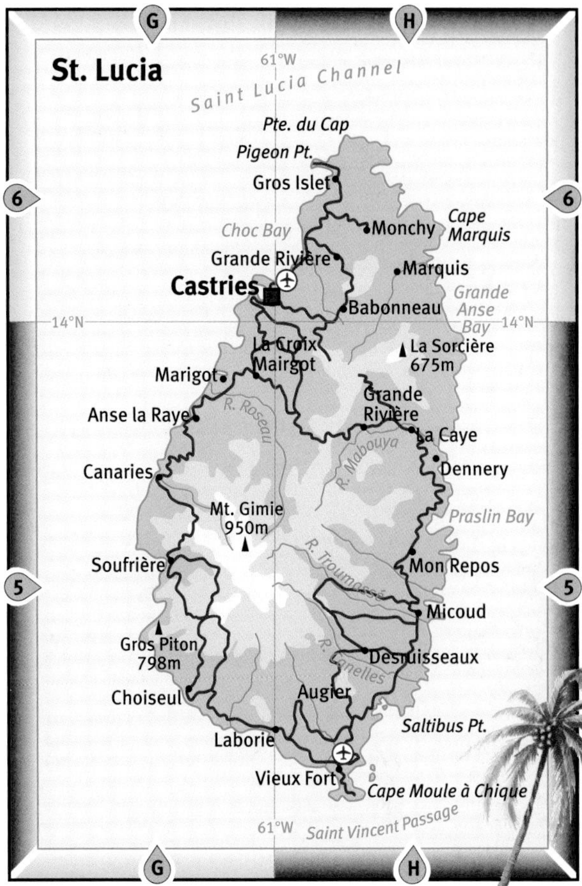

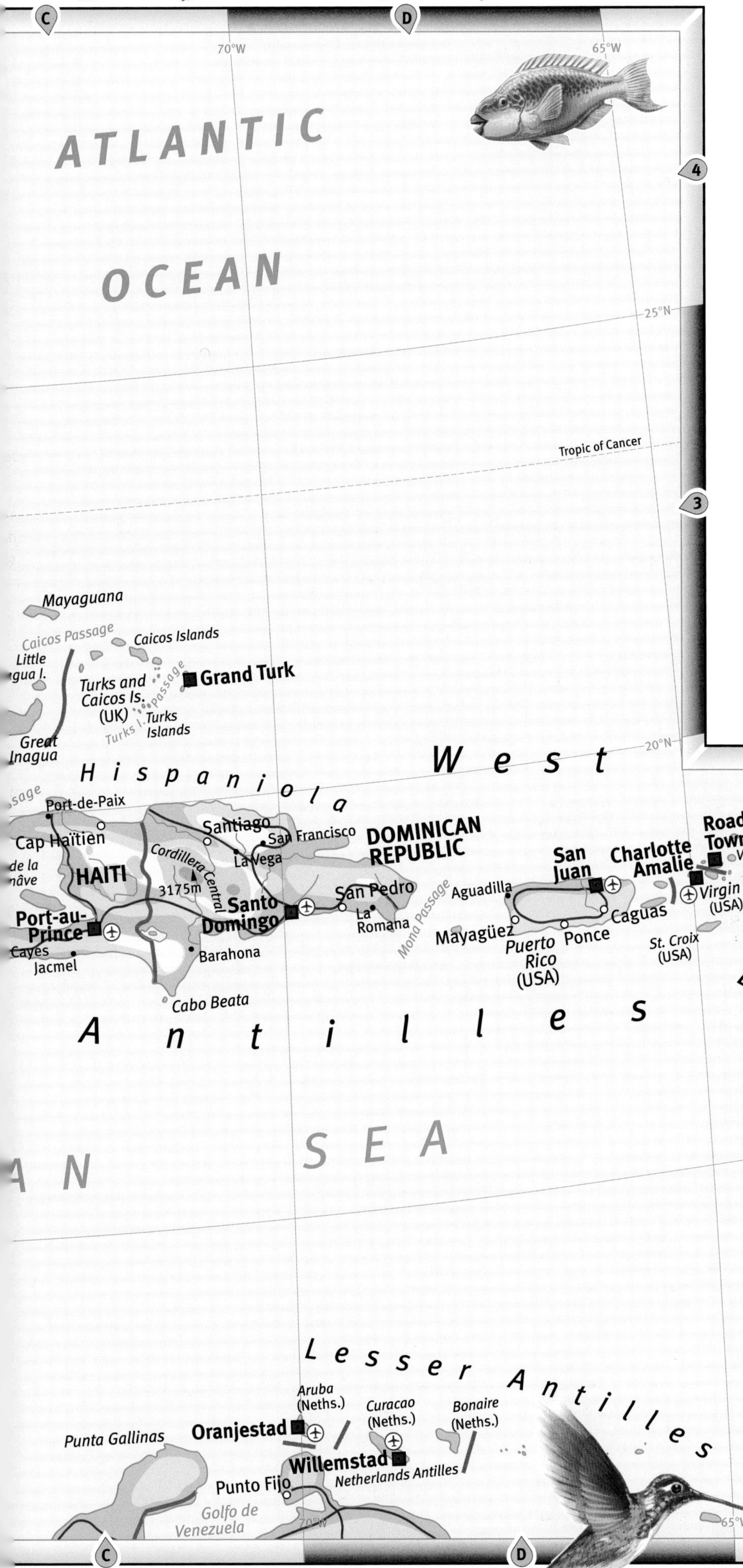

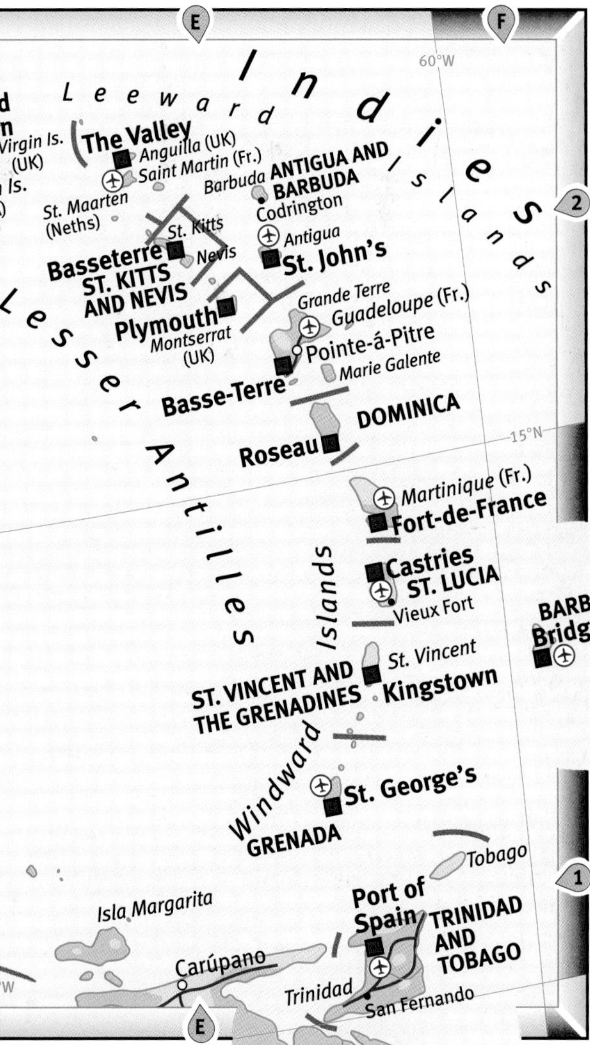

St. Lucia

Saint Lucia Channel
61°W
14°N
Pte. du Cap
Pigeon Pt.
Gros Islet
Monchy
Cape Marquis
Choc Bay
Grande Rivière
Marquis
Castries
Babonneau
Grande Anse Bay
La Croix Maingot
La Sorcière 675m
Marigot
Grande Rivière
Anse la Raye
R. Roseau
La Caye
R. Mabouya
Dennery
Canaries
Mt. Gimie 950m
Praslin Bay
R. Troumassée
Soufrière
Mon Repos
Micoud
Gros Piton 798m
R. Canelles
Desruisseaux
Choiseul
Augier
Saltibus Pt.
Laborie
Vieux Fort
Cape Moule à Chique
Saint Vincent Passage

The Caribbean

70°W
65°W
60°W
25°N
20°N
15°N
Tropic of Cancer
ATLANTIC OCEAN
Mayaguana
Caicos Passage
Caicos Islands
Little Inagua I.
Turks and Caicos Is. (UK)
Grand Turk
Turks I. Passage
Turks Islands
Great Inagua
Hispaniola
West Indies
Port-de-Paix
Cap Haïtien
Santiago
San Francisco
La Vega
Cordillera Central
3175m
HAITI
DOMINICAN REPUBLIC
Port-au-Prince
Santo Domingo
San Pedro
La Romana
Barahona
Cayes
Jacmel
Cabo Beata
Mona Passage
Aguadilla
Mayagüez
San Juan
Puerto Rico (USA)
Ponce
Caguas
Charlotte Amalie
Virgin Is. (USA)
Road Town
Virgin Is. (UK)
St. Croix (USA)
Leeward Islands
The Valley
Anguilla (UK)
Saint Martin (Fr.)
St. Maarten (Neths)
Barbuda
ANTIGUA AND BARBUDA
Codrington
Antigua
St. John's
St. Kitts
Nevis
Basseterre
ST. KITTS AND NEVIS
Plymouth
Montserrat (UK)
Grande Terre
Guadeloupe (Fr.)
Pointe-á-Pitre
Basse-Terre
Marie Galente
DOMINICA
Roseau
Lesser Antilles
Martinique (Fr.)
Fort-de-France
Castries
ST. LUCIA
Vieux Fort
BARBADOS
Bridgetown
Windward Islands
St. Vincent
ST. VINCENT AND THE GRENADINES
Kingstown
St. George's
GRENADA
Tobago
Port of Spain
TRINIDAD AND TOBAGO
Trinidad
San Fernando
Isla Margarita
Carúpano
Antilles
CARIBBEAN SEA
Lesser Antilles
Aruba (Neths.)
Oranjestad
Curacao (Neths.)
Willemstad
Bonaire (Neths.)
Netherlands Antilles
Punta Gallinas
Punto Fijo
Golfo de Venezuela

South America Landscapes and rivers

CARIBBEAN SEA
Lake Maracaibo
Llanos
River Orinoco
River Magdalena
Cocos Islands
Mt. Roraima 2810m
GUIANA HIGHLANDS
ATLANTIC OCEAN
Equator
Cotopaxi 5896m
Chimborazo 6310m
Galapagos Islands
ANDES
River Negro
River Amazon
Amazon Basin
Rocas Island
River Tapajós
Selvas
River Ucayali
River Madeira
River Tocantins
River São Francisco
Mato Grosso
PACIFIC OCEAN
Lake Titicaca
Lake Poopo
BRAZILIAN HIGHLANDS
River Pilcomayo
River Paraguay
Atacama Desert
Tropic of Capricorn
Gran Chaco
6908m Ojos del Salado
River Paraná
River Uruguay
Aconcagua 6960m
Juan Fernández Islands
Pampas
Rio de la Plata
R. Colorado
R. Negro
Patagonia
Valdés Peninsula
Chiloé Island
Falkland Islands
Tierra del Fuego
Cape Horn
South Georgia
SOUTHERN OCEAN
N
80°W
60°W
40°W
20°W
0°
20°S
40°S
60°S
A
B
C
D
1
2
3
4
Key
land height in metres above sea level
more than 5000m
2000 – 5000m
1000 – 2000m
500 – 1000m
200 – 500m
less than 200 metres
land below sea level
highest peaks with heights in metres
lake
river
Scale One centimetre on the map represents 350 kilometres on the ground.
0
350
700
1050km

Oblique Mercator Projection

CARIBBEAN SEA
NICARAGUA
COSTA RICA
PANAMA
Barranquilla
Maracaibo
Caracas
Valencia
VENEZUELA
Medellin
Georgetown
GUYANA
Paramaribo
SURINAME
Cayenne
French Guiana (France)
Cali
Bogota
COLOMBIA
ATLANTIC OCEAN
Equator
Galapagos Islands (Ecuador)
Quito
ECUADOR
Guayaquil
Iquitos
Belem
Manaus
Fortaleza
Rocas Island (Brazil)
Trujillo
PERU
BRAZIL
Recife
Lima
Salvador
BOLIVIA
Arequipa
La Paz
Santa Cruz
Brásília
Sucre
Belo Horizonte
Rio de Janeiro
PARAGUAY
Antofagasta
São Paulo
Asunción
Curitiba
Tropic of Capricorn
PACIFIC OCEAN
CHILE
Porto Alegre
Cordoba
Rosario
URUGUAY
Santiago
Buenos Aires
Montevideo
Juan Fernandez Is. (Chile)
ARGENTINA
Mar del Plata
Concepcion
N
Stanley
Falkland Islands (UK)
South Georgia (UK)
Punta Arenas
SOUTHERN OCEAN
80°W
60°W
40°W
20°W
100°W
0°
20°S
40°S
60°S
Key
colours show countries
PERU country names are labelled like this
capital cities
other important cities
Compare
Look at the size of the British Isles compared to South America

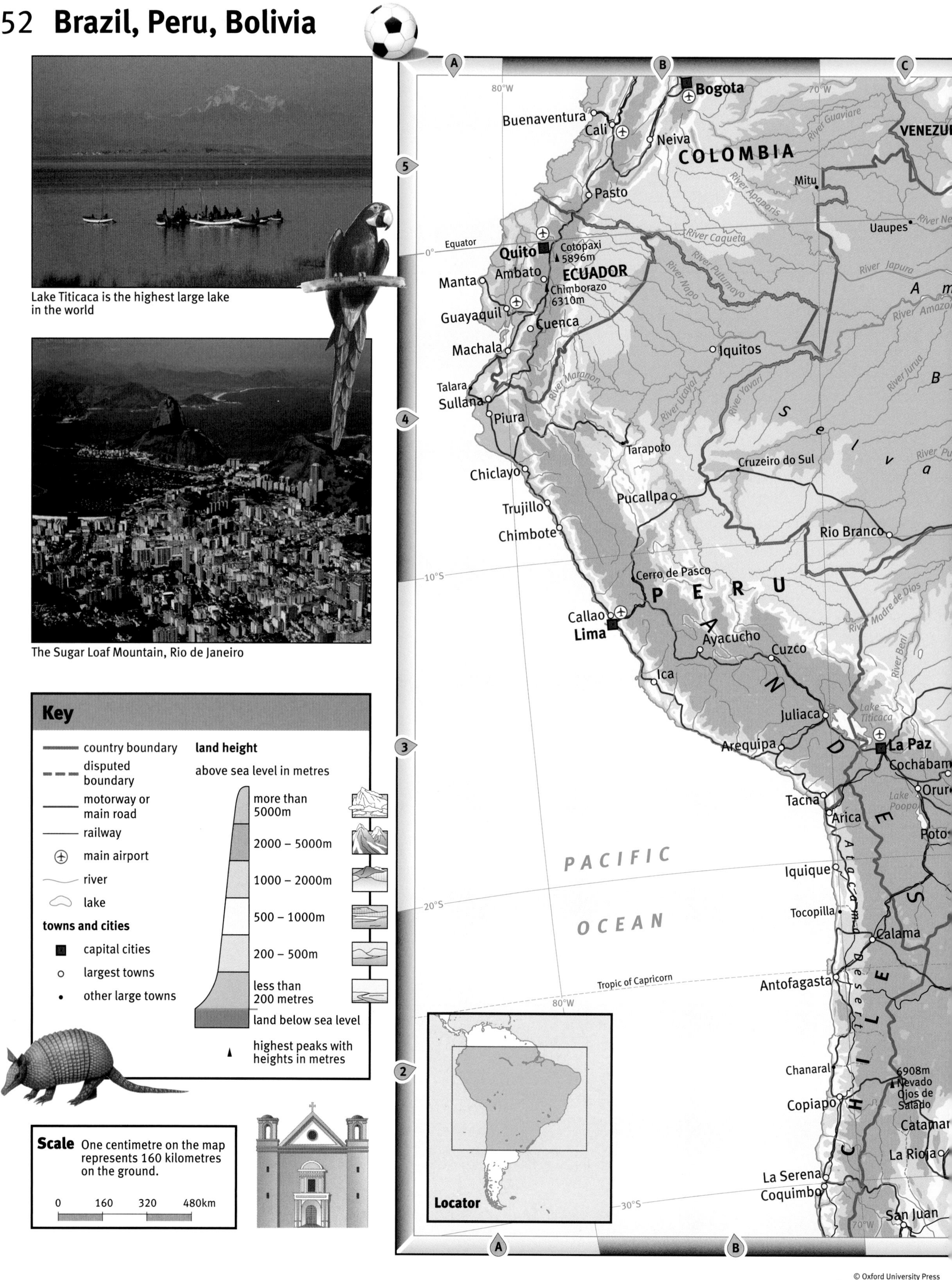

A
B
C
5
4
3
2
80°W
70°W
0°
10°S
20°S
30°S
Equator
Tropic of Capricorn
Bogota
Buenaventura
Cali
Neiva
COLOMBIA
VENEZUE
River Guaviare
River Apaporis
Mitu
Uaupes
Pasto
River Caqueta
River Putumayo
River Napo
River Japura
Quito
Cotopaxi 5896m
ECUADOR
Ambato
Manta
Chimborazo 6310m
Guayaquil
Cuenca
Machala
Iquitos
River Amazon
Talara
Sullana
Piura
River Maranon
River Ucayali
River Yavari
River Jurua
Tarapoto
Chiclayo
Cruzeiro do Sul
River Pu
Trujillo
Pucallpa
Chimbote
Rio Branco
Cerro de Pasco
P E R U
River Madre de Dios
River Beni
Callao
Lima
Ayacucho
Cuzco
A N D E S
Ica
Juliaca
Lake Titicaca
Arequipa
La Paz
Cochabam
Tacna
Lake Poopo
Orur
Arica
Poto
PACIFIC
OCEAN
Iquique
Atacama Desert
Tocopilla
Calama
Antofagasta
Chanaral
6908m Nevado Ojos de Salado
Copiapo
CHILE
Catamar
La Rioja
La Serena
Coquimbo
San Juan
Selva
Key
country boundary
disputed boundary
motorway or main road
railway
main airport
river
lake
towns and cities
capital cities
largest towns
other large towns
land height
above sea level in metres
more than 5000m
2000 – 5000m
1000 – 2000m
500 – 1000m
200 – 500m
less than 200 metres
land below sea level
highest peaks with heights in metres
Scale One centimetre on the map represents 160 kilometres on the ground.
0 160 320 480km
Locator

Lake Titicaca is the highest large lake in the world

The Sugar Loaf Mountain, Rio de Janeiro

Transverse Mercator Projection

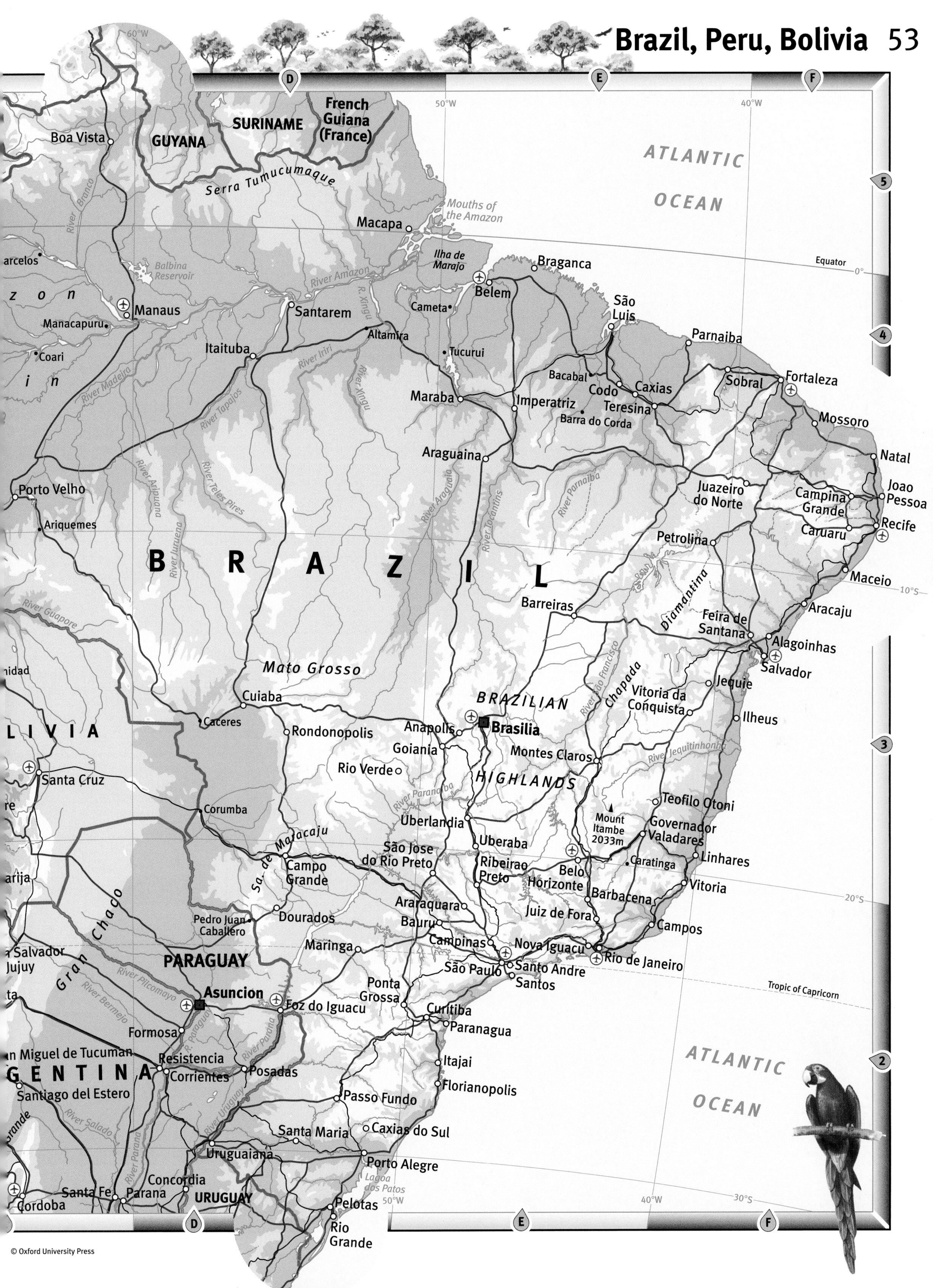

BRAZIL
GUYANA
SURINAME
French Guiana (France)
PARAGUAY
URUGUAY
ATLANTIC OCEAN
Equator
Tropic of Capricorn
Serra Tumucumaque
Mouths of the Amazon
Ilha de Marajo
Balbina Reservoir
River Amazon
River Branco
R. Xingu
River Iriri
River Xingu
River Madeira
River Tapajos
River Aripuana
River Teles Pires
River Juruena
River Araguaia
River Tocantins
River Parnaiba
River São Francisco
River Jequitinhonha
River Paranaiba
River Guapore
River Pilcomayo
River Bermejo
River Paraguay
River Parana
River Uruguay
River Salado
Lagoa dos Patos
Mato Grosso
BRAZILIAN HIGHLANDS
Chapada Diamantina
Sa. de Maracaju
Gran Chaco
Mount Itambe 2033m
Boa Vista
Macapa
Braganca
Belem
Cameta
São Luis
Parnaiba
Manaus
Manacapuru
Coari
Santarem
Altamira
Itaituba
Tucurui
Bacabal
Codo
Caxias
Teresina
Sobral
Fortaleza
Maraba
Imperatriz
Barra do Corda
Mossoro
Araguaina
Natal
Porto Velho
Juazeiro do Norte
Campina Grande
Joao Pessoa
Ariquemes
Petrolina
Caruaru
Recife
Maceio
Barreiras
Aracaju
Feira de Santana
Alagoinhas
Salvador
Jequie
Vitoria da Conquista
Ilheus
Cuiaba
Caceres
Rondonopolis
Anapolis
Brasilia
Goiania
Montes Claros
Rio Verde
Santa Cruz
Corumba
Teofilo Otoni
Uberlandia
Governador Valadares
Uberaba
São Jose do Rio Preto
Campo Grande
Ribeirao Preto
Belo Horizonte
Caratinga
Linhares
Vitoria
Barbacena
Araraquara
Juiz de Fora
Dourados
Pedro Juan Caballero
Bauru
Campos
Campinas
Nova Iguacu
Rio de Janeiro
Maringa
São Paulo
Santo Andre
Santos
Ponta Grossa
Asuncion
Foz do Iguacu
Curitiba
Paranagua
Formosa
Resistencia
Corrientes
Posadas
Itajai
Florianopolis
Passo Fundo
Santa Maria
Caxias do Sul
Uruguaiana
Porto Alegre
Concordia
Santa Fe
Parana
Cordoba
Pelotas
Rio Grande
Santiago del Estero
Jujuy
Tarija
60°W
50°W
40°W
0°
10°S
20°S
30°S
D
E
F
5
4
3
2

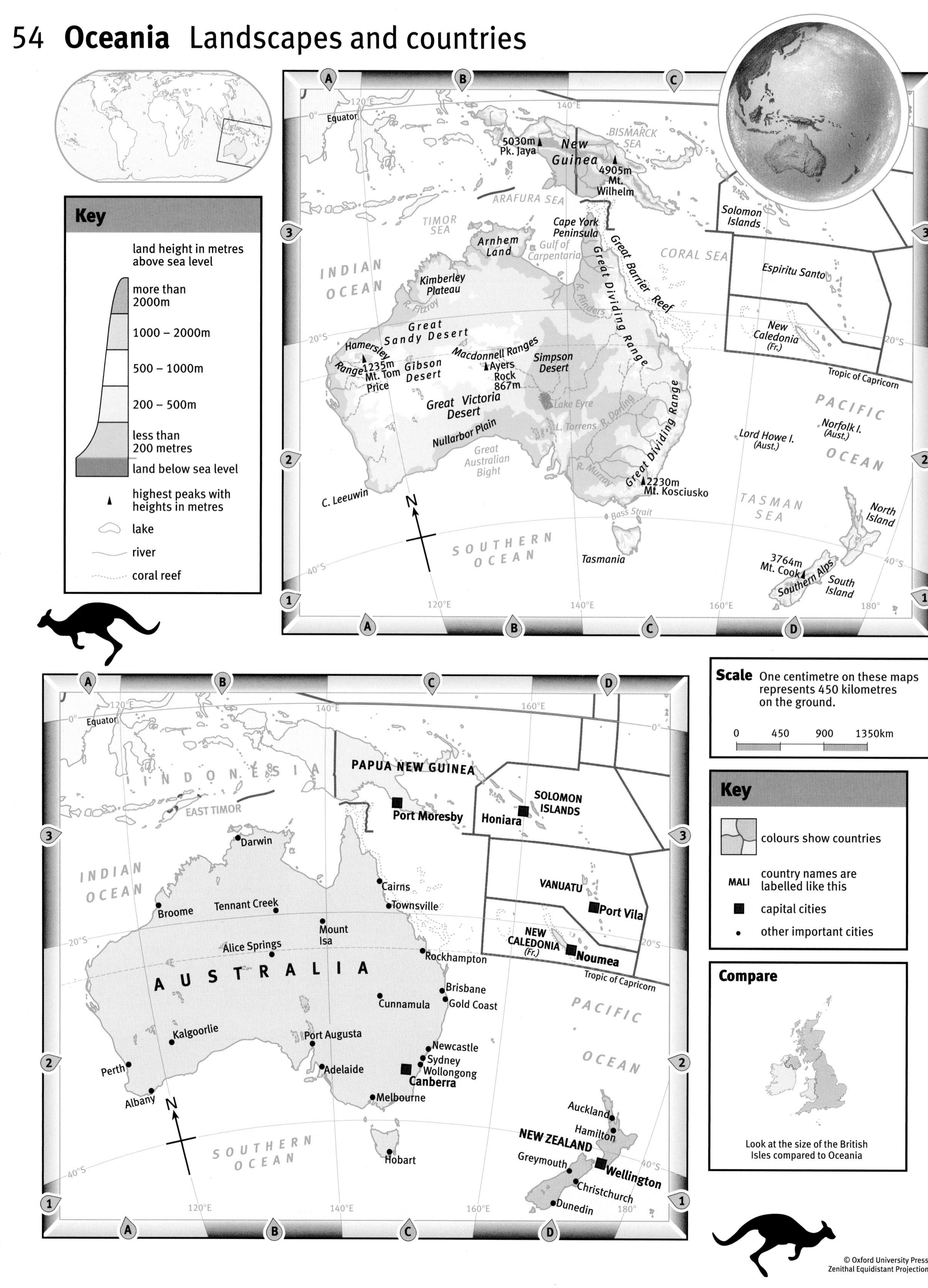
54 Oceania Landscapes and countries
Key
land height in metres above sea level
more than 2000m
1000 – 2000m
500 – 1000m
200 – 500m
less than 200 metres
land below sea level
highest peaks with heights in metres
lake
river
coral reef
Equator
120°E
140°E
160°E
180°
20°S
40°S
A
B
C
D
1
2
3
5030m Pk. Jaya
New Guinea
4905m Mt. Wilhelm
BISMARCK SEA
ARAFURA SEA
TIMOR SEA
Solomon Islands
Cape York Peninsula
Gulf of Carpentaria
Arnhem Land
Great Barrier Reef
CORAL SEA
INDIAN OCEAN
Kimberley Plateau
R. Fitzroy
Great Dividing Range
R. Flinders
Espiritu Santo
New Caledonia (Fr.)
Great Sandy Desert
Hamersley Range
1235m Mt. Tom Price
Gibson Desert
Macdonnell Ranges
Ayers Rock 867m
Simpson Desert
Tropic of Capricorn
Great Victoria Desert
Lake Eyre
R. Darling
L. Torrens
Nullarbor Plain
PACIFIC OCEAN
Lord Howe I. (Aust.)
Norfolk I. (Aust.)
Great Australian Bight
R. Murray
2230m Mt. Kosciusko
C. Leeuwin
N
TASMAN SEA
North Island
Bass Strait
SOUTHERN OCEAN
Tasmania
3764m Mt. Cook
Southern Alps
South Island
INDONESIA
EAST TIMOR
PAPUA NEW GUINEA
Port Moresby
SOLOMON ISLANDS
Honiara
Darwin
Cairns
Townsville
VANUATU
Port Vila
Broome
Tennant Creek
Mount Isa
NEW CALEDONIA (Fr.)
Noumea
Alice Springs
Rockhampton
AUSTRALIA
Brisbane
Gold Coast
Cunnamula
Kalgoorlie
Port Augusta
Newcastle
Sydney
Wollongong
Perth
Adelaide
Canberra
Albany
Melbourne
Auckland
Hamilton
NEW ZEALAND
Hobart
Greymouth
Wellington
Christchurch
Dunedin
Scale One centimetre on these maps represents 450 kilometres on the ground.
0 450 900 1350km
Key
colours show countries
MALI country names are labelled like this
capital cities
other important cities
Compare
Look at the size of the British Isles compared to Oceania
© Oxford University Press
Zenithal Equidistant Projection

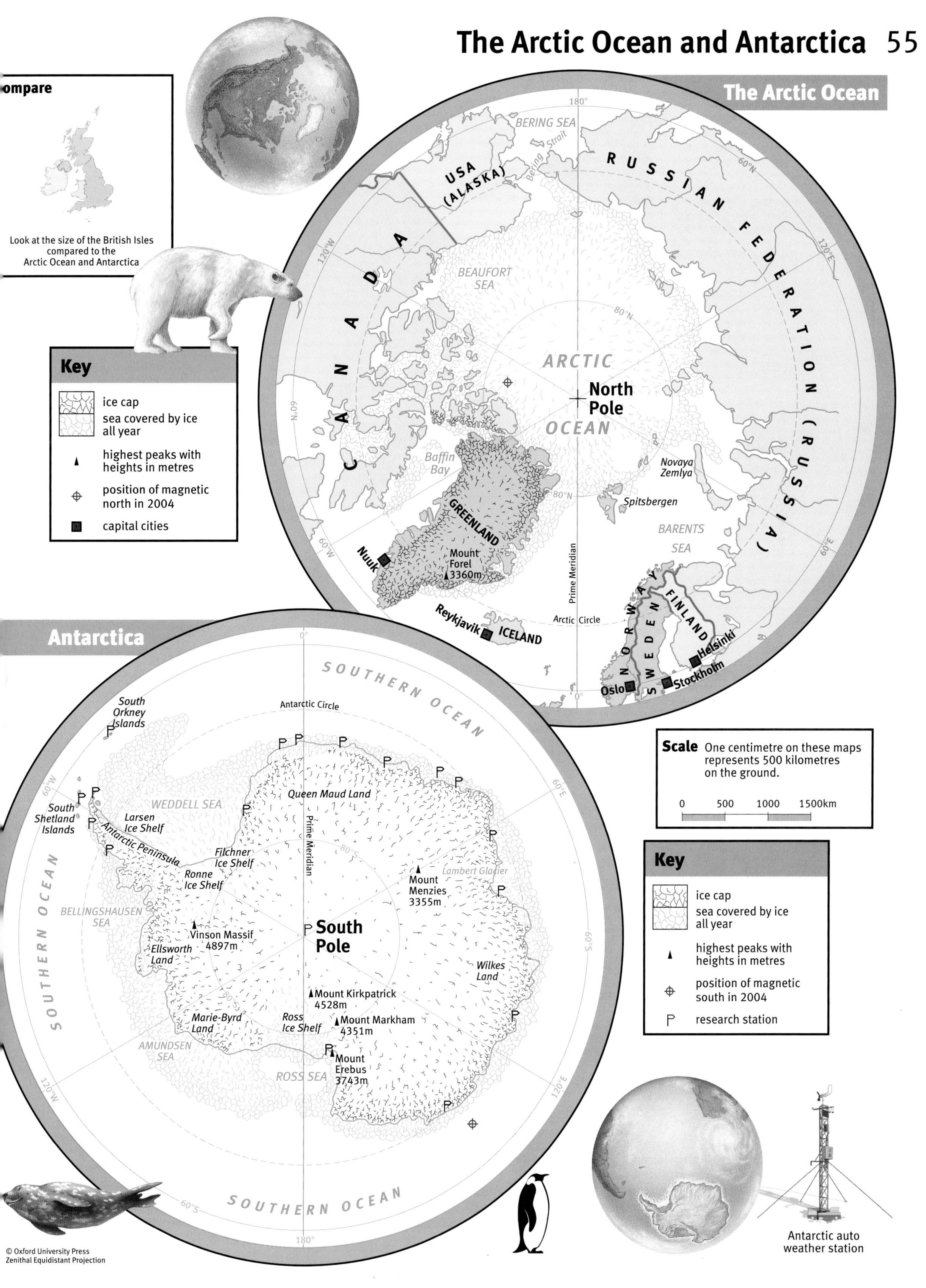

Compare
Look at the size of the British Isles compared to the Arctic Ocean and Antarctica
The Arctic Ocean
Key
ice cap
sea covered by ice all year
highest peaks with heights in metres
position of magnetic north in 2004
capital cities
BERING SEA
Bering Strait
USA (ALASKA)
RUSSIAN FEDERATION (RUSSIA)
CANADA
BEAUFORT SEA
ARCTIC OCEAN
North Pole
Baffin Bay
GREENLAND
Nuuk
Mount Forel 3360m
Novaya Zemlya
Spitsbergen
BARENTS SEA
Prime Meridian
Arctic Circle
Reykjavik
ICELAND
NORWAY
SWEDEN
FINLAND
Oslo
Stockholm
Helsinki
Antarctica
SOUTHERN OCEAN
Antarctic Circle
South Orkney Islands
South Shetland Islands
WEDDELL SEA
Larsen Ice Shelf
Antarctic Peninsula
Queen Maud Land
Filchner Ice Shelf
Ronne Ice Shelf
Lambert Glacier
Mount Menzies 3355m
BELLINGSHAUSEN SEA
Vinson Massif 4897m
Ellsworth Land
South Pole
Wilkes Land
Mount Kirkpatrick 4528m
Marie-Byrd Land
Ross Ice Shelf
Mount Markham 4351m
AMUNDSEN SEA
Mount Erebus 3743m
ROSS SEA
Scale One centimetre on these maps represents 500 kilometres on the ground.
0 500 1000 1500km
Key
ice cap
sea covered by ice all year
highest peaks with heights in metres
position of magnetic south in 2004
research station
Antarctic auto weather station
Zenithal Equidistant Projection

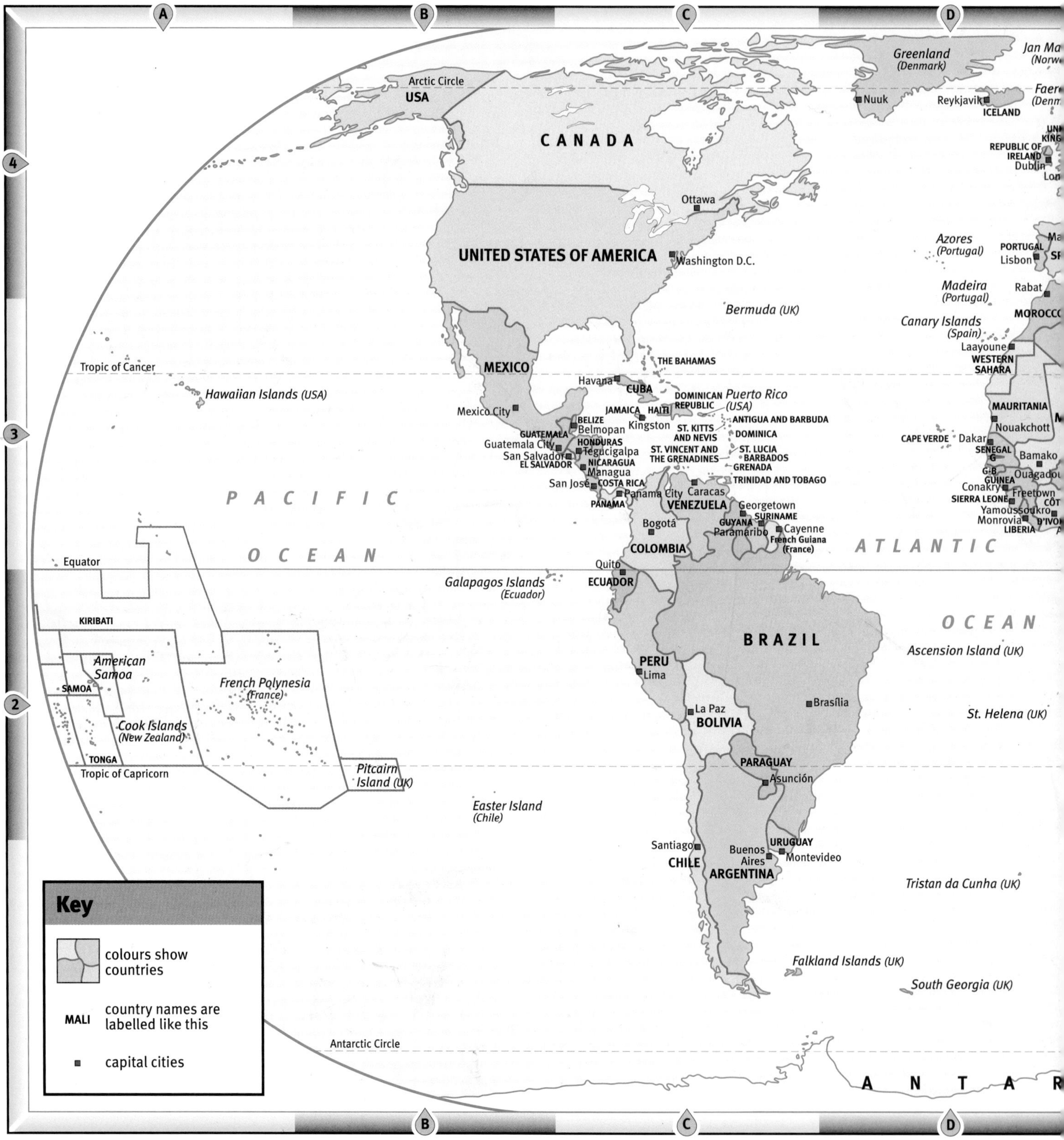

Key

colours show countries

MALI country names are labelled like this

■ capital cities

Abbreviations

A	ALBANIA	CZ	CZECH REPUBLIC	Q	QATAR
AR	ARMENIA	G	THE GAMBIA	R	ROMANIA
AU	AUSTRIA	G-B	GUINEA-BISSAU	S	SLOVAKIA
AZ	AZERBAIJAN	H	HUNGARY	SL	SLOVENIA
B	BELGIUM	IS	ISRAEL	SM	SERBIA AND MONTENEGRO
BE	BENIN	L	LEBANON	SW	SWITZERLAND
BH	BOSNIA-HERZEGOVINA	LI	LITHUANIA	T	TAJIKISTAN
BR	BRUNEI	LU	LUXEMBOURG	TU	TURKMENISTAN
BU	BURKINA	M	FORMER YUGOSLAV REPUBLIC OF MACEDONIA	U	UGANDA
C	CROATIA			UAE	UNITED ARAB EMIRATES
CAR	CENTRAL AFRICAN REPUBLIC	N	NETHERLANDS	ZIM	ZIMBABWE

North America

South America

 Eckert IV Projection

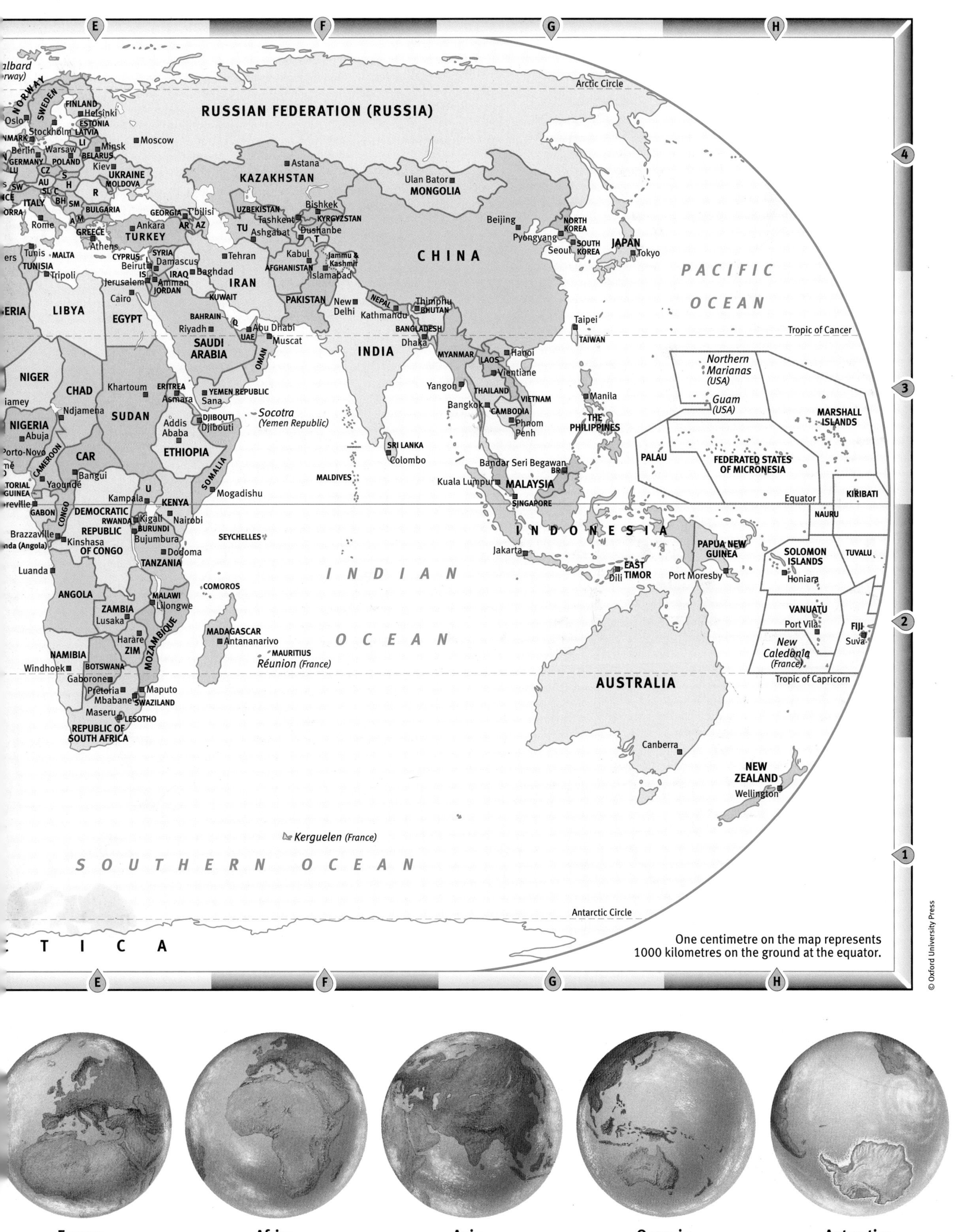
E
F
G
H
Arctic Circle
RUSSIAN FEDERATION (RUSSIA)
NORWAY
SWEDEN
FINLAND
Helsinki
Oslo
Stockholm
ESTONIA
LATVIA
LI
Moscow
Minsk
BELARUS
Berlin
Warsaw
GERMANY
POLAND
CZ
S
Kiev
UKRAINE
MOLDOVA
AU
H
R
ITALY
BH
SM
BULGARIA
Rome
GREECE
Athens
Ankara
TURKEY
GEORGIA
T'bilisi
AR
AZ
Astana
KAZAKHSTAN
UZBEKISTAN
Tashkent
TU
Ashgabat
Bishkek
KYRGYZSTAN
Dushanbe
T
Ulan Bator
MONGOLIA
Beijing
NORTH KOREA
Pyongyang
SOUTH KOREA
Seoul
JAPAN
Tokyo
Tunis
MALTA
TUNISIA
Tripoli
CYPRUS
SYRIA
Beirut
Damascus
IS
Jerusalem
Amman
JORDAN
IRAQ
Baghdad
Tehran
IRAN
Kabul
AFGHANISTAN
Jammu & Kashmir
Islamabad
CHINA
PACIFIC OCEAN
LIBYA
Cairo
EGYPT
KUWAIT
PAKISTAN
New Delhi
NEPAL
Kathmandu
Thimphu
BHUTAN
Taipei
TAIWAN
BAHRAIN
Q
Riyadh
Abu Dhabi
UAE
SAUDI ARABIA
Muscat
OMAN
BANGLADESH
Dhaka
INDIA
MYANMAR
LAOS
Hanoi
Vientiane
Tropic of Cancer
Northern Marianas (USA)
Guam (USA)
MARSHALL ISLANDS
NIGER
CHAD
Khartoum
ERITREA
Asmara
YEMEN REPUBLIC
Sana
SUDAN
NIGERIA
Abuja
Ndjamena
Addis Ababa
DJIBOUTI
Djibouti
Socotra (Yemen Republic)
ETHIOPIA
Yangon
THAILAND
Bangkok
VIETNAM
CAMBODIA
Phnom Penh
Manila
THE PHILIPPINES
PALAU
FEDERATED STATES OF MICRONESIA
SRI LANKA
Colombo
CAR
Bangui
CAMEROON
Yaoundé
SOMALIA
Mogadishu
MALDIVES
Bandar Seri Begawan
BR
Kuala Lumpur
MALAYSIA
SINGAPORE
KIRIBATI
Equator
NAURU
U
Kampala
KENYA
Nairobi
GABON
CONGO
DEMOCRATIC REPUBLIC OF CONGO
RWANDA
Kigali
BURUNDI
Bujumbura
Brazzaville
Kinshasa
SEYCHELLES
INDONESIA
PAPUA NEW GUINEA
SOLOMON ISLANDS
TUVALU
Honiara
Dodoma
TANZANIA
Jakarta
EAST TIMOR
Dili
Port Moresby
Luanda
INDIAN OCEAN
COMOROS
ANGOLA
MALAWI
Lilongwe
ZAMBIA
Lusaka
MOZAMBIQUE
Harare
ZIM
MADAGASCAR
Antananarivo
MAURITIUS
Réunion (France)
VANUATU
Port Vila
FIJI
Suva
New Caledonia (France)
NAMIBIA
Windhoek
BOTSWANA
Gaborone
Pretoria
Maputo
Mbabane
SWAZILAND
Maseru
LESOTHO
REPUBLIC OF SOUTH AFRICA
AUSTRALIA
Tropic of Capricorn
Canberra
NEW ZEALAND
Wellington
Kerguelen (France)
SOUTHERN OCEAN
Antarctic Circle
TICA
One centimetre on the map represents 1000 kilometres on the ground at the equator.
4
3
2
1

Europe

Africa

Asia

Oceania

Antarctica

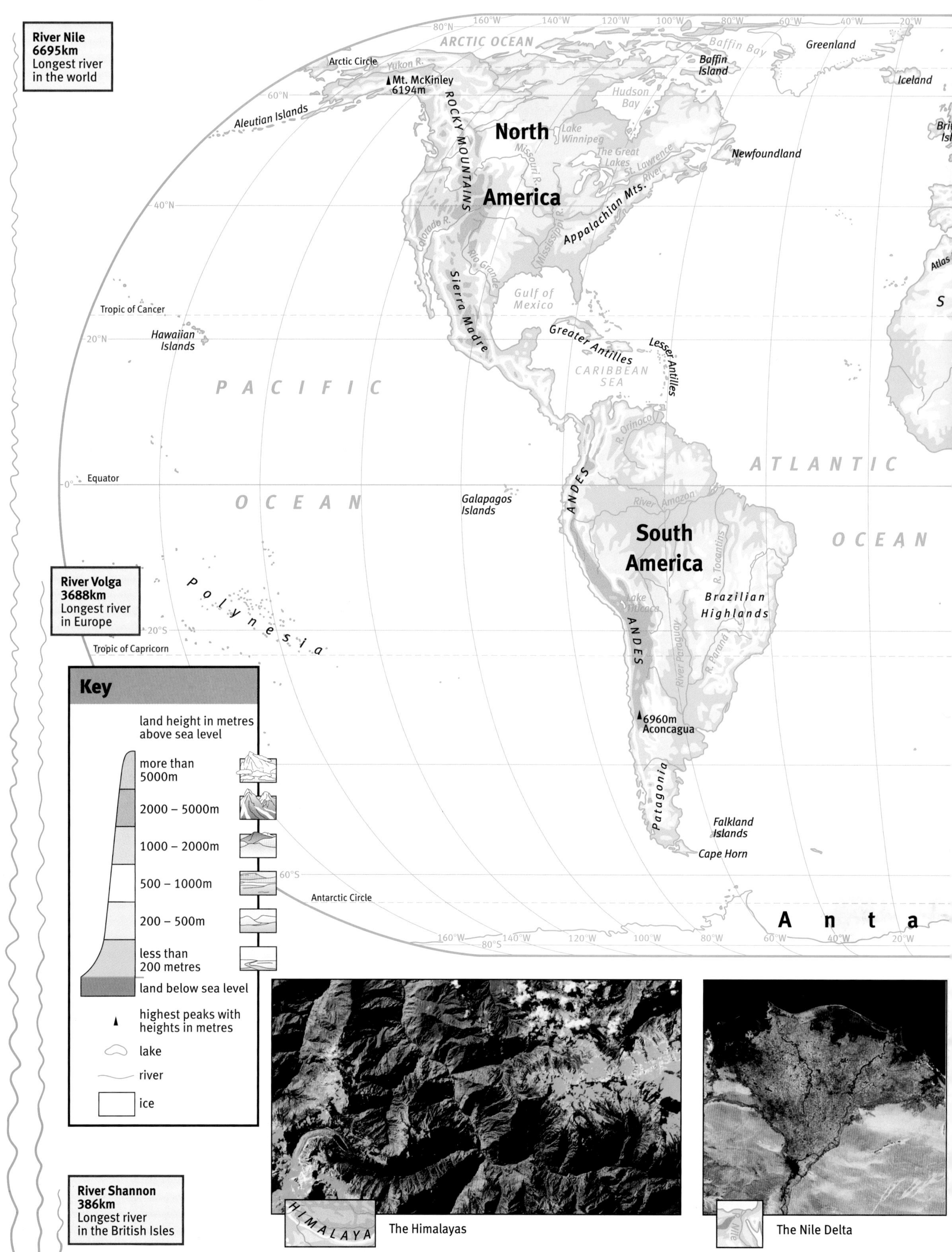
River Nile
6695km
Longest river in the world
River Volga
3688km
Longest river in Europe
River Shannon
386km
Longest river in the British Isles
ARCTIC OCEAN
Arctic Circle
Yukon R.
Mt. McKinley 6194m
Aleutian Islands
ROCKY MOUNTAINS
North America
Lake Winnipeg
Hudson Bay
Baffin Bay
Baffin Island
Greenland
Iceland
Brit Isl
The Great Lakes
St. Lawrence River
Newfoundland
Missouri R.
Appalachian Mts.
Mississippi R.
Colorado R.
Rio Grande
Sierra Madre
Gulf of Mexico
Atlas
Tropic of Cancer
Hawaiian Islands
Greater Antilles
Lesser Antilles
CARIBBEAN SEA
PACIFIC OCEAN
R. Orinoco
ATLANTIC OCEAN
Equator
ANDES
Galapagos Islands
River Amazon
South America
R. Tocantins
Polynesia
Lake Titicaca
Brazilian Highlands
River Paraguay
R. Paraná
Tropic of Capricorn
6960m Aconcagua
Patagonia
Falkland Islands
Cape Horn
Antarctic Circle
Anta
80°N
60°N
40°N
20°N
0°
20°S
60°S
80°S
160°W
140°W
120°W
100°W
80°W
60°W
40°W
20°W
Key
land height in metres above sea level
more than 5000m
2000 – 5000m
1000 – 2000m
500 – 1000m
200 – 500m
less than 200 metres
land below sea level
highest peaks with heights in metres
lake
river
ice
HIMALAYA
Nile
The Himalayas

The Nile Delta

Eckert IV Projection

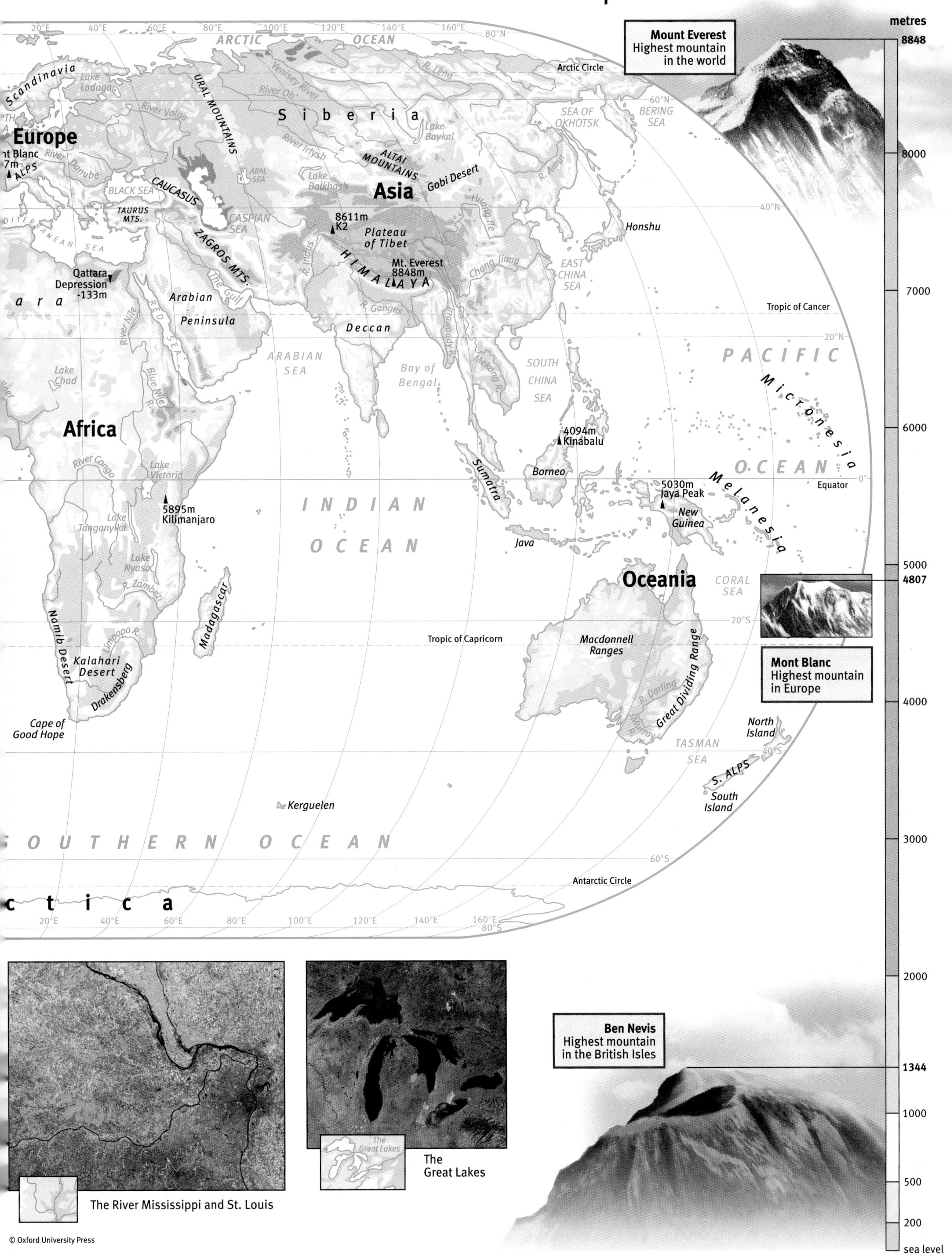
ARCTIC OCEAN
Arctic Circle
Scandinavia
Lake Ladoga
River Ob'
Yenisey River
R. Lena
River Volga
URAL MOUNTAINS
Siberia
Europe
River Danube
ALPS
River Irtysh
Lake Baykal
SEA OF OKHOTSK
BERING SEA
ALTAI MOUNTAINS
Gobi Desert
ARAL SEA
Lake Balkhash
Asia
R. Amur
BLACK SEA
CAUCASUS
TAURUS MTS.
CASPIAN SEA
8611m K2
Plateau of Tibet
Huang He
Honshu
MEDITERRANEAN SEA
ZAGROS MTS.
R. Indus
HIMALAYA
Mt. Everest 8848m
Chang Jiang
EAST CHINA SEA
Qattara Depression -133m
The Gulf
Arabian Peninsula
RED SEA
R. Ganges
Deccan
Irrawaddy R.
Tropic of Cancer
River Nile
ARABIAN SEA
Bay of Bengal
Mekong R.
SOUTH CHINA SEA
PACIFIC OCEAN
Micronesia
Lake Chad
Blue Nile R.
Africa
4094m Kinabalu
River Congo
Lake Victoria
Sumatra
Borneo
Equator
5030m Jaya Peak
Melanesia
New Guinea
5895m Kilimanjaro
INDIAN OCEAN
Lake Tanganyika
Java
Lake Nyasa
R. Zambezi
Madagascar
Oceania
CORAL SEA
Namib Desert
Limpopo R.
Tropic of Capricorn
Macdonnell Ranges
Great Dividing Range
Kalahari Desert
Drakensberg
R. Darling
Murray R.
Cape of Good Hope
North Island
TASMAN SEA
S. ALPS
South Island
Kerguelen
SOUTHERN OCEAN
Antarctic Circle
Antarctica
Mount Everest
Highest mountain in the world
metres
8848
8000
7000
6000
5000
4807
Mont Blanc
Highest mountain in Europe
4000
3000
2000
Ben Nevis
Highest mountain in the British Isles
1344
1000
500
200
sea level
The Great Lakes

The Great Lakes

The River Mississippi and St. Louis

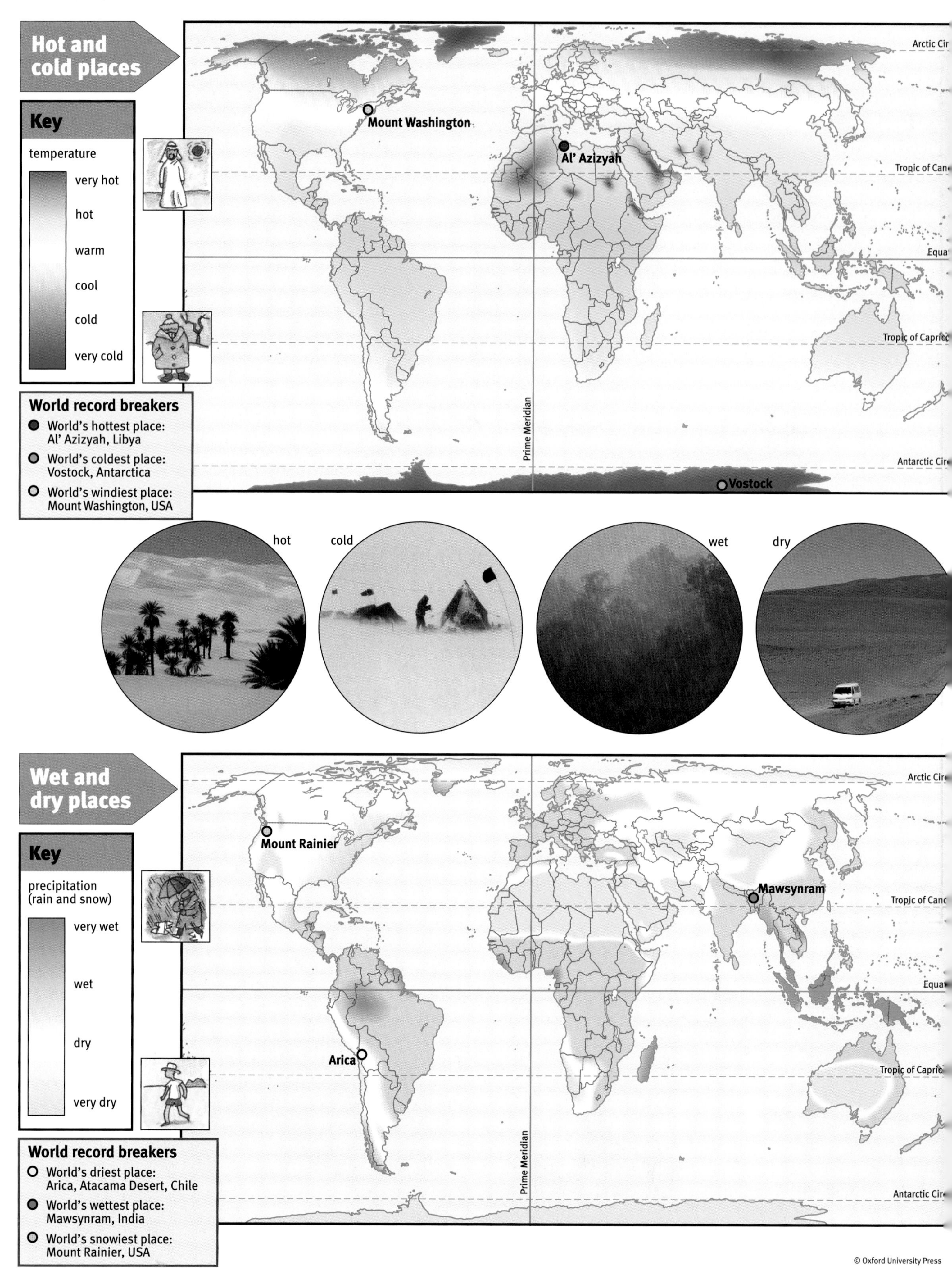
Hot and cold places
Key
temperature
very hot
hot
warm
cool
cold
very cold
World record breakers
World's hottest place: Al' Azizyah, Libya
World's coldest place: Vostock, Antarctica
World's windiest place: Mount Washington, USA
Arctic Cir
Tropic of Can
Equa
Tropic of Capric
Antarctic Cir
Prime Meridian
Mount Washington
Al' Azizyah
Vostock
hot
cold
wet
dry
Wet and dry places
Key
precipitation (rain and snow)
very wet
wet
dry
very dry
World record breakers
World's driest place: Arica, Atacama Desert, Chile
World's wettest place: Mawsynram, India
World's snowiest place: Mount Rainier, USA
Mount Rainier
Mawsynram
Arica
Arctic Cir
Tropic of Canc
Equa
Tropic of Capric
Antarctic Cir
Prime Meridian

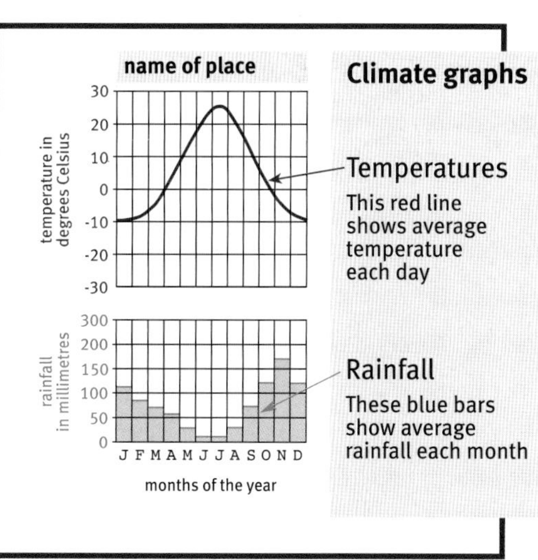
name of place
Climate graphs
temperature in degrees Celsius
Temperatures
This red line shows average temperature each day
rainfall in millimetres
Rainfall
These blue bars show average rainfall each month
J F M A M J J A S O N D
months of the year

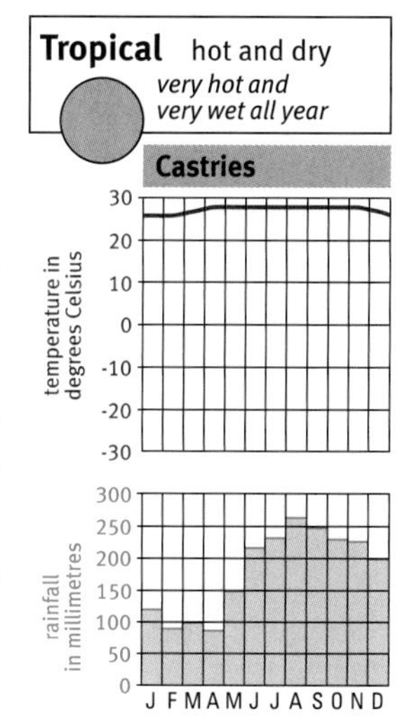
Tropical hot and dry
very hot and very wet all year
Castries
temperature in degrees Celsius
rainfall in millimetres
J F M A M J J A S O N D

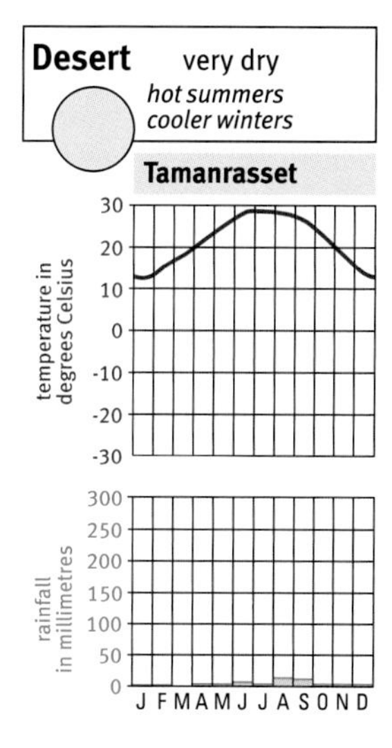
Desert very dry
hot summers cooler winters
Tamanrasset
temperature in degrees Celsius
rainfall in millimetres
J F M A M J J A S O N D

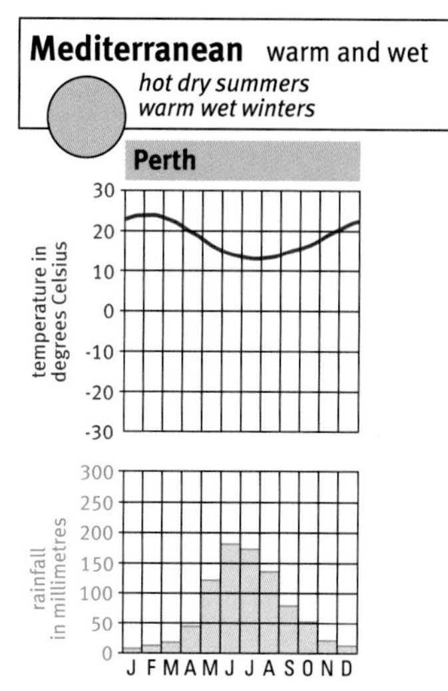
Mediterranean warm and wet
hot dry summers warm wet winters
Perth
temperature in degrees Celsius
rainfall in millimetres
J F M A M J J A S O N D

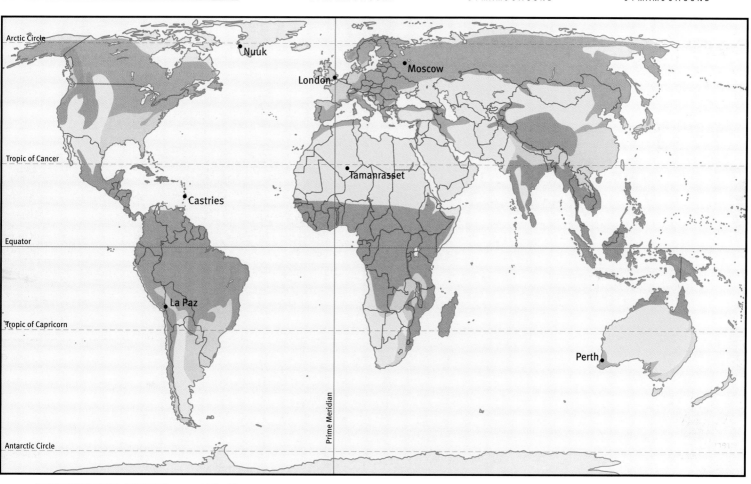

Arctic Circle
Nuuk
Moscow
London
Tropic of Cancer
Tamanrasset
Castries
Equator
La Paz
Tropic of Capricorn
Perth
Prime Meridian
Antarctic Circle

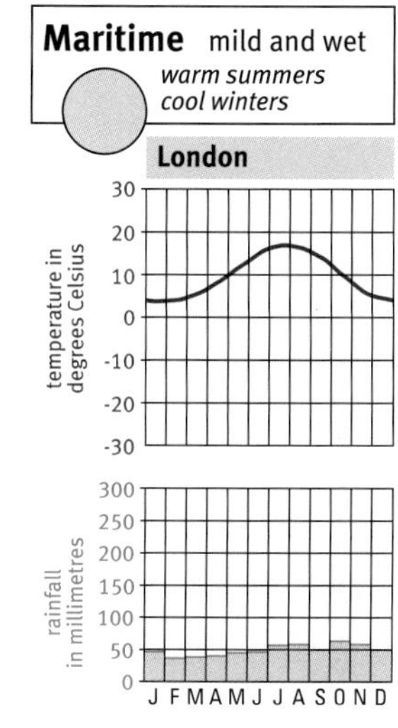
Maritime mild and wet
warm summers cool winters
London
temperature in degrees Celsius
rainfall in millimetres
J F M A M J J A S O N D

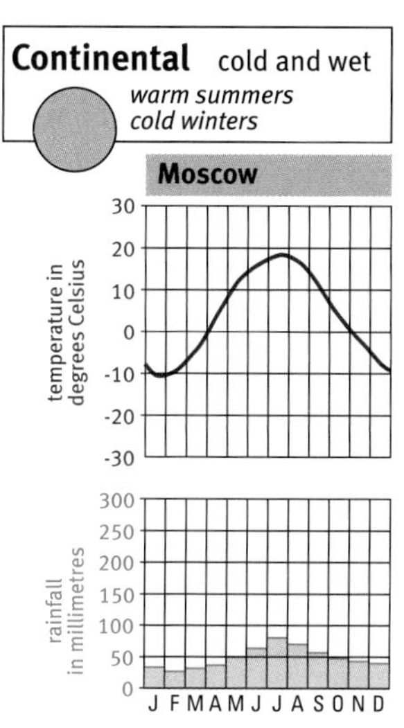
Continental cold and wet
warm summers cold winters
Moscow
temperature in degrees Celsius
rainfall in millimetres
J F M A M J J A S O N D

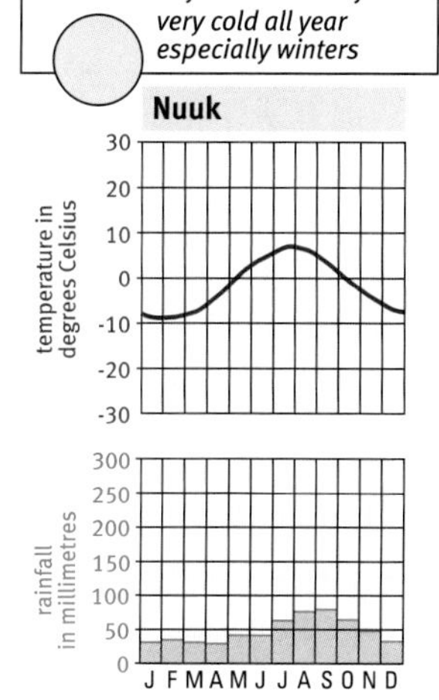
Polar very cold and dry
very cold all year especially winters
Nuuk
temperature in degrees Celsius
rainfall in millimetres
J F M A M J J A S O N D

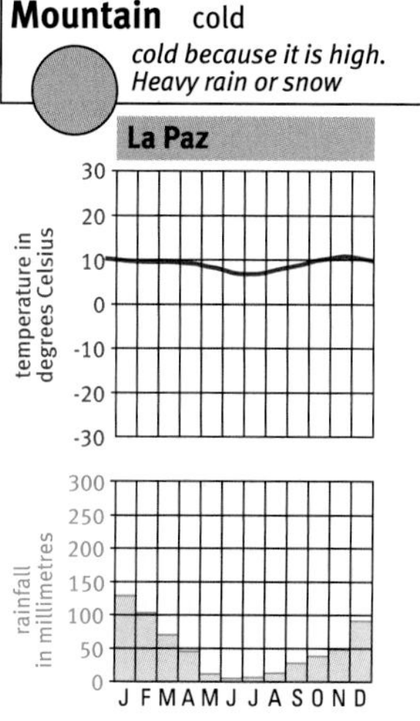
Mountain cold
cold because it is high. Heavy rain or snow
La Paz
temperature in degrees Celsius
rainfall in millimetres
J F M A M J J A S O N D

Eckert IV projection

There are about 6 400 000 000 people in the world.

ARCTIC OCEAN
Arctic Circle
Chicago
New York
Washington D.C.
Philadelphia
San Francisco
Los Angeles
Tropic of Cancer
Mexico City
PACIFIC OCEAN
ATLANTIC OCEAN
Bogotá
Equator
Lima-Callao
Tropic of Capricorn
Rio de Janeiro
São Paulo
Buenos Aires
Antarctic Circle
London

80°N 60°N 40°N 20°N 0° 20°S 40°S 60°S 80°S
160°W 140°W 120°W 100°W 80°W 60°W 40°W 20°W

Key

Population density
people per square kilometre

- over 100
- 5–100
- under 5
- cities with more than six million (6 000 000) people
- country boundary

Population pyramid

If there were just 100 people in the world, this is how old they would be:

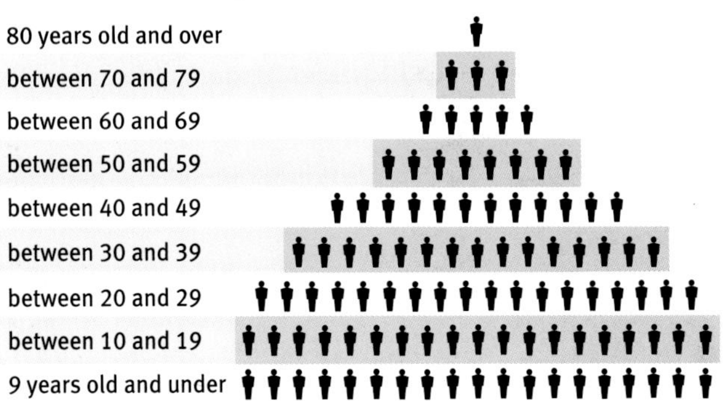
80 years old and over
between 70 and 79
between 60 and 69
between 50 and 59
between 40 and 49
between 30 and 39
between 20 and 29
between 10 and 19
9 years old and under

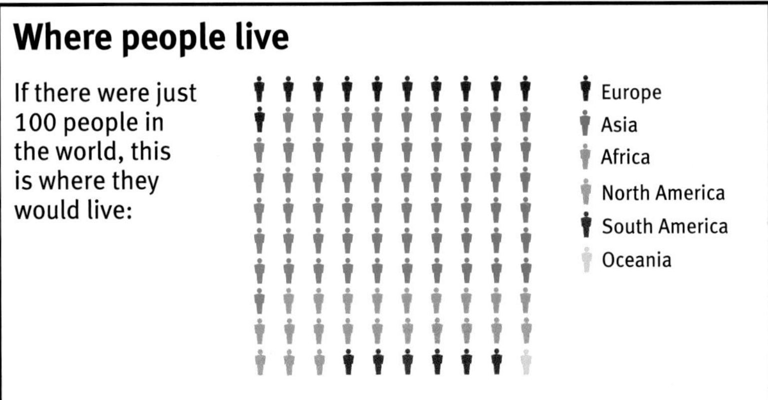
Where people live
If there were just 100 people in the world, this is where they would live:
Europe
Asia
Africa
North America
South America
Oceania

Eckert IV Projection

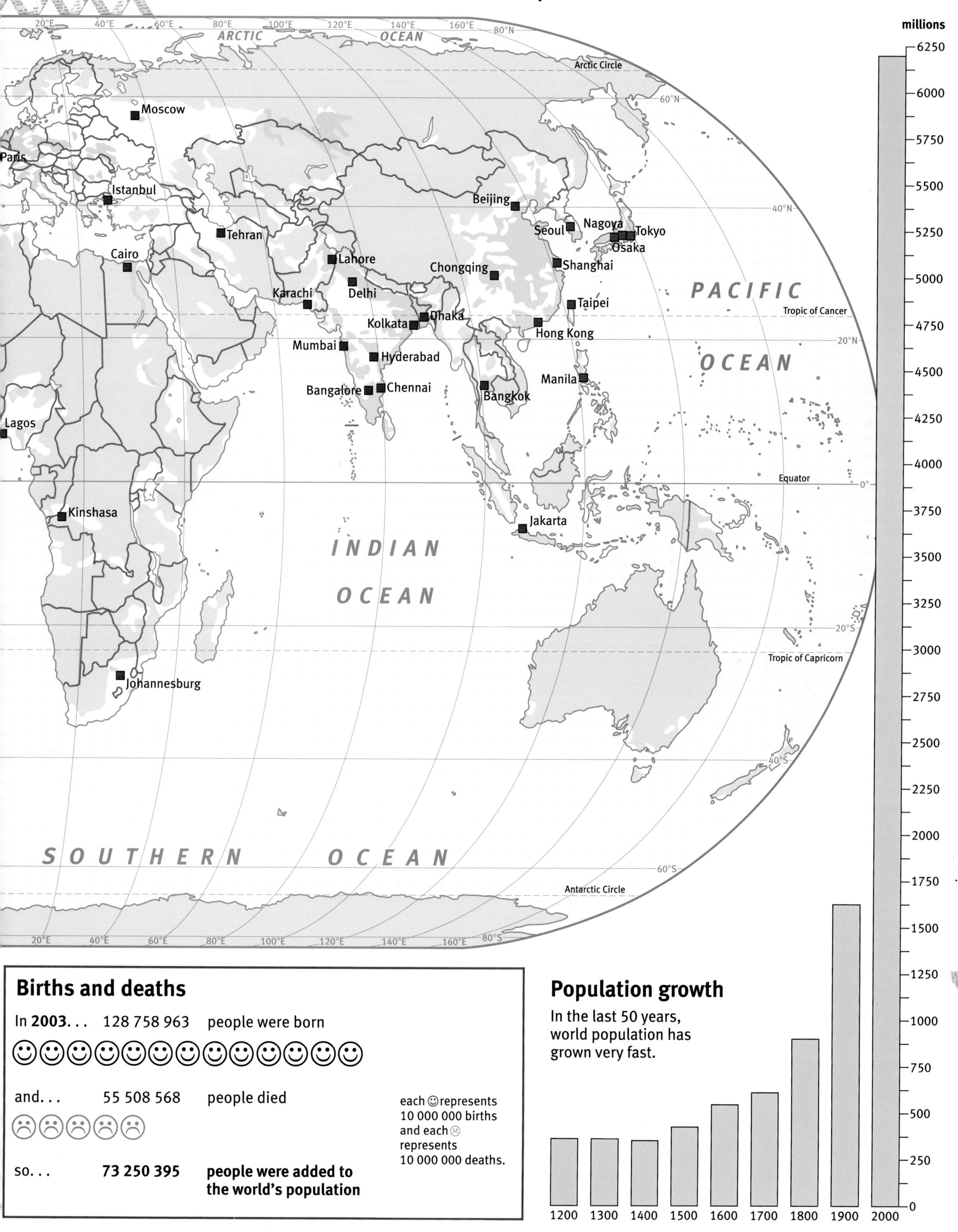
ARCTIC
OCEAN
Arctic Circle
Moscow
Paris
Istanbul
Tehran
Cairo
Lahore
Karachi
Delhi
Beijing
Seoul
Nagoya
Tokyo
Osaka
Shanghai
Chongqing
Taipei
Hong Kong
Dhaka
Kolkata
Mumbai
Hyderabad
Bangalore
Chennai
Bangkok
Manila
Lagos
Kinshasa
Jakarta
Johannesburg
PACIFIC
OCEAN
Tropic of Cancer
Equator
INDIAN
OCEAN
Tropic of Capricorn
SOUTHERN
OCEAN
Antarctic Circle
20°E
40°E
60°E
80°E
100°E
120°E
140°E
160°E
80°N
60°N
40°N
20°N
0°
20°S
40°S
60°S
80°S
millions
6250
6000
5750
5500
5250
5000
4750
4500
4250
4000
3750
3500
3250
3000
2750
2500
2250
2000
1750
1500
1250
1000
750
500
250
0
1200
1300
1400
1500
1600
1700
1800
1900
2000

Births and deaths

In **2003**. . . 128 758 963 people were born

☺☺☺☺☺☺☺☺☺☺☺☺☺

and. . . 55 508 568 people died

☹☹☹☹☹

so. . . **73 250 395** **people were added to the world's population**

each ☺ represents 10 000 000 births and each ☹ represents 10 000 000 deaths.

Population growth

In the last 50 years, world population has grown very fast.

tropical forest
deciduous forest
coniferous forest
ARCTIC OCEAN
Arctic Circle
80°N
160°W
140°W
120°W
100°W
80°W
60°W
40°W
20°W
60°N
40°N
Tropic of Cancer
20°N
PACIFIC
OCEAN
ATLANTIC
OCEAN
Equator
0°
20°S
Tropic of Capricorn
40°S
60°S
Antarctic Circle
80°S
desert
semi desert

Key

- **coniferous forest** trees have leaves all year
- **deciduous forest** trees drop their leaves in winter
- **tropical forest** tall trees growing close together
- **savannah** tall trees and scattered trees
- **temperate grassland** prairies, steppes, pampas and veld
- **semi desert** short grass and small dry bushes
- **desert** sand and stones with few plants
- **tundra** moss and bog with some short trees
- **ice** no plants
- **mountains** thin soils and steep slopes

Eckert IV Projection

savannah
temperate grassland
ARCTIC OCEAN
Arctic Circle
PACIFIC OCEAN
Tropic of Cancer
Equator
INDIAN OCEAN
Tropic of Capricorn
SOUTHERN OCEAN
Antarctic Circle
20°E
40°E
60°E
80°E
100°E
120°E
140°E
160°E
80°N
60°N
40°N
20°N
0°
20°S
40°S
60°S
80°S
tundra
mountains
ice

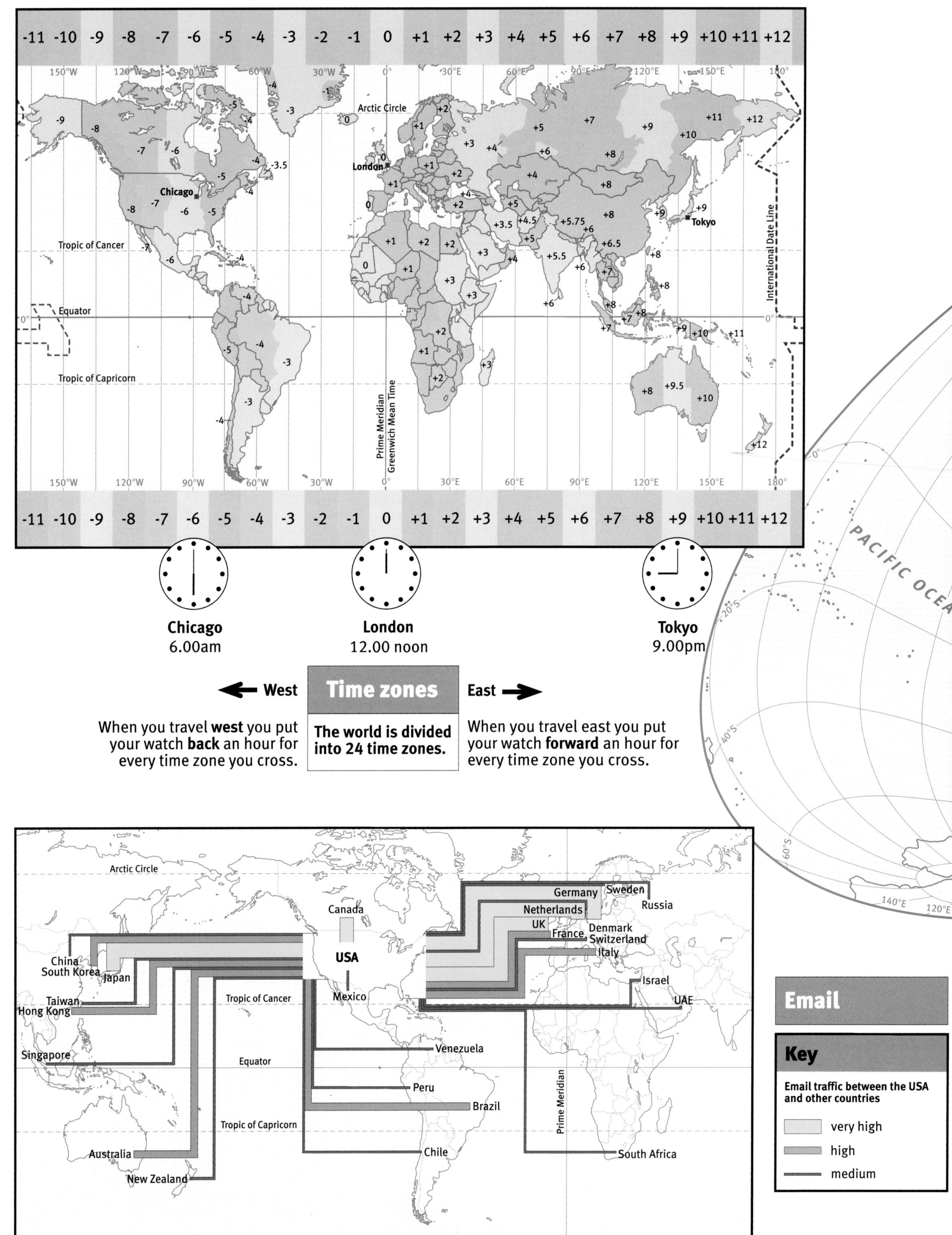
-11 -10 -9 -8 -7 -6 -5 -4 -3 -2 -1 0 +1 +2 +3 +4 +5 +6 +7 +8 +9 +10 +11 +12
150°W 120°W 90°W 60°W 30°W 0° 30°E 60°E 90°E 120°E 150°E 180°
Arctic Circle
Tropic of Cancer
Equator
Tropic of Capricorn
London
Chicago
Tokyo
International Date Line
Prime Meridian
Greenwich Mean Time
-3.5
+3.5
+4.5
+5.5
+5.75
+6.5
+9.5
Chicago
6.00am
London
12.00 noon
Tokyo
9.00pm
West
Time zones
East
When you travel **west** you put your watch **back** an hour for every time zone you cross.
The world is divided into 24 time zones.
When you travel east you put your watch **forward** an hour for every time zone you cross.
PACIFIC OCEAN
20°S
40°S
60°S
140°E
120°E
Arctic Circle
Canada
USA
Mexico
Germany
Sweden
Russia
Netherlands
UK
Denmark
France
Switzerland
Italy
Israel
UAE
China
South Korea
Japan
Taiwan
Hong Kong
Singapore
Tropic of Cancer
Equator
Tropic of Capricorn
Venezuela
Peru
Brazil
Chile
Australia
New Zealand
Prime Meridian
South Africa
Email
Key
Email traffic between the USA and other countries
very high
high
medium

Gall Projection

The distance round the Earth at the Equator is 40 075 kilometres (24 846 miles)

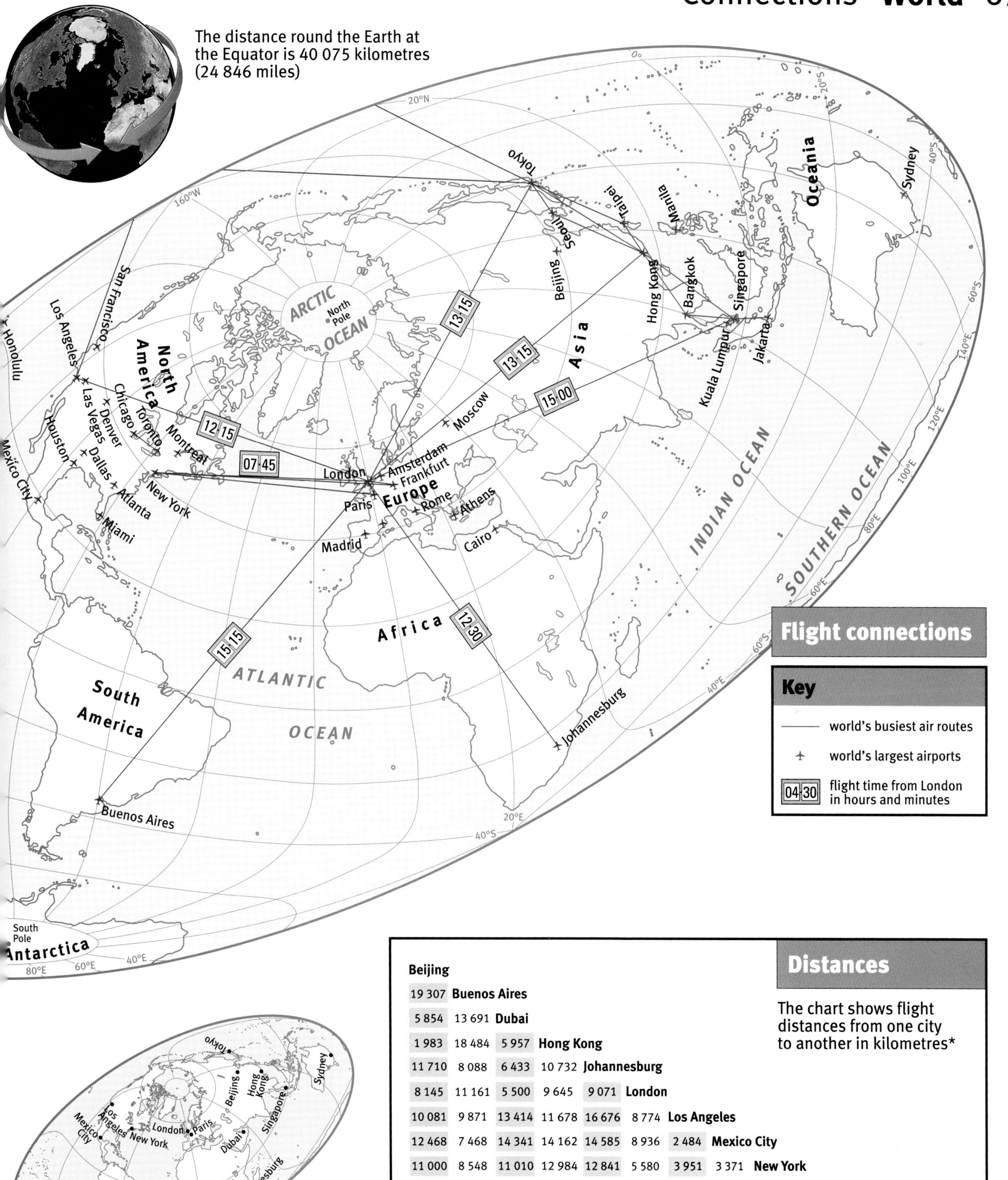
ARCTIC OCEAN
North Pole
North America
South America
Europe
Asia
Africa
Oceania
Antarctica
South Pole
ATLANTIC OCEAN
INDIAN OCEAN
SOUTHERN OCEAN
Honolulu
Los Angeles
San Francisco
Las Vegas
Chicago
Denver
Toronto
Montreal
Houston
Dallas
Atlanta
New York
Miami
Mexico City
Buenos Aires
London
Amsterdam
Frankfurt
Paris
Rome
Madrid
Athens
Cairo
Moscow
Johannesburg
Beijing
Seoul
Tokyo
Taipei
Manila
Hong Kong
Bangkok
Singapore
Kuala Lumpur
Jakarta
Sydney
Dubai
12 15
07 45
13 15
13 15
15 00
15 15
12 30
20°N
40°S
60°S
20°S
20°E
40°E
60°E
80°E
100°E
120°E
140°E
160°W
Flight connections
Key
world's busiest air routes
world's largest airports
04 30 flight time from London in hours and minutes

Distances

The chart shows flight distances from one city to another in kilometres*

	Beijing	Buenos Aires	Dubai	Hong Kong	Johannesburg	London	Los Angeles	Mexico City	New York	Paris	Singapore	Sydney
Buenos Aires	19 307											
Dubai	5 854	13 691										
Hong Kong	1 983	18 484	5 957									
Johannesburg	11 710	8 088	6 433	10 732								
London	8 145	11 161	5 500	9 645	9 071							
Los Angeles	10 081	9 871	13 414	11 678	16 676	8 774						
Mexico City	12 468	7 468	14 341	14 162	14 585	8 936	2 484					
New York	11 000	8 548	11 010	12 984	12 841	5 580	3 951	3 371				
Paris	8 226	11 097	5 242	9 613	8 732	338	9 032	9 210	5 839			
Singapore	4 468	15 904	5 841	2 661	8 860	10 871	14 146	16 630	15 533	10 758		
Sydney	8 949	11 800	12 056	7 374	11 040	16 992	12 073	12 969	15 989	16 962	6 300	
Tokyo	2 113	18 388	7 984	2 903	13 547	9 581	8 823	11 355	10 871	9 726	5 322	7 823

* To change kilometres to miles multiply by 0.62

Oblique Aitoff Projection

Country data files

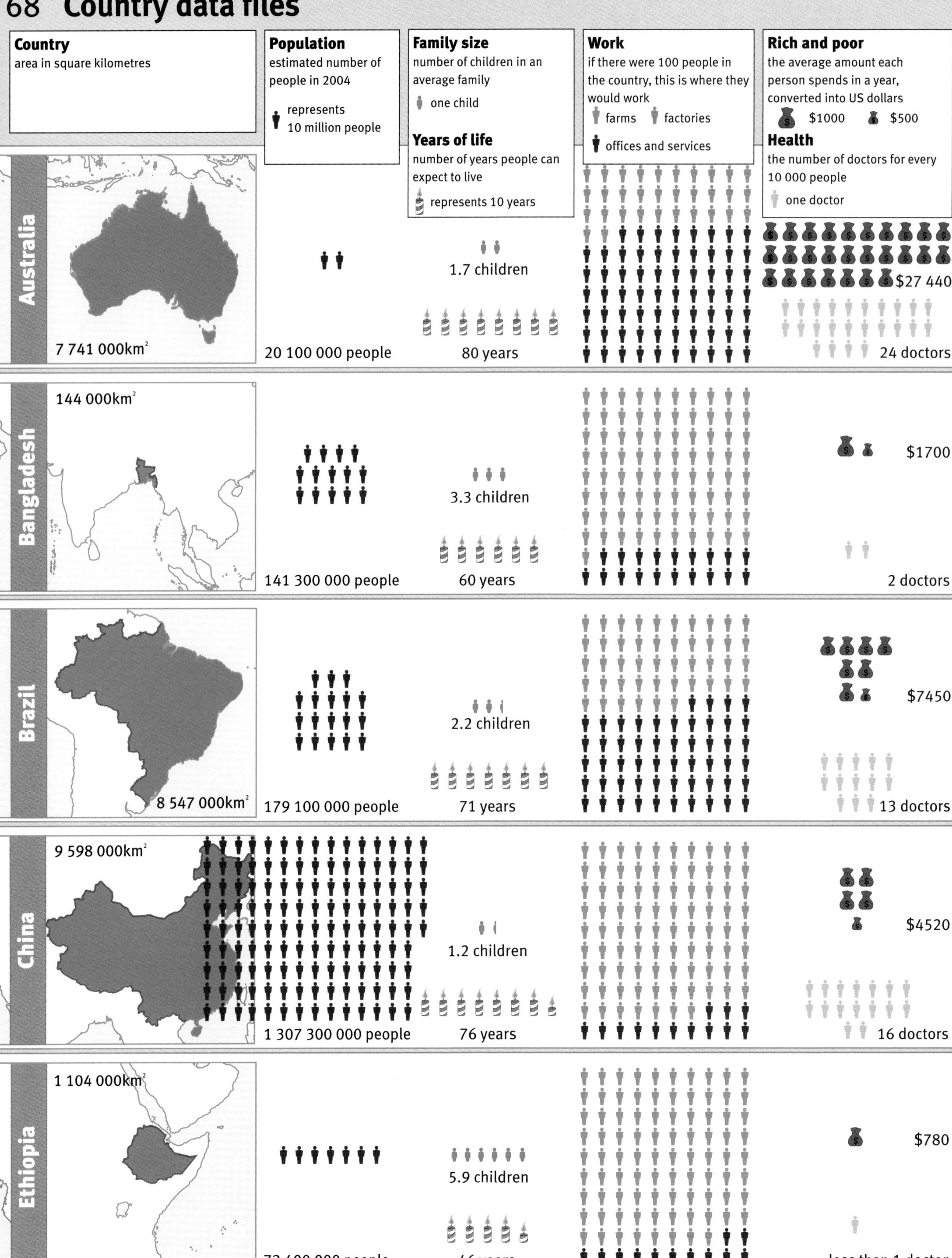
Country
area in square kilometres
Population
estimated number of people in 2004
represents 10 million people
Family size
number of children in an average family
one child
Years of life
number of years people can expect to live
represents 10 years
Work
if there were 100 people in the country, this is where they would work
farms
factories
offices and services
Rich and poor
the average amount each person spends in a year, converted into US dollars
$1000
$500
Health
the number of doctors for every 10 000 people
one doctor
Australia
7 741 000km²
20 100 000 people
1.7 children
80 years
$27 440
24 doctors
Bangladesh
144 000km²
141 300 000 people
3.3 children
60 years
$1700
2 doctors
Brazil
8 547 000km²
179 100 000 people
2.2 children
71 years
$7450
13 doctors
China
9 598 000km²
1 307 300 000 people
1.2 children
76 years
$4520
16 doctors
Ethiopia
1 104 000km²
72 400 000 people
5.9 children
46 years
$780
less than 1 doctor

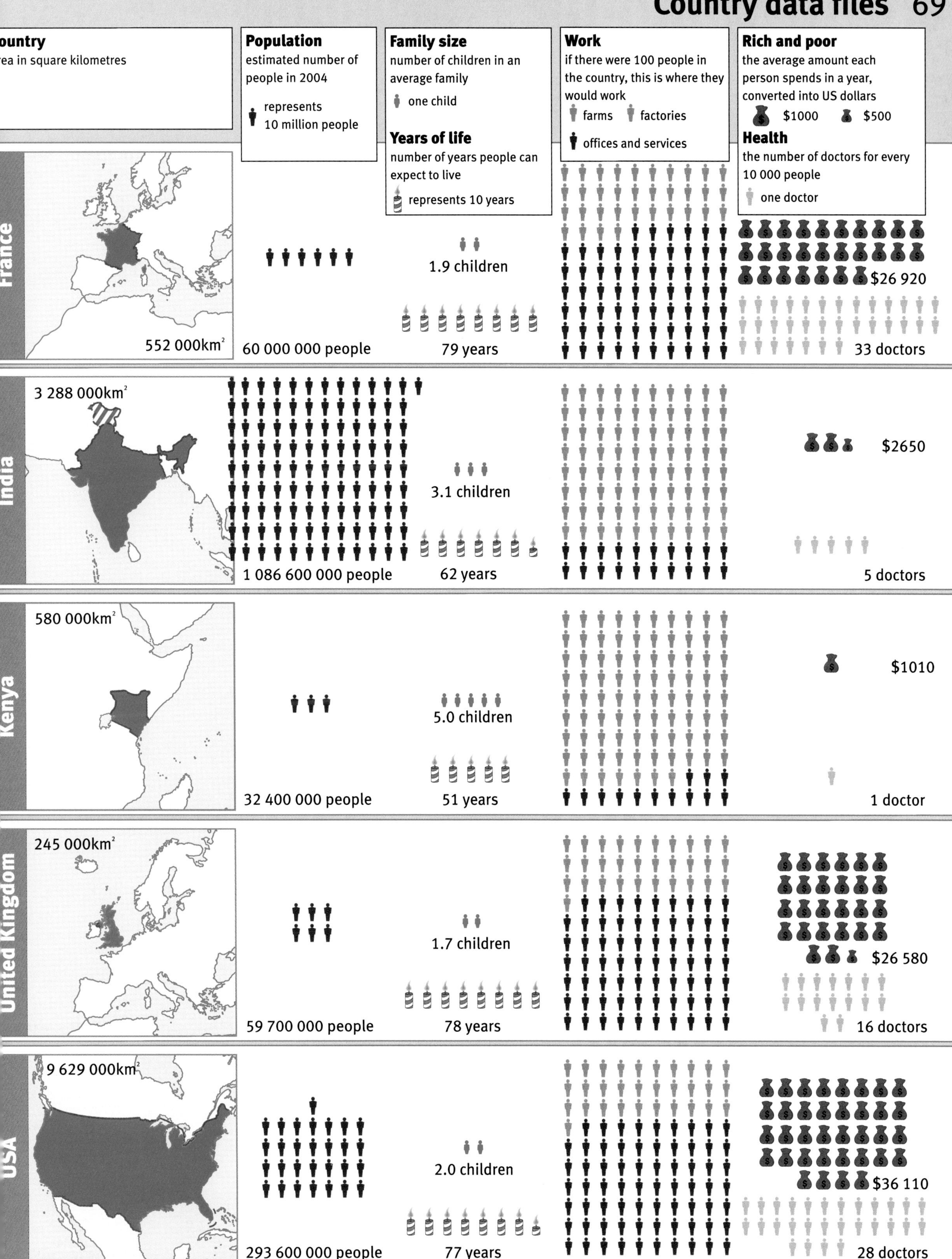
Country
rea in square kilometres
Population
estimated number of people in 2004
represents 10 million people
Family size
number of children in an average family
one child
Years of life
number of years people can expect to live
represents 10 years
Work
if there were 100 people in the country, this is where they would work
farms
factories
offices and services
Rich and poor
the average amount each person spends in a year, converted into US dollars
$1000
$500
Health
the number of doctors for every 10 000 people
one doctor
France
552 000km²
60 000 000 people
1.9 children
79 years
$26 920
33 doctors
India
3 288 000km²
1 086 600 000 people
3.1 children
62 years
$2650
5 doctors
Kenya
580 000km²
32 400 000 people
5.0 children
51 years
$1010
1 doctor
United Kingdom
245 000km²
59 700 000 people
1.7 children
78 years
$26 580
16 doctors
USA
9 629 000km²
293 600 000 people
2.0 children
77 years
$36 110
28 doctors

Index

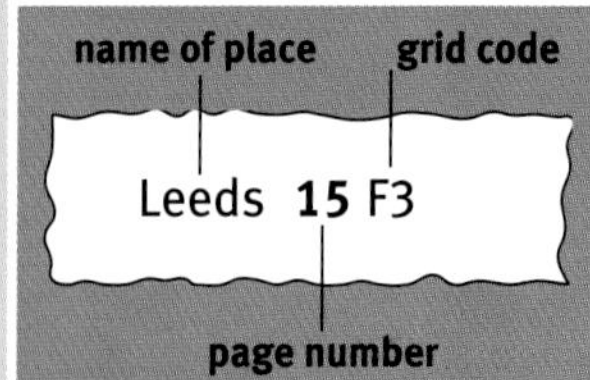
name of place
grid code
Leeds 15 F3
page number

A

Aberdeen **11** G2
Aberystwyth **14** C2
Abidjan **41** A4
Abu Dhabi **36** A3
Abuja **41** B4
Accra **41** A4
Aconcagua *mountain* **50** B2
Adana **33** G2
Addis Ababa **41** C4
Adelaide **54** B2
Aden, Gulf of **34** B3
Adriatic Sea **32/33** E3
Aegean Sea **33** F2
Afghanistan **35** C4
Ahmadabad **37** C3
Albania **33** E3/F3
Albany **54** A2
Aldabra Islands **41** D3
Aldeburgh **17** F3
Alderney *island* **19** E1
Aleppo **35** A4
Aleutian Islands **44** A3
Alexandria **42** B3
Algeria **41** A5/B5
Algiers **41** B5
Alice Springs *town* **54** B2
Alloa **13** E3
Almaty **35** C5
Alps *mountains* **32** D3
Alaska, Gulf of **44** B3
Altai Mountains **38** C4
Amazon, River **52/53** C4/D4
Amlwch **14** C3
Amman **35** A4
Amsterdam **32** D4
Amur, River **39** F5
Anatolian Plateau **30** D1
Anchorage **45** B4
Andaman Islands **37** E2
Andaman Sea **34** D3
Andes *mountains* **50** B1/B4
Andorra **32** D3
Angara River **34** D5/E5
Anglesey *island* **14** C3
Angola **41** B3/C3
Angola Plateau **40** B3
Anguilla **49** E2
Ankara **33** G2
Annan, River **13** E2
Antananarivo **41** D3
Antarctica **55**
Antigua and Barbuda **49** E2
Antofagasta **52** B2
Antrim **12** B1
Antrim Mountains **12** B1/B2
Appalachian Mountains **47** E2
Appennines *mountains* **32** E3
Arabian Peninsula **34** B4
Arabian Sea **36/37** B2
Arafura Sea **54** B3
Aral Sea **34** B5/C5
Ararat, Mount **30** E1
Arbroath **13** F3
Arctic Ocean **55**
Arequipa **52** B3
Argentina **51** B1/B2
Arkansas River **46/47** D2
Armagh **12** B1
Armenia **35** B5
Arnold **15** F2
Arran *island* **12** C2
Aruba **49** C1/D1
Arun, River **17** D2
Ascension Island **41** A3
Ashford **17** E2
Ashgabat **35** B4
Asmara **41** C4
Astana **35** C5
Asuncion **53** D2
Atacama Desert **52** B2/B3
Athens **33** F2
Atlanta **47** E2
Atlantic Ocean **30** B2
Atlas Mountains **40** A5/B5
Auckland **54** D2
Australia **54** A2/C3
Austria **32/33** E3
Aviemore **11** F2
Avon, River **15** F2
Ayers Rock *mountain* **54** B2
Aylesbury **17** D2
Ayr **12** D2
Azerbaijan **35** B5
Azov, Sea of **33** G3

B

Baffin Bay **44** F4/G4
Baffin Island **44** E4/F4
Baghdad **35** B4
Bahamas, The **48/49** B3/C3
Bahrain **35** B4
Baku **35** B5
Balearic Islands **32** D2/D3
Bali *island* **34** E2
Balkhash, Lake **34** C5
Ballybofey **12** A1
Ballymena **12** B1
Ballymoney **12** B2
Baltic Sea **32/33** E4
Bamako **41** A4
Banbridge **12** B1
Banbury **15** F2
Bandar Seri Begawan **35** E3
Bandung **35** E2
Bangalore **37** C2
Bangkok **35** E3
Bangladesh **37** D3/E3
Bangor Northern Ireland **12** C1
Bangor Wales **14** C3
Bangui **41** B4
Banjul **41** A4
Banks Island **44** C4/D4
Bann, River **12** B1
Barbados **49** F1
Barcelona **32** D3
Barents Sea **34** A6/B6
Barking **17** E2
Barmouth **14** C2
Barnet **17** D2
Barnstaple **18** C3
Barra *island* **10** B1/B2
Barranquilla **51** B4
Barrow-in-Furness **13** E1
Barrow, River **21**
Barry **14** D1
Basildon **17** E2
Basingstoke **19** F3
Basseterre **49** E2
Basse-Terre **49** E2
Bass Strait **54** C1/C2
Bath **19** E3
Baykal, Lake **34** E5
Beachy Head *cape* **17** E1
Beaufort Sea **44** B4/C4
Bedford **15** G2
Beijing **38** E3
Beira **41** C3
Beirut **35** A4
Belarus **33** F4
Belem **53** E4
Belfast **12** C1
Belfast Lough *estuary* **12** C1
Belgium **32** D4
Belgrade **33** F3
Belize **45** E1
Belmopan **45** E1
Belo Horizonte **53** E2
Benbecula *island* **10** B2
Ben Cruachan *mountain* **12** C3
Bengal, Bay of **37** D2/E2
Benghazi **41** C5
Benin **41** B4
Ben Nevis *mountain* **10** D1
Benue, River **40** B4
Ben Wyvis *mountain* **10** E2
Bering Sea **34** J5
Bering Strait **34** J6
Berlin **32** E4
Bermuda *island* **45** F2
Bern **32** D3
Berneray *island* **10** B2
Berwick-upon-Tweed **13** F2
Bexley **17** E2
Bhutan **37** D3/E3
Birkenhead **14** D3
Birmingham **15** F2
Biscay, Bay of **32** C3
Bishkek **35** C5
Bismarck Sea **54** C3
Bissau **41** A4
Blackburn **14** E3
Black Mountains **14** D1/D2
Blackpool **14** D3
Black Sea **33** G3
Blackwater, River **21**
Blue Nile River **40** C4
Blyth **13** G2
Bodmin Moor **18** C2
Bognor Regis **17** D1
Bogota **52** B5
Bolivia **52/53** C3
Bolton **14** E3
Bordeaux **32** C3
Borneo *island* **34** E2/E3
Bornholm *island* **32** E4
Bosnia-Herzegovina **33** E3
Boston UK **15** G2
Boston USA **47** F3
Bothnia, Gulf of **30** C3/D3
Botswana **41** C2
Bournemouth **19** F2
Boyne, River **21**

Bradford **15** F3
Braemar **11** F2
Brahmaputra River **37** E3
Brasilia **53** E3
Bratislava **33** E3
Brazil **52/53**
Brazilian Highlands **53** E3
Brazzaville **41** B3
Brecon **14** D1
Brecon Beacons *mountains* **14** D1
Brent **17** D2
Bressay *island* **11** H5
Bridgend **14** D1
Bridgetown **49** F1
Bridgnorth **15** E2
Bridgwater **18** D3
Bridlington **13** H1
Brighton **17** D1
Brisbane **54** C2
Bristol **19** E3
Bristol Channel **18** C3/D3
Bromley **17** E2
Broome **54** B3
Brunei **35** E3
Brussels **32** D4
Bucharest **33** F3
Budapest **33** E3
Buenos Aires **51** C2
Bujumbura **41** C3
Bulgaria **33** F3
Bure, River **17** F3
Burkina **41** A4/B4
Burton upon Trent **15** F2
Burundi **41** C3
Bury **15** E3
Bury St. Edmunds **17** E3
Bute *island* **12** C2
Butt of Lewis *cape* **10** C3
Buxton **15** F3

C

Cabinda *admin.* **41** B3
Cadair Idris *mountain* **14** D2
Caernarfon **14** C3
Caerphilly **14** D1
Cairngorms *mountains* **11** F2
Cairns **54** C3
Cairo **42** C3
Calgary **45** D3
Cali **52** B5
California, Gulf of **44** E2/F3
Cambodia **35** E3
Cambrian Mountains **14** D2
Cambridge **17** E3
Cameroon **41** B4
Cameroun, Mount **40** B4
Campbeltown **12** C2
Canada **45** C4/G3
Canadian Shield **44** E3/F3
Canary Islands **41** A5
Canberra **54** C2
Canna *island* **10** C2
Cannock **15** E2
Cantabrian Mountains **32** C3
Canterbury **17** F2
Cape Town **41** B2
Cape Verde **56** D3
Cape York Peninsula **54** C3
Caracas **51** B4
Cardiff **14** D1
Cardigan **14** C2
Cardigan Bay **14** C2
Caribbean Sea **48/49**
Carlisle **13** F1
Carmarthen **14** C1
Carn Eige *mountain* **10** D2
Carpathians *mountains* **33** F3
Carpentaria, Gulf of **54** B3/C3
Carrickfergus **12** C1
Casablanca **41** A5
Caspian Sea **34** B4/B5
Castleblayney **12** B1
Castle Douglas **13** E1
Castleford **15** F3
Castries **49** G6
Caucasus *mountains* **30** E2
Cayenne **51** C4
Cayman Islands **48** A2/B2
Celebes Sea **34** E3/F3
Central African Republic **41** B4/C4
Central Russian Uplands **30** D2
Ceuta *territory* **32** C2
Chad **41** B4/C4
Chad, Lake **40** B4
Chang Jiang *river* **38** D2/D3
Channel Islands **19** E1
Chari, River **40** B4
Charlotte Amalie **49** E2
Chelmsford **17** E2
Cheltenham **16** B2
Chelyabinsk **35** C5
Chennai **37** D2
Cherwell, River **16** C2
Chester **14** E3
Chesterfield **15** F3
Cheviot Hills **13** F2
Chicago **47** E3

Chile **51** B1/B2
Chiloé Island **50** B1
Chiltern Hills **16/17** C2/D2
Chimborazo *mountain* **52** B4
China **35** D4/F5
Chisinau **33** F3
Chongqing **38** D2
Chorley **14** E3
Christchurch **54** D1
Cirencester **16** C2
Citlaltepetl *mountain* **44** E1
Clydebank **12** D2
Clyde, River **13** E2
Coalville **15** F2
Coast Mountains **44** C3
Cocos Islands **50** A4
Cod, Cape **47** G3
Colchester **17** E2
Coleraine **12** B2
Coll *island* **12** B3
Colombia **51** B3/B4
Colombo **37** C1
Colonsay *island* **12** B3
Colorado Plateau **46** B2
Colorado, River Argentina **50** B2
Colorado River USA **46** B2
Columbia River **46** A3/B3
Colwyn Bay *town* **14** D3
Comoros **41** D3
Conakry **41** A4
Concepcion **51** B2
Congo **41** B3/B4
Congo, Democratic Republic of **41** B3/C4
Congo, River **40** C4
Consett **13** G1
Conwy **14** D3
Cook, Mount **54** D1
Cookstown **12** B1
Copenhagen **32** E4
Coquet, River **13** F2/G2
Coral Sea **54** C3
Corby **15** G2
Cordoba **53** C1
Corsica *island* **32** D3
Costa Rica **45** E1
Côte d'Ivoire **41** A4
Cotopaxi *mountain* **52** B4
Cotswold Hills **16** B2/C2
Coventry **15** F2
Crawley **17** D2
Crete *island* **33** F2
Crewe **14** E3
Croatia **32/33** E3
Cromer **17** F3
Croydon **17** D2
Cuba **48** A3/C3
Cubango, River **40** B3
Cuillin Hills **10** C2
Cumbernauld **13** E2
Cumnock **12** D2
Cunene, River **40** B3
Cunnamula **54** C2
Curacao **49** D1
Curitiba **53** E2
Cwmbran **14** D1
Cyprus **33** G2
Czech Republic **32/33** E3/E4

D

Dakar **41** A4
Dalbeattie **13** E1
Dallas **47** D2
Damascus **35** B4
Danube, River **32/33** E3/F3
Dar es Salaam **41** C3
Darling, River **54** C2
Darlington **13** G1
Dartmoor **18** C2/D2
Dartmouth **18** D2
Dart, River **18** D2
Darwin **54** B3
Davis Strait **44** F4/G4
Dead Sea **34** A4
Deal **17** F2
Death Valley **46** B2
Deccan *plateau* **37** C2
Dee, River Scotland **11** G2
Dee, River Wales **14** D2/D3
Denbigh **14** D3
Denmark **32** D4/E4
Denmark Strait **44** H4
Denver **46** C2
Derby **15** F2
Derwent, River **15** F3
Detroit **47** E3
Deveron, River **11** G2
Devon Island **44** E4
Dhaka **37** E3
Dili **35** F2
Dinaric Alps *mountains* **33** E3
Dingwall **10** E2
Djibouti **41** D4
Djibouti **41** D4
Dniepr, River **33** G4
Dniester, River **33** F3
Dodoma **41** C3

Doha **35** B4
Dolgellau **14** D2
Dominica **49** E2
Dominican Republic **49** C2/D2
Doncaster **15** F3
Donets'k **33** G3
Donets, River **30** C2
Don, River England **15** F3
Don, River Russia **33** H3
Don, River Scotland **11** G2
Dorchester **19** E2
Dornoch Firth *estuary* **11** E2/F2
Douglas **12** D1
Dover **17** F2
Downpatrick **12** C1
Drakensberg *mountains* **40** C2
Dublin **32** C4
Dudley **15** E2
Duero, River **32** C3
Dumbarton **12** D2
Dumfries **13** E2
Duncansby Head *cape* **11** F3
Dundee **13** F3
Dunedin **54** D1
Dunfermline **13** E3
Dungannon **12** B1
Durban **41** C2
Durham **13** G1
Dushanbe **35** C4
Düsseldorf **32** D4
Dyfi, River **14** D2

E

Ealing **17** D2
Earn, River **13** E3
Eastbourne **17** E1
East China Sea **39** F2/F3
East Kilbride **12** D2
Eastleigh **19** F2
East Timor **35** F2
Ebro, River **32** C3
Ecuador **52** A4/B4
Eday *island* **11** G4
Eden, River **13** F1
Edinburgh **13** E2
Edmonton **45** D3
Egypt **42**
Eigg *island* **10** C1
Elbe, River **32** E4
Elbrus, Mount **33** H3
Elburz Mountains **34** B4
Elgin **11** F2
El Giza **42** C2
Ellesmere Island **44** E4/F5
El Salvador **45** E1
Ely **17** E3
Emi Koussi *mountain* **40** B5
Enfield **17** D2
England **8/9**
English Channel **32** C3/C4
Enniskillen **12** A1
Equatorial Guinea **41** B4
Erie, Lake **47** E3/F3
Eritrea **41** C4/D4
Esfahan **35** B4
Esk, River **13** E2
Espiritu Santo *island* **54** D3
Estonia **33** F4
Ethiopia **41** C4/D4
Ethiopian Highlands **40** C4
Etna, Mount **32** E2
Euphrates, River **34** B4
Everest, Mount **38** B2
Evesham **15** F2
Exe, River **18** D3
Exeter **18** D2
Exmoor **18** D3
Exmouth **18** D2
Eyre, Lake **54** B2

F

Fair Isle *island* **11** H4
Falkirk **13** E2
Falkland Islands **51** B1/C1
Falmouth **18** B2
Fareham **19** F2
Farewell, Cape **44** G4
Faroe Islands **30** B3
Federated States of Micronesia **57** H3
Felixstowe **17** F2
Fetlar *island* **11** J5
Fiji **57** H2
Finisterre, Cape **32** C3
Finland **31** D3
Firth of Clyde *estuary* **12** C2/D2
Firth of Forth *estuary* **13** E3/F3
Firth of Lorn *estuary* **12** C3
Fishguard **14** C1
Fitzroy, River **54** B3
Fleetwood **14** D3
Flinders, River **54** C2/C3
Folkestone **17** F2
Forel, Mount **44** H4
Forfar **13** F3
Fortaleza **53** F4
Fort Augustus **10** E2
Fort-de-France **49** E1
Forth, River **12/13** D3/E3

Fort William **10** D1
Foula *island* **11** G5
Foyle, River **12** A1
France **32** C3/D3
Fraserburgh **11** G2
Fraser River **44** C3
Freetown **41** A4
French Guiana **51** C4
Frisian Islands **32** D4
Frome, River **19** E2
Fuji, Mount **39** G3
Fukuoka **39** G3

G

Gabon **41** B3/B4
Gaborone **41** C2
Galapagos Islands **51** A3
Galashiels **13** F2
Gambia, The **41** A4
Ganges, River **37** C3/D3
Gateshead **13** G1
Georgetown **51** C4
George Town **48** A2
Georgia **31** E2
Germany **32** D3/E4
Ghana **41** A4
Gibraltar *territory* **32** C2
Gibraltar, Strait of **30** B1
Gillingham **17** E2
Girvan **12** D2
Glasgow **12** D2
Glenrothes **13** E3
Gloucester **16** B2
Goat Fell *mountain* **12** C2
Gobi Desert **38** C4/D4
Gold Coast *town* **54** C2
Good Hope, Cape of **40** B2
Göteborg **32** E4
Gotland *island* **33** E4
Grampian Mountains **11** E1/F1
Grand Turk **49** C3
Grantham **15** G2
Gravesend **17** E2
Great Australian Bight *bay* **54** B2
Great Barrier Reef **54** C2/C3
Great Basin **46** B2
Great Bear Lake **44** C4/D4
Great Britain *islands* **21**
Great Dividing Range **54** C2/C3
Greater Antilles *islands* **48/49** A3/D2
Great Malvern **15** E2
Great Ouse, River **17** D3/E3
Great Plains **44** D3
Great Salt Lake **46** B3
Great Slave Lake **44** D4
Great Victoria Desert **54** B2
Great Yarmouth **17** F3
Greece **33** F2/F3
Greenland **45** F4/H4
Greenland Sea **30** B3
Greenock **12** D2
Grenada **49** E1
Greymouth **54** D1
Grimsby **15** G3
Guadalajara **45** D2
Guadeloupe **49** E2
Guam **57** H3
Guangzhou **38** E2
Guatemala **45** E1
Guatemala **45** E1
Guayaquil **52** A4
Guernsey *island* **19** E1
Guiana Highlands **50** B4/C4
Guildford **17** D2
Guinea **41** A4
Guinea-Bissau **41** A4
Guinea, Gulf of **40** A4/B4
Guyana **51** C4

H

Haiti **48/49** C2
Halifax Canada **47** G3
Halifax UK **15** F3
Hamburg **32** E4
Hamersley Range *mountains* **54** A2
Hamilton New Zealand **54** D2
Hamilton UK **12** D2
Hanoi **38** D2
Harare **41** C3
Harbin **39** F4
Harlow **17** E2
Harris *island* **10** B2/C2
Harrogate **15** F3
Harrow **17** D2
Hartland Point *cape* **18** C3
Hartlepool **13** G1
Harwich **17** F2
Hastings **17** E1
Havana **48** A3
Havant **16** D1
Havering **17** E2
Hawick **13** F2
Hay-on-Wye **14** D2
Hekla, Mount **30** B3
Helsinki **33** F5
Hereford **14** E2
Herm *island* **19** E1
Herma Ness *cape* **11** J5
Hexham **13** F1
Hillingdon **17** D2
Himalaya *mountains* **37** C4/D3
Hindu Kush *mountains* **34** C4
Hispaniola *island* **49** C2
Hobart **54** C1
Hô Chi Minh **35** E3
Hoggar Mountains **40** B5
Hokkaido *island* **39** H4
Holyhead **14** C3
Holy Island **13** G2
Honduras **45** E1
Hong Kong **38** E2
Honiara **54** C3
Honshu *island* **39** G3/H4
Horn, Cape **50** B1
Horsham **17** D2
Hounslow **17** D2
Houston **47** D1
Hoy *island* **11** F3
Huang He *river* **38** D3/E3
Huddersfield **15** F3
Hudson Bay **44** E3/E4
Hudson River **44** F3
Hudson Strait **44** F4
Humber, River **15** G3
Hungary **33** E3/F3
Huron, Lake **47** E3
Hyderabad **37** C2

I

Ibiza *island* **32** D2
Iceland **31** A3/B3
Ilfracombe **18** C3
Ilkeston **15** F2
India **36/37**
Indian Ocean **34** D2
Indonesia **35** E2/F2
Indus, River **36/37** B3/C4
Inner Hebrides *islands* **10** C1/C2
Inverness **11** E2
Iona *island* **12** B3
Ionian Sea **33** E2
Ipswich **17** F3
Iquitos **52** B4
Iran **35** B4
Iraq **35** B4
Ireland *island* **21**
Irrawaddy River **38** C1/C2
Irtysh, River **34** C5
Irvine **12** D2
Islamabad **37** C4
Islay *island* **12** B2
Isle of Man **12** D1
Isle of Wight **19** F2
Isles of Scilly **18** A1
Israel **35** A4
Istanbul **33** F3
Italy **32/33** D3/E3
Izmir **33** F2

J

Jakarta **35** E2
Jamaica **48** B2
Jammu and Kashmir *state* **37** C4
Japan **39** F2/H4
Japan, Sea of **39** G3/G4
Java *island* **34** E2
Java Sea **34** E2
Jaya Peak *mountain* **54** B3
Jedda **35** A4
Jersey *island* **19** E1
Jerusalem **35** A4
Johannesburg **41** C2
John o'Groats **11** F3
Jordan **35** A4
Juan Fernandez Islands **51** B2
Jura *island* **12** B2/C3
Jura *mountains* **30** C2
Jylland *peninsula* **30** C2

K

K2 *mountain* **37** C4
Kabul **36** B4
Kalahari Desert **40** B2/C2
Kalgoorlie **54** B2
Kaliningrad *admin.* **33** F4
Kamchatka *peninsula* **34** G5/H5
Kampala **41** C4
Kansas City **47** D2
Karachi **36** B3
Kasai, River **40** B3
Kathmandu **37** D3
Kazakhstan **35** B5/D5
Kazakh Upland **34** C5
Kendal **13** F1
Kenya **43**
Kenya, Mount **43** B2
Keswick **13** E1
Kettering **15** G2
Kharkov **33** G3
Khartoum **41** C4
Kidderminster **15** E2
Kielder Water *lake* **13** F2
Kiev **33** G4
Kigali **41** C3
Kilimanjaro, Mount **43** B2
Kilmarnock **12** D2
Kimberley Plateau **54** B3
Kinabalu **34** E3
King's Lynn **17** E3
Kingston Jamaica **48** B2
Kingston UK **17** D2
Kingston upon Hull **15** G3
Kingstown **49** E1
Kinshasa **41** B3
Kiribati **56/57**
Kirkcaldy **13** E3
Kirkcudbright **12** D1
Kirkwall **11** G3
Kola Peninsula **30** D3/E3
Kolkata **37** D3
Kolyma, River **34** G6
Kosciusko, Mount **54** C2
Krakow **33** F4
Kuala Lumpur **35** E3
Kunlun Shan *mountains* **38** B3
Kuril Islands **35** G5
Kuwait **35** B4
Kuwait **35** B4
Kyle of Lochalsh **10** D2
Kyrgyzstan **35** C5
Kyushu *island* **39** G3

L

Laayoune **41** A5
Laccadive Islands **37** C1/C2
Ladoga, Lake **33** G5
Lagan, River **12** B1
Lagos **41** B4
Lahore **37** C4
Lake District *geog. reg.* **13** E1/F1
Lammermuir Hills **13** F2
Lancaster **13** F1
Land's End *cape* **18** B2
Lanzhou **38** D3
Laos **35** E3/E4
La Paz **52** C3
Lappland **30** D3
Larne **12** C1
Latvia **33** F4
Lebanon **35** A4
Leeds **15** F3
Leeuwin, Cape **54** A2
Leeward Islands **49** E2
Leicester **15** F2
Lena, River **34** F6
Lerwick **11** H5
Lesotho **41** C2
Lesser Antilles *islands* **49** D1/E2
Letterkenny **12** A1
Lewis *island* **10** C3
Liard River **44** C3/C4
Liberia **41** A4
Libreville **41** B4
Libya **41** B5/C5
Liechtenstein **32** D3
Liffey, River **21**
Lifford **12** A1
Lilongwe **41** C3
Lima **52** B3
Limpopo, River **40** C2
Lincoln **15** G3
Lincoln Wolds *hills* **15** G3
Lisbon **32** C2
Lisburn **12** B1
Lithuania **33** F4
Little Minch *sound* **10** C2
Liverpool **14** E3
Livingston **13** E2
Ljubljana **32** E3
Llandovery **14** D1
Llandudno **14** D3
Llanelli **14** C1
Llangollen **14** D2
Loch Awe *lake* **12** C3
Loch Fyne *lake* **12** C2/C3
Loch Linnhe *lake* **12** C3
Loch Lomond *lake* **12** D3
Loch Ness *lake* **10** E2
Loch Rannoch *lake* **12** D3
Loch Shin *lake* **10** E3
Loch Tay *lake* **12** D3
Lofoten Islands **30** C3
Logan, Mount **44** B4
Loire, River **32** D3
Lomé **41** B4
London **17** D2
Londonderry **12** A1
Long Eaton **15** F2
Lord Howe Island **54** C2
Los Angeles **46** B2
Loughborough **15** F2
Lough Foyle *estuary* **12** A2
Lough Neagh *lake* **12** B1
Louth **15** G3
Lower Lough Erne *lake* **12** A1
Lowestoft **17** F3
Lualaba, River **40** C3
Luanda **41** B3
Lundy *island* **18** C3
Lune, River **13** F1
Lurgan **12** B1
Lusaka **41** C3
Luton **17** D2
Luxembourg **32** D3
Luxembourg **32** D3
Luzon *island* **34** F3
Lyme Bay **19** E2
Lyme Regis **18** E2
Lyons **32** D3
Lytham St. Anne's **14** D3

M

Mablethorpe **15** H3
Macclesfield **15** E3
Macdonnell Ranges *mountains* **54** B2
Macedonia, Former Yugoslav Republic of **33** F3
Mackenzie River **44** C4
Madagascar **41** D2/D3
Madeira *islands* **41** A5
Madeira, River **53** C4
Madrid **32** C3
Magdalena, River **50** B4
Maidstone **17** E2
Malabo **41** B4
Malawi **41** C3
Malay Peninsula **34** E3
Malaysia **35** E3
Maldives **35** C3
Malé **35** D3
Mali **41** A4/A5
Malin Head *cape* **12** A2
Mallaig **10** D2
Mallorca *island* **32** D2
Malta **32** E2
Malton **13** H1
Managua **45** E1
Manama **35** B4
Manaus **53** C4
Manchester **15** E3
Manila **35** F3
Maputo **41** C2
Maracaibo **51** B4
Maracaibo, Lake **50** B4
Mar del Plata **51** C2
Margate **17** F2
Marrakech **41** A5
Marseilles **32** D3
Marshall Islands **57**
Martinique **49** E1
Maseru **41** C2
Mashhad **35** B4
Massif Central *mountains* **32** D3
Mato Grosso *geog. reg.* **53** D3
Mauritania **41** A4/A5
Mauritius **57** F2
Mbabane **41** C2
McKinley, Mount **44** B4
Medan **35** D3
Medellín **51** B4
Mediterranean Sea **32/33** D2/G2
Medway, River **17** E2
Mekong River **38** D2
Melbourne **54** C2
Melilla *territory* **32** C2
Mendip Hills **19** E3
Menorca *island* **32** D2/D3
Mersey, River **14** E3
Merthyr Tydfil **14** D1
Merton **17** D2
Mexico **45** D2/E1
Mexico City **45** E1
Mexico, Gulf of **44** E2
Miami **47** E1
Michigan, Lake **47** E3
Middlesbrough **13** G1
Milan **32** D3
Milford Haven **14** B1
Milton Keynes **15** G2
Mindanao *island* **34** F3
Mindoro *island* **34** F3
Minehead **18** D3
Mingulay *island* **10** B1
Minneapolis **47** D3
Minsk **33** F4
Mississippi River **47** D2
Missouri River **46/47** B3/D2
Moffat **13** E2
Mogadishu **41** D4
Moldova **33** F3
Mombasa **43** B2
Monaco **32** D3
Monadhliath Mountains **11** E2/F2
Monaghan **12** B1
Mongolia **38** C4/E4
Monmouth **14** E1
Monrovia **41** A4
Mont Blanc *mountain* **32** D3
Monterray **47** C1
Montréal **47** F3
Montrose **13** F3
Montserrat **49** E2
Moray Firth *estuary* **11** E2/F2
Morecambe **13** F1
Morocco **41** A5
Moroni **41** D3
Moscow **33** G4
Montevideo **51** C2
Motherwell **13** D2
Mount Isa *town* **54** B2
Mourne Mountains **12** B1
Mozambique **41** C2/C3
Mozambique Channel **40** C2/D3
Mull *island* **12** B3/C3
Mull of Galloway *cape* **12** D1
Mull of Kintyre *cape* **12** C2
Mumbai **37** C2
Munich **32** E3
Murray, River **54** C2
Muscat **36** A3
Myanmar **38** C1/C2

N

Nairobi **43** B2
Namib Desert **40** B2
Namibia **41** B2/B3
Naples **32** E3
Nassau **48** B3
Nasser, Lake **42** C1
Nauru **57** H2
Ndjamena **41** B4
Neath **14** D1
Negro, River Argentina **50** B2
Negro, River Brazil **52/53** C4
Nene, River **17** D3/E3
Nepal **37** D3
Netherlands **32** D4
Newark-on-Trent **15** G3
Newbury **19** F3
Newcastle **54** C2
Newcastle upon Tyne **13** G1
New Delhi **37** C3
Newfoundland *island* **44** G3
New Guinea *island* **54** B3/C3
New Orleans **47** D1
Newport **14** E1
New Quay **14** C2
Newquay **18** B2
Newry **12** B1
Newtown **14** D2
Newtownabbey **12** C1
Newtownards **12** C1
New York **47** F3
New Zealand **54** D1/D2
Niamey **41** B4
Nicaragua **45** E1
Nicaragua, Lake **44** E1
Nicobar Islands **35** D3
Nicosia **33** G2
Nidd, River **13** G1
Niger **41** B4
Nigeria **41** B4
Niger, River **40** A4/B4
Nile, River **42** C1/C3
Nith, River **13** E2
Nizhniy-Novgorod **33** H4
Northallerton **13** G1
Northampton **15** G2
North Channel **12** C1/C2
North Downs *hills* **17** D2/E2
North Dvina, River **30** E3
Northern Ireland **12** A1/C1
Northern Marianas **57** H3
North Esk, River **11** G1
North European Plain **33** E4/F4
North Island **54** D2
North Korea **39** F3/F4
North Ronaldsay *island* **11** G4
North Sea **32** D4
North Uist *island* **10** B2
Northwest Highlands **10** D2/E3
North York Moors **13** H1
Norway **31** C2/C3
Norwich **17** F3
Nottingham **15** F2
Nouakchott **41** A4
Noumea **54** D2
Novosibirsk **35** D5
Nullarbor Plain **54** B2
Nuuk **45** G4
Nyasa, Lake **40** C3

O

Oban **12** C3
Ob', River **34** C6
Oder, River **32/33** E4
Odessa **33** G3
Ohio River **47** E2
Ojos del Salado *mountain* **52** C2
Okhotsk, Sea of **34** G5
Okovango Swamp **40** C3
Oldham **15** E3
Olympus, Mount **33** F3
Omagh **12** A1
Oman **35** B3/B4
Omsk **35** C5
Onega, Lake **33** G5
Ontario, Lake **47** F3
Oporto **32** C3
Orange, River **40** B2/C2
Oranjestad **49** C1
Orinoco, River **50** B4
Orkney Islands **11** F3/G4
Osaka **39** G3
Oslo **32** E4
Oswestry **14** D2
Ottawa **47** F3

Index

Ouagadougou **41** A4
Oubangui, River **40** B4
Ouse, River **15** F3
Outer Hebrides *islands* **10** B1/C3
Oxford **16** C2

P

Pabbay *island* **10** B2
Pacific Ocean **58/59**
Paisley **12** D2
Pakistan **36/37** B3/C4
Palau **57** H3
Palembang **35** E2
Panama **45** E1/F1
Panama City **45** F1
Papa Westray *island* **11** G4
Papua New Guinea **54** C3
Paraguay **53** C2/D2
Paraguay, River **53** D2
Paramaribo **51** C4
Paraná, River **50** B2/C2
Paris **32** D3
Parry Islands **44** D4
Peace River **44** D3
Pechora, River **30** E3
Peipus, Lake **33** F4
Peloponnese *islands* **33** F2
Pemba Island **43** B1
Pennines *hills* **13** F1
Penrith **13** F1
Pentland Firth *sound* **11** F3
Penzance **18** B2
Perm **35** B5
Perth Australia **54** A2
Perth UK **13** E3
Peru **52** B3/B4
Peterborough **15** G2
Peterhead **11** H2
Philadelphia **47** F2
Philippines **35** F3
Phnom Penh **35** E3
Phoenix **46** B2
Pilcomayo, River **53** C2/D2
Pindus Mountains **33** F2/F3
Pittsburgh **47** F3
Plymouth Montserrat **49** E2
Plymouth UK **18** C2
Poland **32/33** E4/F4
Pontypool **14** D1
Poole **19** F2
Poopo, Lake **52** C3
Popocatepetl *mountain* **44** E1
Po, River **32** D3/E3
Portadown **12** B1
Port Augusta **54** B2
Port-au-Prince **49** C2
Portland **46** A3
Portland Bill *cape* **19** E2
Port Moresby **54** C3
Porto Alegre **53** D1
Port-of-Spain **49** E1
Porto Novo **41** B4
Portree **10** C2
Portsmouth **19** F2
Port Talbot **14** D1
Portugal **32** C2/C3
Port Vila **54** D3
Prague **32** E4
Preston **14** E3
Pretoria **41** C2
Príncipe *island* **40** B4
Puebla **45** E1
Puerto Rico **49** D2
Punta Arenas **51** B1
Pusan **39** F3
Pwllheli **14** C2
Pyongyang **39** F3
Pyrénées *mountains* **32** D3

Q

Qatar **35** B4
Quantock Hills **18** D3
Québec **47** F3
Queen Charlotte Islands **44** C3
Quezon City **35** F3
Quito **52** B4
Qullai Garmo *mountain* **34** C4

R

Raasay *island* **10** C2
Rabat **41** A5
Ras Dashen Terara *mountain* **40** C4
Rathlin Island **12** B2
Reading **16** D2
Recife **53** F4
Redbridge **17** E2
Redcar **13** G1
Redditch **15** F2
Redhill **17** D2
Red Sea **40** C5/D4
Reigate **17** D2
Republic of Ireland **32** C4
Republic of South Africa **41** B2/C2
Reykjavik **31** A3
Rhine, River **32** D3
Rhodes *island* **33** F2
Rhondda **14** D1
Rhône, River **32** D3
Rhum *island* **10** C1/C2
Ribble, River **15** E3
Richmond **13** G1
Rift Valley **40** C3/C4
Riga **33** F4
Rio de Janeiro **53** E2
Rio de la Plata *river* **50** C2
Rio Grande **46/47** C2/D1
Ripon **13** G1
Riyadh **35** B4
Road Town **49** E2
Rocas Island **51** D3
Rochdale **15** E3
Rockhampton **54** C2
Rocky Mountains **44** C3/D2
Romania **33** F3
Rome **32** E3
Roraima, Mount **50** B4
Rosario **51** B2
Roseau **49** E2
Rostov-on-Don **33** G3
Rotherham **15** F3
Rotterdam **32** D4
Rousay *island* **11** F4/G4
Royal Tunbridge Wells **17** E2
Rugby **15** F2
Runcorn **14** E3
Russian Federation **35** A5/J6
Ruwenzori, Mount **40** C3/C4
Rwanda **41** C3
Rybinsk Reservoir **33** G4
Ryukyu Islands **39** F2

S

Sacremento **46** A2
Sahara Desert **40** A5/C5
St. Abb's Head *cape* **13** F2
St. Albans **17** D2
St. Andrews **13** F3
St. Austell **18** C2
St. Bees Head *cape* **13** E1
St. David's Head *cape* **14** B1
St. George's **49** E1
St. George's Channel **14** A1/B2
St. Helena *island* **41** A3
St. Helens **14** E3
St. Ives **18** B2
St. John's **49** E2
St. Kilda *island* **10** A2
St. Kitts and Nevis **49** E2
St. Lawrence, Gulf of **44** F3/G3
St. Lawrence River **44** F3
St. Louis **47** D2
St. Lucia **49** G5/H6
St. Peter Port **19** E1
St. Petersburg **33** G4
St-Pierre & Miquelon *islands* **45** G3
St. Vincent and the Grenadines **49** E1
St. Vincent, Cape **32** C2
Sakhalin *island* **34** G5
Salisbury **19** F3
Salisbury Plain *hills* **19** F3
Salt Lake City **46** B3
Salvador **53** F3
Salween River **38** C2
Samoa **56** A2
Sana **35** B3
Sanday *island* **11** G4
San Diego **46** B2
San Francisco **46** A2
San José **45** E1
San Juan **49** D2
San Marino **32** E3
San Salvador **45** E1
Santa Cruz **53** C3
Santa Cruz Islands **54** D3
Santiago **51** B2
Santo Domingo **49** D2
São Francisco, River **53** E3
São Paulo **53** E2
São Tomé **41** B4
São Tomé and Principe **41** B4
Sapporo **39** H4
Sarajevo **33** E3
Sardinia *island* **32** D2/D3
Sark *island* **19** E1
Saskatchewan River **44** D3
Saudi Arabia **35** B3/B4
Sawel *mountain* **12** A1
Scafell Pike *mountain* **13** E1
Scalloway **11** H5
Scalpay *island* **10** C2
Scandinavia **30** C3
Scarborough **13** H1
Scotland **8/9**
Scunthorpe **15** G3
Seattle **46** A3
Seine, River **32** D3
Semarang **35** E2
Senegal **41** A4
Senegal River **40** A4
Seoul **39** F3
Serbia and Montenegro **33** E3/F3
Severn, River **16** B2/B3
Seville **32** C2
Seychelles **57**
Sgurr Mór *mountain* **10** D2
Shanghai **39** F3
Shannon, River **21**
Shapinsay *island* **11** G4
Sheerness **17** E2
Sheffield **15** F3
Shenyang **39** F4
Shetland Islands **11** H4/J5
Shiraz **35** B4
Shrewsbury **14** D2
Siberian Lowland **34** C5/D6
Sicily *island* **32** E2
Sidlaw Hills **13** E3/F3
Sierra Leone **41** A4
Sierra Madre Occidental *mountains* **44** D2
Sierra Madre Oriental *mountains* **44** D2
Sierra Nevada *mountains* **46** A2/B2
Sinai, Mount **42** C2
Singapore **35** E3
Skegness **15** H3
Skipton **15** E3
Skopje **33** F3
Skye *island* **10** C2/D2
Sleat, Sound of **10** D2
Slieve Donard *mountain* **12** C1
Slough **17** D2
Slovakia **33** E3/F3
Slovenia **32** E3
Snaefell *mountain* **12** D1
Snake River **46** B3
Snowdon *mountain* **14** C3
Soar, River **15** F2
Socotra **35** B3
Sofia **33** F3
Solihull **15** F2
Solomon Islands **54** C3/D3
Solway Firth *estuary* **13** E1
Somalia **41** D4
Sound of Jura **12** C2/C3
Southampton **19** F2
South China Sea **38/39** E1
South Downs *hills* **17** D1
Southend-on-Sea **17** E2
Southern Alps *mountains* **54** D1
Southern Ocean **55**
Southern Uplands *mountains* **12/13** D2/E2
South Esk, River **13** F3
South Georgia *island* **51** D1
South Korea **39** F3
Southport **14** D3
South Ronaldsay *island* **11** G3
South Island **54** D1
South Uist *island* **10** B2
Southwold **17** F3
Spain **32** C2/C3
Spalding **15** G2
Sperrin Mountains **12** A1
Spey, River **11** F2
Spurn Head *cape* **15** H3
Sri Lanka **35** D3
Stafford **15** E2
Stanley **51** C1
Start Point *cape* **18** D2
Stirling **13** E3
Stockholm **33** E4
Stockport **15** E3
Stockton-on-Tees **13** G1
Stoke-on-Trent **15** E3
Stornoway **10** C3
Strabane **12** A1
Strait of Dover **17** F1/F2
Strangford Lough *estuary* **12** C1
Stranraer **12** C1
Stratford-upon-Avon **15** F2
Stromness **11** F3
Stronsay *island* **11** G4
Stroud **19** E3
Sucre **53** C3
Sudan **41** C4
Suir, River **21**
Sulawesi *island* **34** E2/F2
Sumatra *island* **34** D3/E2
Sumburgh Head *cape* **11** H4
Sunderland **13** G1
Superior, Lake **47** D3/E3
Surabaya **35** E2
Suriname **51** C4
Sutton **17** D2
Sutton Coldfield **15** F2
Swale, River **13** G1
Swanage **19** F2
Swansea **14** D1
Swaziland **41** C2
Sweden **31** C2/C3
Swindon **19** F3
Switzerland **32** D3
Sydney **54** C2
Syria **35** A4

T

Tabriz **35** B4
Tagus, River **32** C2
Taipei **39** F2
Taiwan **39** F2
Tajikistan **35** C4
Tallinn **33** F4
Tamar, River **18** C2
Tanganyika, Lake **40** C3
Tanzania **41** C3
Tapajos, River **53** D4
Tarbat Ness *cape* **11** F2
Tashkent **35** C5
Tasmania *island* **54** C1
Tasman Sea **54** D2
Taunton **18** D3
Taurus Mountains **33** G2
Taw, River **18** D2
Tay, River **13** E3
T'bilisi **31** E2
Tees, River **13** F1/G1
Tegucigalpa **45** E1
Tehran **35** B4
Teifi, River **14** C2
Teign, River **18** D2
Telford **14** D2
Teme, River **16** B3
Tennant Creek *town* **54** B3
Tennessee River **47** E2
Test, River **19** F3
Thailand **35** D3/E3
Thailand, Gulf of **34** E3
Thames, River **19** F3/G3
Thar Desert **37** C3
The Cheviot *mountain* **13** F2
The Fens *geog. reg.* **17** D3/E3
The Great Lakes **47** D3/F3
The Gulf **34** B4
The Minch *sound* **10** C3/D3
Thetford **17** E3
The Valley **49** E2
The Wash *estuary* **17** E3
Thimphu **37** D3
Thurso **11** F3
Thurso, River **11** F3
Tianjin **38** E3
Tibesti Mountains **40** B5
Tibet, Plateau of **38** B3/C3
Tien Shan *mountains* **38** A4/B4
Tierra del Fuego *island* **50** B1
Tigris, River **34** B4
Timor *island* **34** F2
Timor Sea **54** B3
Tiranë **33** E3
Tiree *island* **12** B3
Titicaca, Lake **52** C3
Tiverton **18** D2
Tocantins, River **53** E3/E4
Togo **41** B4
Tokyo **39** G3
Tom Price, Mount **54** A2
Tonga **56** A2
Torbay **18** D2
Toronto **47** F3
Torrens, Lake **54** B2
Townsville **54** C3
Trent, River **15** F2/G3
Trevose Head *cape* **18** B2
Trinidad and Tobago **49** E1
Tripoli **41** B5
Trowbridge **19** E3
Trujillo **52** B4
Truro **18** B2
Tunis **41** B5
Tunisia **41** B5
Turkana, Lake **43** B3
Turkey **31** D1/E2
Turkmenistan **35** B4/C4
Turks and Caicos Islands **49** C3
Tuvalu **57** H2
Tweed, River **13** E2/F2
Tynemouth **13** G2
Tyne, River **13** G1
Tyrrhenian Sea **32** E2/E3
Tywi, River **14** D1

U

Ucayali, River **52** B4
Uganda **41** C4
Ujung Pandang **35** E2
Ukraine **33** F3/G4
Ulan Bator **38** D4
Ullapool **10** D2
Ullswater *lake* **13** F1
Ulva *island* **12** B3
United Arab Emirates **35** B4
United Kingdom **32** C4/C5
United States of America **46/47**
Unst *island* **11** J5
Upper Lough Erne *lake* **12** A1
Ural Mountains **30** E2/E3
Ure, River **13** G1
Uruguay **51** C2
Uruguay, River **50** C2
Urumqi **38** B4
Usk, River **14** D1
Uzbekistan **35** B5/C5

V

Vaal, River **40** C2
Valdés Peninsula **50** B1
Valencia Portugal **32** C2
Valencia Venzuela **51** B4
Valletta **32** E2
Vancouver **46** A3
Vancouver Island **44** C3
Vänern, Lake **32** E4
Van, Lake **30** E1
Vanuatu **54** D3
Varanasi **37** D3
Vättern, Lake **32** E4
Venezuela **51** B4
Victoria Island **44** D4
Victoria, Lake **40** C3
Vienna **33** E3
Vientiane **38** D1
Vietnam **35** E3/E4
Vilnius **33** F4
Virgin Islands UK **49** E2
Virgin Islands USA **49** D2/E2
Vistula, River **33** E4/F4
Volga, River **33** H4
Volgograd **33** H3
Volta, Lake **40** A4/B4
Vyrnwy, River **14** D2

W

Wales **14**
Walsall **15** F2
Waltham Forest *town* **17** D2
Walvis Bay *town* **41** B2
Warrenpoint **12** B1
Warrington **14** E3
Warsaw **33** F4
Warwick **15** F2
Washington **13** G1
Washington D.C. **47** F2
Watford **17** D2
Waveney, River **17** F3
Wear, River **13** F1
Welland, River **15** G2
Wellington **54** D1
Wells-next-the-Sea **17** E3
Welwyn Garden City **17** D2
Wensum, River **17** F3
West Bromwich **15** F2
Western Sahara **41** A5
West Indies *islands* **49** D2/E1
Weston-super-Mare **18** E3
Westray *island* **11** F4/G4
Weymouth **19** E2
Whalsay *island* **11** H5/J5
Whernside *mountain* **13** F1
Whitby **13** H1
Whitehaven **13** E1
White Nile River **40** C4
White Sea **30** D3
Whitney, Mount **46** B2
Wick *lake* **11** F3
Wicklow Mountains **21**
Widnes **14** E3
Wigan **14** E3
Wigtown **12** D1
Wilhem, Mount **54** C3
Willemstad **49** D1
Winchester **19** F3
Windermere *lake* **13** F1
Windhoek **41** B2
Windsor **17** D2
Windward Islands **49** E1
Winnipeg **47** D3
Winnipeg, Lake **44** E3
Wisbech **17** E3
Witham, River **15** G3
Woking **17** D2
Wollongong **54** C2
Wolverhampton **15** E2
Worcester **15** E2
Workington **13** E1
Worksop **15** F3
Worthing **17** D1
Wrath, Cape **10** D3
Wrexham **14** E3
Wuhan **38** E3
Wye, River **14** D2

X

Xi'an **38** D3
Xiamen **39** E2

Y

Yamoussoukro **41** A4
Yangon **38** C1
Yaounde **41** B4
Yell *island* **11** H5
Yellow Sea **39** F3
Yemen Republic **35** B3
Yenisey River **34** D6
Yeo, River **19** E2
Yeovil **19** E2
Yerevan **35** C5
Yes Tor *mountain* **18** C2
York **15** F3
Yorkshire Wolds *hills* **13** H1
Yucatan Peninsula **44** E1/E2
Yukon River **44** B4

Z

Zagreb **32** E3
Zagros Mountains **34** B4
Zambezi, River **40** C3
Zambia **41** C3
Zanzibar *island* **40** C3
Zimbabwe **41** C2/C3

World Flags

Afghanistan

Albania

Algeria

Andorra

Angola

Antigua and Barbuda

Argentina

Armenia

Australia

Austria

Azerbaijan
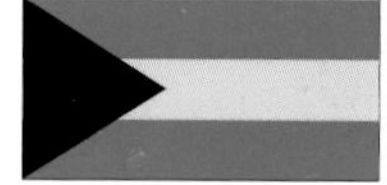
Bahamas
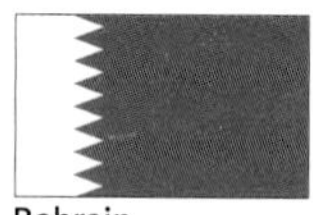
Bahrain
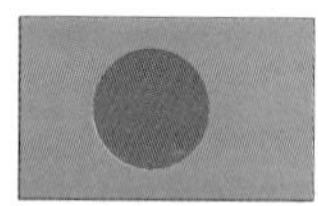
Bangladesh

Barbados

Belarus

Belgium

Belize

Benin
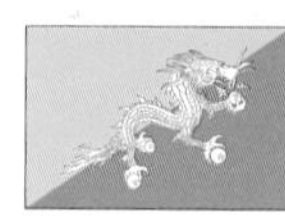
Bhutan

Bolivia

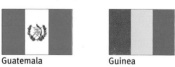

Bosnia-Herzegovina

Botswana

Brazil

Brunei
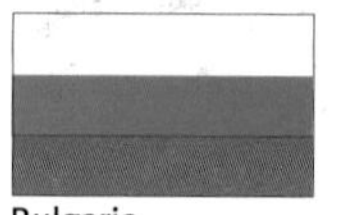
Bulgaria

Burkina

Burundi

Cambodia

Cameroon

Canada

Cape Verde

Central African Republic
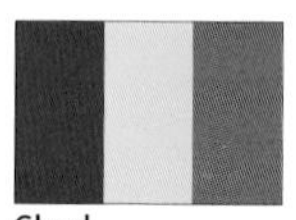
Chad

Chile

China
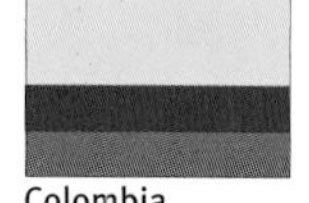
Colombia

Comoros

Congo

Congo, Dem. Rep.
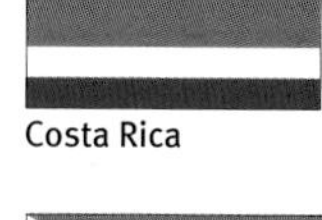
Costa Rica
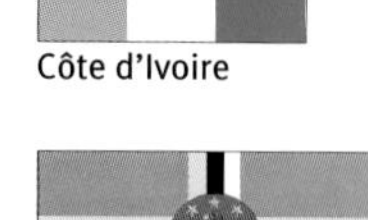
Côte d'Ivoire

Croatia
Cuba
Cyprus
Czech Republic
Denmark
Djibouti
Dominica

Dominican Republic

East Timor

Ecuador

Egypt

El Salvador

Equatorial Guinea

Eritrea

Estonia
Ethiopia
Fiji
Finland
France
French Guiana
Gabon

Gambia
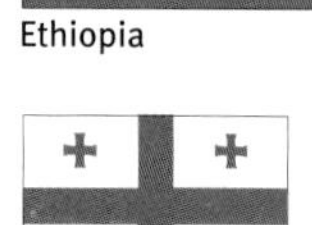
Georgia

Germany

Ghana

Greece

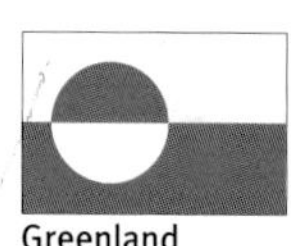
Greenland

Grenada

Guatemala
Guinea
Guinea-Bissau
Guyana
Haiti
Honduras
Hungary

Iceland
India

Indonesia

Iran

Iraq

Ireland
Israel

Italy
Jamaica
Japan
Jordan
Kazakhstan
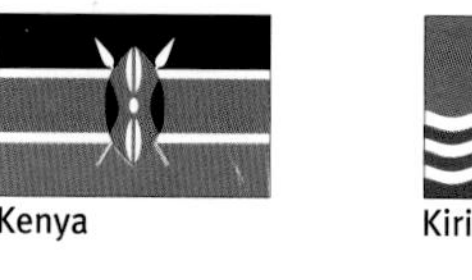
Kenya

Kiribati

Kuwait

Kyrgyzstan
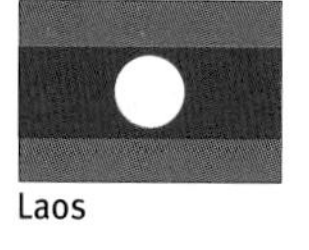
Laos
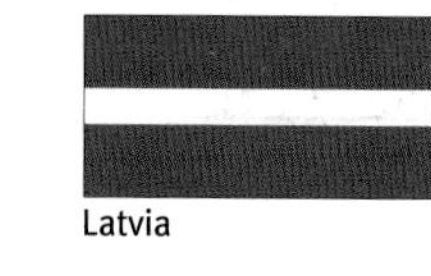
Latvia

Lebanon
Lesotho
Liberia